The Stigma Trap

The Stigma Trap

College-Educated, Experienced, and Long-Term Unemployed

OFER SHARONE

OXFORD
UNIVERSITY PRESS

OXFORD
UNIVERSITY PRESS

Oxford University Press is a department of the University of Oxford. It furthers
the University's objective of excellence in research, scholarship, and education
by publishing worldwide. Oxford is a registered trade mark of Oxford University
Press in the UK and certain other countries.

Published in the United States of America by Oxford University Press
198 Madison Avenue, New York, NY 10016, United States of America.

© Oxford University Press 2024

Library of Congress Cataloging-in-Publication Data
Names: Sharone, Ofer, author.
Title: The stigma trap : college-educated, experienced, and long-term
unemployed / Ofer Sharone.
Description: New York, NY : Oxford University Press, 2024. |
Includes bibliographical references. |
Identifiers: LCCN 2023032473 (print) | LCCN 2023032474 (ebook) |
ISBN 9780190239244 (hardback) | ISBN 9780190239268 (epub) |
ISBN 9780190239275
Subjects: LCSH: College graduates—Employment—United States. |
Unemployed—United States. | Unemployment—United States—Psychological aspects. |
Stigma (Social psychology) | Downward mobility (Social sciences)
Classification: LCC HD6278.U5 S49 2024 (print) | LCC HD6278.U5 (ebook) |
DDC 331.11/4—dc23/eng/20230831
LC record available at https://lccn.loc.gov/2023032473
LC ebook record available at https://lccn.loc.gov/2023032474

DOI: 10.1093/oso/9780190239244.001.0001

Printed by Sheridan Books, Inc., United States of America

This book is dedicated to my children: Avilev, Eliyah, and Talia.

Contents

1

Stigma and the Myth of Meritocracy

After receiving a PhD in mathematics from MIT, Larry spent three decades working in the tech industry, most recently in the area of speech recognition. And today, in his late fifties and after a prolonged bout of unemployment, Larry is a cashier at a department store, earning just above the minimum wage.

Are you wondering how, with a degree from MIT and all that experience, Larry couldn't find a job—any job—in tech?

When I share a story like Larry's, most people look perplexed and want to know more about Larry's *particular* case. The questions they ask presume that there must be some explanation specific to Larry—some reason this happened to him but wouldn't happen to most people, including them. I rarely get asked about the hiring system or the widespread stigmas that might cause highly educated and skilled workers to somehow end up long-term unemployed or stuck in poverty-wage retail jobs. The questions I'm asked—and equally the questions I am *not* asked—reveal that, at some level, most of us implicitly believe in the myth of meritocracy. Sure, we are aware of all the ways in which people are unfairly advantaged or disadvantaged, but still, our surprise at a story like Larry's betrays how tenaciously we hold on to the belief that if you do the "right" things, study hard, go to a good college, and get a good job, you'll do okay. Your career will not suddenly go off a cliff. This belief may be comforting, but it is just plain wrong. Even with all those things done right, your career can go off a cliff. It already has for millions of American workers.

In this book, we will meet college-educated white-collar workers, some with advanced degrees from top universities like MIT and Harvard, who get shut out of jobs that pay middle-class wages. This fate is not unique to college-educated workers, but focusing on such a set-for-success group reveals that in the United States the careers of even the most privileged workers are precarious.[1] The precarity is financial—prolonged unemployment often entails a loss of one's way of life. But the precarity is also social, relational, and existential. The dark underside of our tenacious belief in meritocracy is the stigmatization of those who experience unemployment or downward mobility. This stigmatization means that an American worker risks more than financial calamity from a protracted period of unemployment. One's closest relationships and sense of self are also very much on the line.

The precariousness of every aspect of workers' lives—from money to identity—is most obvious in the case of the unemployed, but it is not limited to them. The myth of meritocracy, and the stigma trap it sets up, underlie the anxiety-filled lives of most contemporary American workers.[2]

Unemployed Workers and the Stigma Trap

How is it possible for a well-established career of a highly educated worker to go off the rails? While college and advanced degrees are necessary to enter most professional jobs, they do not mean you can retain this employment. Large studies show that if, for whatever reason, college-educated workers become unemployed, they are as likely as any other worker—of whatever level of education—to get trapped in long-term unemployment,[3] and being an experienced older worker means you are in fact *more* likely to get trapped in long-term unemployment.[4]

What creates this trap? It is a largely hidden but ubiquitous force that permeates American society. It is a force powerful enough to make past educational and professional achievements suddenly irrelevant. This force—the focus of this book—is *stigma*.

Once workers become unemployed, regardless of their level of education or past professional achievements, they are stigmatized in the eyes of potential employers. Viewed through the distorting lens of the myth of meritocracy—the false assumption that your position reflects your merit—being unemployed raises suspicions in the eyes of a potential employer that something may be wrong with you. Otherwise, you wouldn't be unemployed.[5] And if, due to these very suspicions and stigmas—or to other biases concerning race or age or, for that matter, just bad luck—an unemployed jobseeker does not find a job within 6 months and becomes long-term unemployed, then the stigma further intensifies, and employers are more likely to assume that something must be seriously wrong with this worker.[6]

Employers' stigmatization of unemployed workers can be seen in studies in which researchers send fake resumes to companies with real job openings. These resumes are identical in terms of the applicants' skills and qualifications and differ only in whether the applicant has a current employment gap. From these studies, we know that employers are far less likely to invite unemployed applicants for interviews, especially if the applicant is over 50.[7]

This book shows that it is not only employers who stigmatize unemployed jobseekers. Stigmatizing beliefs about unemployment can potentially come up when unemployed individuals interact with *anyone* in their lives. The stigma can surface when one tries to network with former colleagues, or when one turns to a spouse or close friend for support. Even career coaches can stigmatize the very people they are supposed to be helping. And finally, the stigma is often internalized and the unemployed individuals begin to stigmatize themselves.[8] To understand the unemployment experience, the challenge of re-employment, and the best means to support jobseekers caught in long-term unemployment requires exploring what I call the *stigma trap*. This trap is set by the ways that stigma surfaces in various parts of the unemployed person's life and by how these cumulative experiences create feedback loops that over time make it harder and harder to escape long-term unemployment.[9]

To delve into the daily experiences of navigating life as someone unemployed, this book draws on interviews with 139 long-term unemployed workers, mostly college educated, all highly experienced, and almost all over the age of 50. The book also draws on interviews with recruiters who review job applications, as well as interviews with some currently employed professionals who are frequently contacted for networking purposes. I describe in detail who was interviewed for this book and the recruitment and interview process in the appendix at the end of this book.

While the rest of this book explores how highly educated workers become trapped in long-term unemployment and the nature of this experience, their struggles represent only a more extreme version of the challenges facing nearly all American workers at one level or another. Navigating life within American capitalism and its deeply held myth of meritocracy means that workers perpetually contend with a risk of stigmatization if they should lose their jobs or experience downward mobility. And, as we will see, stigmatization rarely remains purely external. Ultimately, we tend to internalize the stigma and come to question our own merit.

Stigma is a powerful and pervasive force. Erving Goffman, the sociologist who pioneered the study of stigma, defined it simply as the outcome of classifying someone as an "other" *and* as "inferior" and "tainted," and showed how this classification shapes everyday interactions.[10] The experience of stigma is essentially an "assault on worth,"[11] and the effects of stigma are often cumulative. Stigma's insidious power to undermine the lives of its targets derives from both its ubiquity and internalization.

Remarkably, some of Goffman's descriptions of the experiences of stigmatized individuals from over half a century ago apply with precise accuracy to unemployed jobseekers today. Yet, missing from Goffman's analysis of stigma is a theory of why certain characteristics and not others become the target of stigma. Humans differ from each other in countless ways, and most of these differences are treated with indifference.[12] Why is unemployment considered such an important marker of difference in the United States that unemployed workers tend to experience stigma in every realm of their lives?

Whereas Goffman abstracts stigma from its specific context, the work of Michel Foucault can help us see the intricate connection between the stigma of unemployment and the institutions of neoliberal capitalism. Foucault shows how in places like the United States the neoliberal capitalist market comes to function as an institution of "veridiction," meaning that it is the primary institution relied on to verify the value of anything or anyone.[13] When a person's unemployment is viewed through the lens of neoliberalism, it appears that the market has rendered a verdict that the unemployed person is worthless.[14]

In other words, at the core of the United States' distinctly neoliberal form of capitalism is the myth of meritocracy.[15] A society characterized by neoliberal capitalism is organized in a way that defers to the outcomes of unregulated markets because it implicitly or explicitly assumes that markets are fair, and in particular, that success in the labor market reflects a person's merit.[16] The crucial flipside of the assumption that success reflects merit are the skeptical questions about the talent, attitude, or motivation of anyone who experiences a lack of success in the labor market.[17] Notably we can see the myth of meritocracy at play every time we find ourselves drawing inferences about others like Larry based solely on their employment status or perceived level of career success.

In each chapter of this book we will see stigma show up in a distinct way and examine its effects. In Chapter 2, we are going to hear directly from recruiters who review applications from unemployed workers. Having been assured that they will remain anonymous, these recruiters openly discuss the widely shared stigmas employers hold against unemployed and older workers. From them we will hear the myth of meritocracy stated loud and clear, and we will see how the stigmatization of unemployed and older workers creates difficult barriers to getting a job even for those who graduated from MIT or Harvard and who enjoyed decades of professional success.

When I ask recruiters what is the way out of this trap, their unanimous response is networking. Chapter 3 explores what actually happens when unemployed jobseekers try to take that advice. As we will see, networking for long-term unemployed workers can be a bruising experience because they run up against stigmas and the myth of meritocracy not only with job recruiters but also with their own networks. And while interactions with recruiters often take place through online portals or in formal interviews, networking tends to be more direct and personal, often inflicting painful blows and leaving the unemployed jobseeker feeling like a beggar or a used-car salesman.

Next, Chapter 4 delves into the ways that the experience of long-term unemployment and the stigma attached to it undermine identities—not only our identities as valuable workers but sometimes our identities as viable parents or even as legitimate grown-ups. These multiple identity crises, along with the feeling of constant anxiety and the sense that one is heading toward a cliff, generate a feedback loop. As the emotional crises intensify, the stigma trap becomes even tougher to escape because recruiters treat any hint of negative feelings as a disqualifying red flag. In other words, unemployed workers are stigmatized for being unemployed and then further stigmatized for feeling upset about being stigmatized.

Chapter 5 explores what happens in long-term unemployed jobseekers' more intimate relationships. While some marriages and friendships provide crucial support, even these relationships can be poisoned by stigmatizing myths. Relationship struggles create yet another feedback loop: Not only does one lack support when it is most needed, but given the centrality of relationships to our well-being, the struggles in these relationships become an additional source of emotional turmoil—which in turn makes getting a job even more difficult because recruiters back away from a candidate at the first whiff of turmoil.

What can help? Chapter 6 examines a sociologically informed model of support, where the myth of meritocracy is contested and obstacles that are beyond individual control are openly acknowledged. This chapter will show how support that is informed by a sociological perspective facilitates awareness of the larger societal forces that make such a trap of unemployment. This awareness in turn helps counter the internalization of stigma. Knowing it's not really your fault does not in itself get you hired, but combating self-blame helps unemployed jobseekers' well-being and resilience to continue searching. Finally, Chapter 7 considers the prospects and obstacles for unemployed jobseekers to engage in collective action to challenge the forces that create the stigma trap. It will also reflect on what can be learned from the policies passed during the early stages of the Covid-19 pandemic, and more broadly, discuss the tenacity of the unemployment stigma and how it may be challenged.

The unemployed workers described in this book could be any one of us. In contemporary American society there is no escaping the risk of unemployment. The careers of American workers, regardless of prestigious degrees and impressive work experience, are precarious, and layoffs have become a routine part of life.[18] It was not always like this. In the post–World War II era white-collar workers at large companies could reasonably expect to stay at one company for life. In that era, layoffs of white-collar workers were rare, even during recessions. But by the 1980s job security began to crumble. The rock star CEO of the new era, Jack Welch of General Electric, became the hero of Wall Street by routinely laying off workers regardless of the company's profitability. American capitalism has never looked back.[19] Currently, about three out of four American workers become unemployed at some point in their careers,[20] and in recent decades the percentage of unemployed workers who get trapped in long-term unemployment has been rising.[21] As I write this, there are over a million Americans trapped in long-term unemployment. But the stigma of unemployment means that this group is largely invisible. Stigma individualizes the challenge of unemployment, rendering it a problem with the unemployed individual as opposed to a problem with society. Viewed through this lens long-term unemployment is largely a nonstory in the media and is rarely raised as an issue by politicians running for office.

This book aims to shine a bright light on the story of long-term unemployed workers and the stigmatizing myth of meritocracy at the heart of American capitalism. This spotlight will perhaps help us see with fresh eyes the nature of the stigma trap that ensnares people who are no different from us. They are our neighbors, our former colleagues, our friends, our spouses, and perhaps ourselves. Looking with fresh eyes that are untainted by stigma is a critical first step to sparking our collective imagination for how to build a more fair and compassionate society.

2

The Trap

Advanced Degree from Harvard, Experienced, and Long-Term Unemployed?

It often starts with an unusual email on an otherwise ordinary day. Doug's story is typical. He is a 56-year-old project manager in information technology. Soon after arriving at work, Doug was asked to come down to his manager's office where he found his manager and the human resources (HR) director: "They just sat me down and said, 'Thank you for all your hard work and it's done.' They didn't say any more." Twenty-two years of giving his all to his company—and forging deep connections with coworkers—ended in that brief meeting.[1]

Despite such painful endings, the search for new work typically begins with optimism.[2] My interviewees had had long and successful careers and assumed that employers would value and recognize their qualifications and they would be hired quickly. But this assumption often proves unfounded, and, in time, what begins as confidence turns to bewilderment and eventually to insidious self-doubt. Tina, who is in her late 50s and most recently worked in publishing, describes her experience: "You send in your application and it's amazing. You hear absolutely nothing." The lack of response usually leaves jobseekers feeling that there must be something wrong with the way they present themselves. Tim, a tech manager in his mid-50s, expresses a frustration that was typical of my interviewees:

The thing that really kills me is you never find out why you didn't get it. You're never able to make adjustments because they never tell you what happened. Ever. Something goes into a black box. You don't get any feedback on why something didn't happen. And to me, I feel like I'm a person that tries to get along with people. I'll do whatever somebody wants, but I've got to know what they want. What is it that you're judging me on? And then I will do that thing, but if you don't tell me what you're judging me on, how do I know what to do?

Tim's reaction reveals a frustration at the heart of many jobseekers' experiences, who end up feeling foiled by the lack of actionable feedback that would allow them to adjust their strategy. Sharon, who is in her mid-40s and worked in finance, expresses the widely shared idea that if she were only given an "honest answer," she could solve the problem:

> I am a person who is very analytical. I am a problem-solver. I'm an out-of-the-box thinker and usually can think my way out of any situation. This one is different because you receive next to no feedback in this process. I have no data to make any adjustments. No one tells you why you aren't being chosen—an honest answer which you can act on. I am just *blindly* tweaking my resume, my LinkedIn profile, and changing the types of jobs I am going for. Any adjustments I make, I'm just *flying blind*. I have no idea whether I am making things better or worse.

The assumption implicit in Tim's and Sharon's frustrations is that the hiring system is, at least in part, a rational evaluation of skills and experiences, and a merit-based matching of what the applicant has to offer to what the employer needs. That (supposedly) being the case, the jobseeker is left thinking that there must be some disconnect between the skills the employer is looking for and the skills that come across to the employer from his or her resume or social media profile. That's how it seemed to Tammy, an office manager in health care:

> It's just so hard because you don't get any feedback. . . . They're just too busy to be bothered so they don't want to tell you, "You know, this skill was lacking." Or "We wanted somebody that had more experience in such and such." I have no idea. Do I change my resume? Do I change my LinkedIn? I don't know.

The assumption of merit-based hiring makes the stream of rejections particularly confusing and dispiriting. Tina does not understand why she keeps being rejected when, as she puts it, she is applying "for jobs that I really am *very qualified for.*" Similarly, Larry does not understand why he is not getting invited for interviews with companies that "say they want people who have the math background and the programming background, the business background and so on—all the things I have. And yet, I don't get anybody biting."

The assumption is that hiring is mostly based on skills and experience—but what if it *isn't*? This was the view of one unusual jobseeker, Sandra, who had a different perspective. Unlike the other jobseekers I've discussed, Sandra had also been on the hiring side in her work as a director of fundraising at a university. As she had experienced it, hiring did not strictly compare experiences and skills but was shaped much more by random factors such as who the hiring manager happens to like, or which resume happens to be near the top of the pile. She explains:

> Sometimes you hire the other person and it's just that I *liked* the other person better. There wasn't anything wrong with candidate B. It's just candidate A had a nicer smile. It's like dating. . . . Or you have a stack of resumes. You can't read them all or you'll drive yourself crazy. You're only going to read the first 25. And there's probably somebody great in the next 500.

Sandra's understanding of the importance of liking a candidate, regardless of skills or credentials—what hiring managers often refer to as having a good gut feeling or "chemistry"—is well documented by prior research,[3] as is the arbitrariness that arises when recruiters have many more applications than they can assess with any care.

Sandra is correct to point to factors that lead to arbitrariness in hiring. But the dearth of positive responses to the highly experienced, educated, and credentialed candidates I interviewed also has another key explanation. Ironically, the same assumption of meritocracy—of hiring generally based on skills—that was implicit in jobseekers' confused and frustrated reactions is also being made by recruiters. When this assumption is applied to assessing unemployed jobseekers—especially those over 50 and who are long-term unemployed—it results in their systematic exclusion. In the rest of this chapter, we will get an under-the-hood view—from the recruiters themselves—of the stigmas and practices that create the application black hole that sucks up so many qualified people's job applications without a trace.

Recruiters and the Stigma of Unemployment

To better understand the trap of unemployment, I spoke with 20 recruiters about how they review job applications. Almost the first thing out of every recruiter's mouth is the sense of being overwhelmed. Linda explains:

> I know jobseekers are often frustrated when they don't get a reply. . . . But at some point the volume becomes so high, it's hard. The non-replies are not personal. . . . It's just lack of time.

Time-crunched recruiters are faced with the task of whittling a large stack of resumes down to a manageable few and to do that, they rely on shortcuts. In particular, they keep an eye out for easy-to-spot "red flags"—something that in their mind can allow them to reject the candidate on the spot without spending any more time.[4] These red flags act as shortcuts to the applicant review process, and it is in these shortcuts that we see the power of stigmas that often lead to the automatic rejection of unemployed jobseekers without consideration of their qualifications.

Sandra, the jobseeker quoted above who has experience in hiring, discussed the arbitrariness of the process introduced by factors like whether a hiring manager happens to like a particular candidate. But the hiring system isn't just arbitrary. Stigma means it's systematically tilted against the unemployed workers, and that tilt keeps getting steeper the longer you're unemployed. My interviews with recruiters reveal the stigmas underlying the findings from audit studies that show the lower likelihood of unemployed workers being invited to interviews.[5] In fact, as soon as a worker is laid off, there are some questions raised in the minds of recruiters about *why* that worker was laid off. As recruiter Tara explains:

> There's a perception that people who are out of work or laid off are not the top performers within an organization. The perception from a potential employer would be, "If a company really wanted somebody, they're not going to be laying those folks off. They're going to be laying off possibly the poor performers." Now, that's obviously not always the case. A company could lay off people for a wide variety of reasons. But there is that perception that very often those folks who have been laid off or out of work for any length of time are not going to be the top people out there that a company might want to employ. That's a perception.

The more polite way corporate America typically talks about their bias against unemployed workers is by expressing a preference for "passive jobseekers." This innocuous-sounding term refers to workers who are currently working and not actively looking for work and whom recruiters proactively seek out. Recruiter Richard explains the appeal of such workers: "There is a preference for the passive jobseeker who is gainfully employed such that we're tracking them down [because] the odds are that they will be better candidates. They require more work for us to lure them, but they yield great hires."[6] Claire, another recruiter, explains the allure of the "passive jobseeker":

> A lot of companies have that perception that the candidate who is not actively out there looking is the better candidate versus the one who is knocking on doors and actively in a job search. The "passive seeker" is very much sought after. Their thought is, "These are the best people." There are people who are pretty content in their jobs because their company takes very good care of them, so they're not looking for a job. Another company might be saying, "I want that person because their company is keeping them, they must think highly of them." It's funny because they may not be that different than somebody else who is looking for another job. But just say the word, "It's a passive candidate," and the client's eyes might light up and say, "Oh! That's great,' " which, once again, is so much about perception. The perception is that the passive seeker is the better of the candidates.

The widely shared perception that passive jobseekers are better poses a clear obstacle for unemployed jobseekers and one that has likely become more formidable in recent years. The rise over the past decade of social networking sites like LinkedIn has made passive jobseekers relatively easy and cheap to identify. Recruiter Ray recalled how, in earlier eras, finding passive jobseekers "used to be more time-intensive" and "typically required a referral who knew this person." But today, with a few clicks on LinkedIn, Ray can browse the profiles of everyone working at rival companies and send them a message. Echoing other recruiters, Ray explains the logic of pursuing passive jobseekers: "We want to hire someone who is working. The sense is that if someone is good, they would be working. Those laid off are the least needed." Ray personally thinks this logic is "crap," recalling his own experience: "I was a top-performer and the whole group was laid off." Nevertheless, he feels that he needs to follow the wishes and logic of his employer clients.

Whether it is initially due to a bias against laid-off workers, a preference for passive jobseekers, or simply some initial bad luck and the randomness of the hiring process, once a jobseeker does not find a job within 6 months, a new barrier to employment rises which likely dwarfs the others. Studies reveal that jobseekers with equal qualifications and experiences but who are unemployed longer than 6 months face much lower odds of being invited to interviews.[7] The recruiters I interviewed had no difficulty explaining the employer logic behind that. Tara, for example, puts it this way:

> I think if it gets beyond 9 months, a year or more, that's when it really becomes a larger issue. . . . Companies start to think, "Maybe not only did your former employer not want you, but now you've been looking, why haven't you been hired? What's the matter with you that you haven't been hired?"

Chad agrees: "Yeah, 6 months is kind of a magic number to [employers]. Somebody who is an all-star candidate would be swept up, picked up, hired inside of 6 to 9 months. So they get scared of that candidate, they back off of that candidate, they do not want the risk being associated with that candidate."

The pernicious nature of this stigma is that it creates the very conditions that amplify it. As employers "back off" from the candidate who is 6 months unemployed they make it very likely that this candidate will become 9 months or a year unemployed, which in turn leads employers to respond even more negatively to the candidate. Recruiter Claire observes: "As times goes on, that perception grows bigger and bigger. It's not just focused on the fact that you were laid off. It's focused on, 'Why hasn't anyone else hired you?' That becomes more the issue at that time, especially for the long term." Chad is equally blunt:

> You see that the last time they held a job was a year ago. So immediately a question comes to mind, "Well, why is that?" Employers start to internally rely on other people's opinions and experience beyond their own, to help them with their decision making. They look at this person and say, "They haven't been employed for a year and they're looking. So obviously, other recruiters, other hiring managers, have already made that call for them, that this person for some reason is not hirable or else they would have already been hired in the last year."

In addition to any stigmas recruiters themselves attribute to long-term unemployed jobseekers, they are driven by what they know or assume their clients—the hiring managers—will think of an applicant who has been out of work for a lengthy period. Recruiter Rachel, who acknowledges the pernicious and unfair effects of the circular logic that makes candidates not "hirable" because they haven't been hired, nonetheless explains that "even if I really wanted to, I cannot help." As an interviewer I had a hard time formulating a follow-up question to this statement by Rachel. As I thought about how this logic creates a nearly impossible situation for jobseekers, Rachel filled in the silence: "If I were hiring, I'd be hiring people based on capabilities. But what I'm describing is not me, *it's what the market says.*" By discussing these outcomes as reflecting the market, Rachel distances herself from what she sees are unfair results. By treating the market as an actor who "says" things, we can see how it is conceived of as an impartial arbiter of value[8] and how this conceals the very human and stigma-informed decision-making process driving these market outcomes.

Tara, like Rachel and many of the other recruiters who agreed to interview with me, is sensitive to the plight of unemployed jobseekers and how stigmas lead potential employers to overlook their skills and capabilities, but she also recognizes that not all her recruiter colleagues feel the same way. From her experience, the pervasive stigma against unemployed jobseekers is the result of the limited life experiences of both hiring managers and recruiters who "were not impacted [by the recession], who did not lose their jobs, [who] don't realize how bad it is out there for the people who are out of work. So their view is, 'Why are they out of work so long?'" As we will see in later chapters, it is not only hiring managers and recruiters who harbor these views but nearly everyone in the long-term unemployed jobseeker's life.

"What Have You Been Doing?"

Over time, jobseekers become more aware of and concerned about employer stigmas against the long-term unemployed. For Tammy, who has been looking for work for over a year, "the thing that scares me is when they see that you haven't been employed for a while, they don't even look at your stuff." Tim refers to the duration of his unemployment as his "biggest concern" because "the longer you're out from a permanent position, the more people are looking skeptically at you." Given these reasonable concerns, among the most upsetting experiences of unemployed jobseekers is being asked to explain their employment gaps or what they have been doing during the gap. For recruiters who interview jobseekers with employment gaps, asking about this gap seems like an obvious thing to do. Dan puts it this way: "I might see a gap and wonder what you were doing then. You haven't worked for 2 years."

Recruiter Ray explains that how the jobseeker has been using the time makes a difference. If someone took a year off 'to do game development,' that's different from someone, *just* not finding job."[9] But the same question that seems obvious to recruiters signals the recruiters' cluelessness to jobseekers. For example, Tina, who has been looking for work for almost a year, finally got an interview. She describes what happened: "The HR person said: 'Oh! Well, what have you been doing?' And I wanted to slap her. It's like, 'What do you think I've been doing?' But people don't realize that looking for a job is a job."

Being asked about their employment gap was among the most frustrating questions for jobseekers because it made plain that hiring managers or recruiters simply could not comprehend that someone might try for a year to find work and still fail, without anything really being wrong with them. Doug, who had been looking for 2 years, puts it this way: "One of the challenges is responding to the question, 'What have you been doing all this time'? It's hard to explain yourself. They only see, "Oh, your last job was 2 years ago. What have you been up to since then?" Tammy described the anger that this question evokes due to the implicit stigmatizing judgment beneath it. Here is how she discussed her experience at an interview: "The first question is, 'So, what have you been doing the last couple of years?' I just could not believe it. I felt like smashing his face in. This guy has got *no clue what's going on*." To have a chance at being hired, unemployed jobseekers must, of course, suppress their rage and respond in an articulate and convincing way that no, they have not been a couch potato, and no, there is nothing wrong with them.

Ironically, these frustrated jobseekers trying to keep from slapping the interviewer are the lucky ones who even got an interview. In most cases there are no interviews and no questions, just a systematic screening out. Recruiter Linda explains that recruiters seldom take the time to understand what jobseekers have been doing during their gap because it does not actually matter: "When the person who has been out of work for 6 months competes with all the people who have relevant recent experience and are currently working, this person loses. People who are *capable* of doing the job are competing with people who are *doing* the job and they lose." When I ask Linda whether it matters if the reason for the gap is due to staying home to care for a young baby or due to inability to find work, she explains: "It can make a difference if we start talking to the person. But in most cases, the person will never even be considered. If there were enough people matching the job who are currently working, the person who is out of job—*their resume will not even be opened*. They will not get any communication to enable them to explain why they have been out of work." Ultimately, it comes down to whether recruiters have the *bandwidth* to even consider hiring an unemployed worker. Linda is very blunt about this:

> I'm not saying that the person who is working currently is better in the long run. But nobody has the bandwidth [to do the] comparison. If the person is already working and is doing the job well and fits, *why would I look elsewhere?* We get an incredible volume of people applying to jobs. So with the amount of information coming at me, and to do my job, I have no capacity or desire to be looking at people who have been out of work for a while. So people who have been out of work for a year or more, typically they're not even considered. I post a job and I get applications from other countries, from people who have nothing to do with what I posted. The person who has been out of work will be sort of in that category that we don't even read. . . . It's not that we sit down and discriminate against somebody. It's just that a very high volume of applications comes at us, and we can spot the promising profile and then we work with them.

Roger echoes Linda's point: "We deal with hundreds of candidates a week. So [recruiters] feel, 'If I can find someone just as qualified and maybe is currently employed or even just recently lost their job,' they're gonna default to that person." Thus, well-educated, well-qualified, highly experienced candidates are unceremoniously lumped with candidates who, in Linda's words, "have nothing to do with what I posted." Hearing Roger describe employers' default rejection of longer-term unemployed workers, and Linda discussing having "no capacity or desire" to look at candidates who are out of work, puts in stark relief the obstacles that long-term unemployed jobseekers face.

A final irony is that if the economy improves and the unemployment rate goes down, the stigma against those who have been trapped in long-term unemployment increases. Claire explains:

> In the last few years, as the economy has grown stronger, it's tougher for the folks who have been out for a year or more. Again, companies will be looking at a resume and saying, "Gee, you've been out this length of time. The economy is strong. Why is that? What's the matter that other companies aren't hiring you at this time?" Once again, it's the perception of the longer you're out, the more there is the feeling that there's something the matter with this person, this resume. "Other people don't want you."

Roger agrees that if the economy is not in a recession, recruiters will con-
clude that "this person for some reason is not hirable or else they would have
already been hired."

The recruiters I interviewed seemed unaware that, at the time of our
interviews, more than a third of all unemployed workers were long-term
unemployed—a historically high level. It appears that recruiters' sense of the
broader employment conditions is simply based on the overall unemployment rate, which masks issues like the long-term unemployment trap.[10]

Over time, after experiencing these formidable obstacles to re-
employment, jobseekers who had held higher-level positions often decide to
broaden their search to pursue more plentiful but lesser-paying, and lower-
level jobs in their fields. But what awaits them next is perhaps the most cruel
of all the obstacles and the one that most makes a mockery of the idea of
meritocracy.

Upside-down Meritocracy: Rejecting Workers for Being Too Skilled

The most ironic obstacle facing the unemployed workers I studied is their
own prior success. Many individuals have typically worked for decades in
a career and have advanced to relatively high levels. When they lose a job,
they typically begin by looking for similar positions. Over time, however,
with mounting financial pressures and concerns about their lengthening
employment gap, a lot of these jobseekers reassess and consider broad-
ening their searches. Those who had been successful in their field and had
held highly coveted jobs recognize that there are far fewer high-level job
openings than lower-level ones. Susan, an HR conflict resolution specialist
in her late 50s, explains: "It's like a pyramid, you know? If you're in a field
and you get X number of years, you get up toward the top and there are only
a couple of positions. I've got more than 20 years of experience and there
just aren't a lot of jobs that are looking for that level of experience." While
a lower-level job would involve adjusting to lower pay and some setback
to one's professional identity, given the scarcity of high-level jobs and the
intense competition for such jobs, most jobseekers do eventually expand
their searches to include lower-level jobs, often ones they had held in at
prior stages of their career.[11]

Brian's story is illustrative. He began his career as an engineer in a small company, and by the age of 59 he had climbed his way to the position of director of engineering. There are very few director of engineering positions and many more engineering jobs. Yet Brian has learned that when he applies for engineering positions, "it can be a hard sell because I've already been there. I've already matriculated up the ladder from an engineer into a leader at a company. And there's the notion I've heard that employers are looking for someone on the way up the ladder, not on the way down." Michelle is 61-years-old and likewise worked her way up to become an executive director at a nonprofit. She is now is applying for lower-level coordinator positions but is getting nowhere. In a recent phone interview, halfway through the conversation, her interviewer asked: "So you've had all this great leadership management experience, why do you want this coordinator job?" Michelle did her best to reassure the interviewer that she was truly interested in being a coordinator: "Well, I've been a manager. I've been up there sitting in an office making rules. But what I really like to do is work with the volunteers, helping directly manage those programs on that level. That's what I'd really like to do.' Hang up, don't hear back from him." Whereas Michelle's interview ended abruptly, Nathan, a 60-year-old program director in the field of community education, was explicitly told at an interview that his resume made him seem too "heavy": Nathan explained: "I'm not overweight, so I knew that heavy was not about my physical size. We did talk and 'heavy' turned out to be a code word for 'over-qualified.'"

The recruiters I interviewed were quite open about rejecting applicants for being too experienced and skilled. They worried that such applicants would soon be bored and would leave at the first opportunity. Recruiter Sherry explains that even if an applicant says they "want to get some data-entry job, the concern there is that we'll teach them to do data entry and they will move on because it's boring." Wilma, another recruiter, offers an explanation focusing on perceptions of an applicant's likelihood of being "happy":

I would hear from corporate recruiters, "We're not looking for somebody who has got 20 years of experience. They're going to be over-qualified. They're going to be bored in this job. They're not going to be happy in this job." How do they know that? That's just their perception and I think, very often, that's what they're hearing from a hiring manager: "I don't want a 20–25 years of experience person."

Employers are essentially guessing what will make jobseekers happy or not. Regardless of the fact that jobseekers are expressing an interest in the position by applying and regardless of how compelling a case they might make in their cover letters that this is a job that they would very much like, their level of experience means that recruiters presume the opposite.

It is important to see how age is inextricably connected to the issue of over-qualification. With age comes experience, which, in this upside-down world of hiring, is held against the jobseeker. Recruiter Chad explains:

> If I'm looking for someone with only 5 years' experience and I see your picture and you're older, I'm gonna move on. *You don't want this job.* You don't want to compete with kids with 5 years of experience. That's not the job for you. You're helping me not bother you in a situation that I know isn't right for you. You shouldn't be interviewing for that job.

Jobseekers, of course, beg to differ and want an opportunity to convince recruiters like Chad that, actually, they do really want this job, but the overlapping presumptions that come with age and experience mean that they will probably never get a chance to make their case.

Nearly all the jobseekers I interviewed for this book were caught in this almost impossible trap, including those with skills that were highly in demand in fields such as software engineering and accounting. For example, having risen from software engineering positions to management, here is how Stacy describes the bind of over-qualification: "If I say, 'OK, fine. I'll just take a lower-level software engineering job,' then people are like, 'Well, what are you doing? You were this high-level guy. Now you want to be a low-level guy? You're just going to leave as soon as you find a better job.'" Ryan, an accountant who rose to higher levels of management, bumped up against a similar concern that he would jump ship as soon as a better opportunity arose in this field:

> There are plenty of accounting jobs out there. I'll take an accounting job. I don't have a problem with that. It's a significant drop in income, but at least it's a steady income. But [employers] believe that I would jump at the next chance that would come along that would be closer to what I have been. So that's the fear of an employer if I take a lower job. If something comes along that's more what I used to do, I'd leave. And that's not the case, but I have to convince them that that's not the case.

Ryan explains that, contrary to employers' assumptions, he would actually prefer a long-term position and steady income, even if it means a pay cut, but he does not know how to rebut employers' assumptions about his preferences. Gail has attempted to push back and explain her interest to employers, but to no avail: "I've had [employers] tell me that with my prior pay level, they're not going to even interview me because I wouldn't be interested." In reality Gail *is* interested: "I'm actually willing to take a lot less money than what they expect. Give me a chance! I'll tell you if I'm not interested." But jobseekers are almost never given this chance. Wilma, the recruiter, confirms that employers presume that workers would not be willing to take a significant pay cut. She believes that if a person "makes $75,000 and the last time they were making $100,000, that person will leave and get a job that is more at the level of their experience and their salary range." Acting on this assumption, employers tend not even to ask jobseekers about their salary expectations; they simply presume and reject.

Steven's story is typical. He started his career as a high school guidance counselor and by his late 50s worked his way up to being a school principal. But since there are very few principal jobs available and competition for these few jobs is fierce, Steven decided to aim for the relatively more plentiful guidance counseling jobs. But he found this route closed:

> Counselor jobs, they wouldn't even look at me. I got feedback all the time from people off the record saying, "You're waaay too expensive, overqualified for this position." But *they didn't even ask*. I would have liked it. I didn't look at it that way! And I certainly don't see a counselor as "less than." But that's how they saw it and I hardly ever got interviewed for a counselor position.

It is not clear how one can escape this trap. Steven explains that the reason he never got interviews is the employer's assumption that "they can pay so much less by hiring a person right out of college than somebody with years of experience." The fact that Steven, just like Gail and Ryan, actually does not mind the lower pay does not matter because employers' preemptive rejections leave him with no effective way of communicating it:

> You're in the position where you don't want to advertise in your cover letter, "Listen, I'll take peanuts." It's a hard thing to really get across that you don't really need to be paid top level. I think a lot of people look at my resume

and it's been principal administration for 15 years. And I think a lot of people don't think I'd be happy. I'd be thrilled! People make assumptions, you know? [A former colleague] told me, "Put it in your letter. Find a way to put that down in your letter. A way that's effective and comes across the way you mean it to." So I have said that "I'd like to return to my first love" and "understanding the budget restraints that schools are under, I'm willing to negotiate salary." That's the best I could figure. It's dreadful. It's a real bind.

James found himself in the same trap. He had been "principal software engineer," but now he says he "wouldn't mind taking a cut in salary to get into a company." Yet, like Steven and Gail, James learned that his past success now poses an enormous obstacle: "I'd take a bigger cut in pay than most people would consider. . . . But you can't just go and tell a prospective employer that you would be willing to do that. That usually doesn't work. They don't believe you, or else they think, 'Oh, this guy is a real loser.'"

Jobseekers like James are actually in a double bind. If they seek jobs with salaries commensurate with their level of experience, they are "too expensive." If they seek jobs with lower salaries, it is assumed that they would not be happy or must be a "loser." Either way, they are rejected out of hand.

Most jobseekers have no idea how to rebut employers' presumption that they will be bored, unhappy, and prone to leave at the first opportunity. Sandra expresses the typical confusion and frustration:

Since I've been in an executive director role, no matter what position I'm hired for now, people think I'll be too "directorish." At one company, an interviewer told me, "You really know it all," but she didn't say it like "We're really impressed." But what are you supposed to do on a resume? Should I have written something like "I don't really know anything"?

Some career coaches do indeed suggest doing something equivalent to what Sandra raised as an absurdity and advise jobseekers to downplay their qualifications and perhaps even remove advanced degrees from their resumes. Jobseekers, however, often find this advice upsetting. Brian, for example, reports his reaction to the advice he received from a coach: "I had one [coach] tell me that I should change my job title. That I shouldn't list director of engineering. I'm like, 'But that was my job title. I'm not going to be deceptive about something when I'm looking to establish relationships with people.'" Other jobseekers take the advice and remove some of their most impressive experiences and credentials from their resumes, but then run into other problems such as more resume gaps or undermining their own sense of integrity. When Daniel, a neuroscientist in his mid-50s, applies for lower-level jobs than he's had in the past, "I immediately take my PhD out. I just leave the very basic, very minimal experiences." But it makes him feel outraged: "I think it is a shame. I'm just such a mess. So just trying to pretend that I'm not a scientist. . . . I don't want to stop being genuine in who I am. This is who I am, no matter what, whether I get a job or not! I'm not going to change it. So I have a problem."[12] In Chapter 3, which is focused on networking, I will revisit the important issue Daniel raises regarding feeling compelled to act in ways that he does not experience as genuine to who he is.

In certain fields, such as technology, short-term contract jobs can provide a tempting way out. When hiring for contract positions, employers' concerns about over-qualification and a worker getting bored and leaving do not come into play. But contract jobs create a different kind of trap. Recruiter Sherry explains that "if the person has been contracting, they're not a good match for a full-time job. . . . People who are contractors do not match full-time job descriptions just because it's assumed that they are likely to switch jobs again." This leaves workers who take contract jobs potentially stuck in contract jobs, which means a perpetual state of job search and precarity.[13]

Stepping back, we can see that the obstacle of over-qualification is both real and immensely ironic for a system that claims to be meritocratic. Degrees and experience exhibiting merit are great—until they are not. This aspect of the trap leaves Tammy dumbfounded: "I don't know what else to say. *I've done everything right.* I have a great resume. Maybe it's too great and scares people away?" I am not sure what one should call a hiring system in which experience is seen as "too great" and "scares" employers, but certainly not a meritocracy.

Being Simultaneously Over- and Under-Qualified

To avoid the over-qualification trap, some jobseekers consider switching to a new field in which their work experience will not be held against them. In some cases, switching to a new field is also a deliberate attempt to find work that is more enjoyable and meaningful, even if starting fresh inevitably means a lower position and less pay. Tonya, for example, had been in HR for 20 years. Senior-level HR positions are not common, and when applying for lower-level HR jobs, Tonya was of course told she was over-qualified. So she decided to "break into something entirely different—event planning. . . . I thought I'd turn my hobby into maybe a job." But whereas for HR jobs she was told that she was over-qualified when, seeking event planning positions the door was shut for being under-qualified:

> I'm told that I am not qualified because I don't have any paid experience in event planning. So I'm stuck. . . . I'm looking to break into a field in an entry-level position and I'm a person who's got all this other experience. I have no idea how to do this successfully. I went on an interview for the exact job I wanted. I was so excited and [the interviewer] looked at me like I had ten heads. He asked me: "What are you doing?" I said to him. "What I'm offering you is a gift. I'm offering you a reliable person. I'll be here, I'll do whatever it is. I don't care. I just need experience." And he just thought I was insane.

The recruiters interviewing Tonya would not look at the skills she had gained in HR and imagine how they might transfer to event planning, even though it seems rather obvious. Instead, they simply focused on her lack of experience in event planning. As we examine this obstacle, it is important to notice how—just as in the case of over-qualification—age plays an important role.

My interviews with recruiters shed light on why employers reject older career changers. Sherry put it this way: "Ninety-five percent of what matters is a very close match to the job description in terms of *recent experience*." Sherry thinks it is only in "rare cases where a person who has been doing one kind of job would be considered a fit for another kind of job." Recruiter Claire shares a similar understanding of how employers view older career changers:

> I have had people say, "I really want to do something different." That's always challenging because, even though there's a good job market right now, companies like to find people who already are skilled in the particular area where their job opening is. If there's a finance job, they want somebody who has got a good accounting and finance background. If somebody wants to make a complete career change, I have to be honest with them that it's a lot harder . . . *especially if you've been working in a particular field for 10, 15, 20 years.*

Claire's statement that switches are "especially" hard for experienced workers was a repeated theme and made clear just how much the obstacle to making a career change is linked to the workers' age. When I asked Claire to clarify she was blunt:

> When you've got a lot of years of experience, especially *when you're not in your 20s and 30s*, maybe you're in your 40s and 50s, trying to make that career transition can be very difficult. . . . Companies are not interested. They want to find somebody who has got experience in the particular area they're looking for.

Jobseekers are baffled by the trap of being simultaneously over-qualified for some jobs and under-qualified for others. The absurdity of the situation is crystalized in the peculiar situation that Sharon found herself in. Sharon initially saw her layoff as an opportunity to switch roles within finance. Instead of continuing to do accounting for investors, she was excited to help individuals choose their investments. To pursue this goal, she spent time and money to obtain further training and obtained a widely recognized certificate in investment management. Yet, three years after gaining this certificate, she has not found any job in finance—either in her old role or in her hoped-for new one:

> Even though I have the professional certification, people say, "We want to see experience" and I don't have direct experience. . . . I have related experience. In some cases, I've done some of the same tasks that I would be expected to do in the new field, it's just that I haven't done it in that context. So for them, it's not real experience. It's like, "Have you done this task in the same context as I'm looking?" If the answer is "no," you can't get anywhere.

Training not only got Sharon nowhere in terms of changing careers within finance, but ironically made it *more* difficult when trying to get back to her old field of financial accounting. The training and certification in investment management, she reports, "raises eyebrows" among her former financial accounting colleagues and makes them question her commitment to her former field. She sums up her situation this way: "The certification that I earned has effectively closed the door to the old world and has not helped me break into the new world. So I'm sort of stuck in the middle." To make matters worse, because the training and attempted career change took time,

Sharon is now facing the obstacle that "people think something is wrong with me because I haven't worked in a long time." Sharon can't go back and she can't move forward. She is a Harvard graduate with decades of experience in finance at top firms, but now she is working at a nearly minimum-wage retail job just to survive.

Social Networks and the Strategic Straitjacket

As we have seen older unemployed jobseekers are trapped by obstacles in every direction, whether they pursue jobs similar to their former jobs, lower-down jobs in their field, or seek to switch fields. Making it even harder to escape this trap is that fact that today's jobseekers cannot effectively pursue two different escape paths, hoping that at least one will succeed. They must choose. This forced strategic choice is the result of social networking technologies.

Here is the conundrum: Jobseekers can only have one social networking profile. If that profile focuses on their prior field, they stand no chance of breaking into a new field. If it focuses on the newly targeted field, they stand no chance of getting back into their old field. As Recruiter Sherry explains:

> [A jobseeker's] resume and LinkedIn profile must be consistent. If these are different, that is a huge red flag. *It's the first thing we check.* So if now you're changing fields, your LinkedIn needs to reflect this. Even if you have 20 years of amazing experience in this other field and you are very proud of it, you need to let it go and emphasize experience in the new field, if any. That's a very tough switch to make.

Recruiter Brian emphasized that without a singular focus, it looks to recruiters as if the jobseeker doesn't know what he or she wants. If, for example, you have experience in both engineering and marketing and would be happy (and well-qualified) to work in either, "You do have to make it easy for recruiters and tell them what you want. If you want a marketing job, you need to focus really hard on marketing. One hundred percent. Don't try to find a job in either one, whichever one comes first."

The upshot is that unemployed jobseekers not only have a limited set of strategies—none of them particularly likely to succeed—but must choose just one of them. Keith's case is illustrative. He had been a restaurant chef but, hoping for more autonomy over his schedule, decided to try to become a self-employed "home-chef." He created a social networking profile with the top line saying "home chef;" his description of past jobs highlights relevant experiences. While being a home chef is Keith's top preference, given the difficulty of obtaining any position he is also open to restaurant chef positions. But now his social networking profile makes that unlikely:

> I am foreclosing going back to the restaurant business by declaring that I am a personal chef. There are jobs that I might apply for and am qualified for. So the LinkedIn profile does close off some doors. You can write a different resume depending on the job you apply for, [but] on LinkedIn it's the same resume to every person.

Keith cannot simultaneously have a profile in which his title is "home-chef" and make a compelling case that he is committed to working in a restaurant; like other unemployed jobseekers he finds himself in a strategic straitjacket.[14]

Degree from MIT and Unemployed: The Role of Age Bias

We have already seen the important role of age as an indirect obstacle for unemployed jobseekers. Older workers with more years of experience in a given field are more likely to be deemed over-qualified for all but the highest-level position that they have attained in that field, and under-qualified for any job that is not in their established field. But on top of these indirect effects, large studies reveal pervasive, straight-up age discrimination,[15] which helps explain why being over 50—regardless of education and skills—is the best predictor of getting trapped in long-term unemployment.[16]

To understand why employers discriminate based on age, I asked the recruiters I interviewed if they can explain the findings of these studies. Sherry was not at all surprised and was quite blunt: "Yes, on average, I would say that, sure, older workers are discriminated against." She was forthcoming about her own stereotypes and those of hiring managers: "An older person would probably not have energy and enough learning ability to compete with young people." Another recruiter, Tara, agrees with these stereotypes and explains that, for this reason, "You rarely see a job posting where an employer is looking for a candidate with 15 years of experience. Most job postings have a limited range of desired years of experience, typically no more than 5 to

8 years." She pauses, and then says with an uneasy tone, "If the applicant has more [years of experience than that], it's a problem."

When I asked *why* being more experienced is seen as a negative and not a positive, Tara offered the following reasoning: "Employers usually want someone who has growth potential, not someone who will be bored with it because they have been doing it for a while." She then adds that it's also "a revenue thing. Employers don't want to pay higher salaries. This is a key factor." Thinking of the jobseekers I had interviewed—the ones at the receiving end, so to speak, of this assumption—I asked if this barrier would be there even for a candidate who had graduated from MIT or Harvard and had worked at highly respected firms. Without hesitation, Tara responded: "Yes. You may have an MIT or Harvard advanced degree, but if you've been working 20 years—you're older and unemployed—that's very hard, that person would have a very hard time."

All the recruiters I interviewed discussed age discrimination in remarkably similar terms. Chad echoed Tara and Sherry and uses virtually the same words when telling me that regardless of education and credentials "people who are older have a harder time." Chad's explanation of why such workers have a "harder time" reveals the sheer variety of biases that employers harbor regarding older workers:

> The obvious things [employers] talk about are this person is expensive and this person is not as energetic or exciting. This person is at the sunset of their career. How long are they actually gonna work for us? We're gonna invest time in them and then they're gonna say they're gonna retire. This person may complain about traveling, they may complain about rigorous activities. This person may not want to do things with the rest of the organization because they have a different personal lifestyle. They don't fit into the corporate culture where we're young and running around and going to community events. Or everybody can go do a marathon together or something. There's a corporate fit issue. So they've got a lot of negative possibilities. It's a core bias.

The "core" bias against age, as Chad calls it, seems impervious to evidence that debunks it. For example, research has long showed that contrary to the typical concern of employers, older workers actually tend to stick around *longer* than younger workers and that age is not predictive of performance.[17]

Jobseekers tend to be aware of the effects of age discrimination if for no other reason than that they have personally experienced the stark contrast between applying for jobs as a 50-plus worker and applying for jobs when they were younger. Some have also seen age discrimination from the hiring side of the table. Jose believes age is "the prime, number-one issue" because "I know myself, as a hiring manager, and even my wife, she was hiring a nurse and she said, "You know, that one was a little too old.'" Ryan likewise says that he knows "for sure" that age is a key barrier because "that's what we *do* when we hire people! We ask, how old is this person?"

Older jobseekers know they are being discriminated against but don't know what to do about it. Consider, for example, the first concern which Chad describes as "obvious" that older workers are more "expensive." Anthony, a sales engineer, imagines employers look at his resume and thinking, "We're dealing with a 50-plus guy. He's going to cost us too much money to come in because he's too experienced." How does one get out of that trap? Recruiter Chad suggests a solution:

> [Jobseekers] almost have to be direct about the being expensive issue. You almost have to take that concern away and say, "I know that you've got a budget for this opportunity. I wouldn't be sitting here in front of you or asking about this job if I didn't think I was in your budget." Period. You need to make it clear to them that you're within budget.

Only one problem. Such jobseekers don't usually have any chance to explain anything to anybody. They are not typically sat in front of anybody except their application-swallowing computers and hence there is usually no chance to be "direct," as Chad advises, to address this bias. As we saw in the prior discussion of over-qualification, in most cases older jobseekers are excluded in the pre-interview initial screen due to being perceived as expensive *even if* they would be willing to accept a lower salary.

The same problem keeps older jobseekers from addressing employers' skepticism about their competence and energy. As Tom, an electrical engineer in his late 50s, puts it: "I'm so much better than I was 20 years ago. I'm older but I'm so much better." But he doubts employers will look past his age. "There is a bias in how employers evaluate abilities and stamina." Carol feels the same way: "I'm not sure how to convince people that I'm still with it, I still have energy." Recruiter Chad's advice to jobseekers for overcoming "the assumption that somebody is in the sunset of their career" is to "show enthusiasm and energy." But yet again, following this advice is impossible when one is not invited to interviews.[18]

Some jobseekers try to escape the trap by attempting to hide or obfuscate their age. They may hope to get away with not putting a college graduation date on their resume and only list their most recent 15 years of work experience. But such strategies are often impossible to implement and can backfire. Many online applications make one's age unconcealable. Bruce explains that for many online job applications, "in the education line it asks you what year you graduated. And you can't proceed with the online application until you fill that in." Moreover, recruiters express frustration—sometimes even moral outrage—at any perceived attempt to hide one's age. Here is how recruiter Erica responds to this jobseeker strategy:

> If someone who is older is trying to hide their age, the reality is, if they're putting all their experience down, they're not hiding their age. Good recruiters are not stupid. There are some candidates that don't put all their experience down. They put a bunch of stuff and maybe it dates back to, let's say 2002, and then there's nothing. But their job in 2002 was director of finance. Well, if you were a director of finance in 2002, then you were an accountant in 1992. I'm not an idiot! You're not fooling anybody!

What if a jobseeker tries to deal with this problem by changing their title from "director" to a more middle-level position? Recruiter Claire responds this way: "I've seen people do this. But then when we do a background check and we realize they were not truthful, not fully open, it's a problem. You can't do it. I know it's a catch-22. Jobseekers are caught in a hard place, but you can't change titles on resumes."

Another catch-22 involves posting your picture on your social networking profiles. Because jobseekers know that recruiters use social networking sites to find and vet candidates, and know the power of images, they are understandably nervous about posting their pictures. As Marie put it, the picture "definitely opens the door for possible discrimination." Jerry is a 48-year-old tech worker and explains his concern this way:

> I'd say my age and my photograph on LinkedIn could definitely be a factor. . . . In this industry, I mean, why would you hire somebody in their 40s when you could hire somebody in their 20s? You can get a lot more mileage out of the younger person.

Studies show that these concerns are well grounded given the significant attention recruiters pay to images, and the effects of candidate images in hiring decisions.[19] Yet there are powerful pressures on jobseekers to post a picture anyway. Jobseekers fear that if they do not post their picture they will be perceived as trying to hide something.[20] Alex explains: "It's one of these things, I think you have to do it just because it's expected now. If you don't have a picture out there, it may hurt you, because someone may say 'Well, what is this person trying to hide?'" Patricia concurs: "If you put [a picture], it could go against you, but if you do not have it, what are you trying to hide? I feel between a rock and hard place. I don't look like I am in my 20s. . . . You are damned if you do and damned if you don't."

Jobseekers' perceptions of how recruiters may interpret the absence of a picture square with recruiter Chad's frustration with jobseekers who do not post a profile picture:

> For God sakes, get a picture up there! With a big smile. People want to see you. And it breathes life into a humdrum, two-dimensional profile. With the older generation, I understand that they're concerned about the bias creeping in. But here's the thing: . . . No picture says, "Don't call me. I'm not looking for a job. Don't bother me." . . . By not putting the picture, by not putting all your information, you're almost acting coy and not trustworthy. You're not presenting the whole story. The reality is you're 51, okay? You need to sell that as an advantage and not hide it and not try to trick somebody. So when I don't see a picture, it's much worse than seeing a picture of somebody who looks older.

Older jobseekers are indeed stuck. Posting their picture will likely trigger a biased response, but not posting their pictures leads recruiters to perceive them having something to hide or being untrustworthy.

Escaping the Trap?

Older long-term unemployed workers, regardless of their educational background, skill level, or experience, face a daunting set of obstacles. Even the most credentialed professionals, and even those possessing degrees from the most prestigious universities in the world, can discover that their ability to find a new job may be blocked by unforgiving employer stigmas and biases.[21]

When jobseekers cannot find a job similar to the one they lost because of the stigma of unemployment and age discrimination, when they cannot take a lower-level job because they are deemed over-qualified, when they cannot change careers because they are deemed too old to hire with no experience, what is the way out? When I put this question to recruiters, the answer was unanimous: *networking*. Erica, for example, stated bluntly that workers with an unemployment gap "cannot compete" and that networking is the only solution:

> People who cannot compete based on their resumes have to spend more effort and rely more on referrals, connections. . . . One way to go about it is networking. That doesn't mean they need to be very close friends with the people who help them. Like a friend of a friend of a friend, who may know something about their background, may be able to help bring them somewhere and talk some hiring manager into creating a position.

Tara, anther recruiter, agrees that mobilizing one's network is a jobseeker's "best chance" of overcoming the obstacles of being unemployed and older:

> Your best chance of getting into the organization is, do you know someone who works there currently? . . . Someone in that company handing your resume to a hiring manager has a much better chance of getting an interview than somebody who sends their resume to that big, dark hole. Networking and knowing people inside is a big factor.

In Chapter 3, we'll see what actually happens when unemployed jobseekers take this advice.

3

Networking and Feeling Like Beggars and Used-Car Salesmen

Tainted by the stigma of unemployment, subject to age discrimination, and trapped by being seen as over-qualified and under-qualified at the same time, unemployed jobseekers hear three words of advice over and over: network, network, network.

All that word means is to ask others for help in finding a job. As Paul puts it: "Networking means interacting with as many people as possible and letting them know that you're looking for a job."[1] This includes reaching out to former colleagues, alumni of any schools you went to, and friends and neighbors; it also means meeting new people—sometimes at networking events and conferences, but typically by asking the people you already know if there's anyone *they* know.[2]

Older networking studies emphasized the value of finding out about job openings.[3] But that's not really the issue in the current era. Jobseekers report little difficulty learning what's out there from job boards and company websites. What network ties are best for now is getting a referral that can help you stand out from the pile of other applicants.[4] This is especially true for older unemployed jobseekers who hope that a referral will counteract the stigma of an employment gap. Jobseeker Doug puts it this way: "The length of unemployment, the question of 'What's wrong with this person'—I can't overcome that." The most likely way to move past this barrier, he explains, is finding a way to "get people to overlook that [gap] by connecting with my contacts, meeting new contacts, and reminding contacts of my value." Karen likewise emphasizes the importance of network contacts for someone who, like her, is experiencing long-term unemployment: "I recognize I've been out so long that my chances of getting even an interview where I don't have either a push or a recommendation or something from somebody who knows somebody at the employer are very low."[5]

A referral from a network contact may indeed be the most promising approach to avoid being screened out due to the employer stigmas. As we heard from recruiters in Chapter 2, applications with lengthy unemployment gaps are not likely to receive close consideration, but a referral from a network contact does increase the odds that an employer will at the very least take a closer look at the application. But even if networking is sound strategy, the recruiters' glib advice to jobseekers to simply go out there and network overlooks the fact that for unemployed jobseekers, networking can be an excruciating process, not least because it requires contending with the same pernicious force that pervades the accounts in this book: stigma.

The stigma of unemployment is not only in the minds of employers. In American society, it's everywhere—including among the people you are trying to network with. This leads to a set of typical networking experiences that ultimately challenge jobseekers' identities not only as valued professionals but also as self-sufficient adults and moral beings. In short, networking is bruising and often stirs up emotional turmoil—sometimes enough to make the jobseeker quit seeking.

Networking Is Not Only Hard for Introverts

Networking for unemployed jobseekers is inherently difficult, due to stigma and other factors that are essentially built into being long-term unemployed. Yet this is not how many jobseekers see it. In interviews, I often heard jobseekers attribute their networking difficulties to an introverted personality or other character traits they considered to be shortcomings. Here, for example, is how Richard, a 53-year-old software developer, explains his difficulties: "I'm an internal person. . . . I'm not the person out there schmoozing and all those things. Unfortunately, what's going to kill me is that inability." Tom likewise feels that his personality "type" is his greatest obstacle: "Going out and meeting that person cold is really difficult for me. . . . It's Mount Everest to me, it's my biggest barrier. *I'm just not the type that goes out.*"

Introversion certainly doesn't help, but networking was difficult for *all* the jobseekers I interviewed, whatever their personalities. This is most clear in interviews with jobseekers who see themselves as highly social and extroverted, but still find networking difficult as someone who is unemployed. In fact, the commonalities of networking experiences across all kinds of personalities are striking. Consider Jeff, who drives an Uber for financial survival while looking for a professional job:

One of the interesting things about my Uber experience is how much I enjoy the social interaction that takes place. Within the confines of my car, in anything from a five-minute to one-hour ride, I can't tell you how many enjoyable, interesting conversations I've had with my passengers. But that's a completely different type of social interaction than networking *with the specific goal of job seeking in mind*. And in that circumstance, I feel less comfortable. I'm not sure why that is, but I do.

When I ask Jeff to think about the difference, he reflects: "Maybe the root of that is just because of *my own reservations* about myself as a potential employee." Jeff's observation is revealing. He is not introverted. He likes interacting. But networking is a very specific form of interaction—one that is particularly vulnerable and loaded when one is unemployed because it involves reaching out to connect while being perceived by others—as well as perceiving oneself—through the tainted lens of the unemployment stigma.

One way to see that networking when unemployed is a uniquely challenging experience is to compare it to networking when one is employed. Steven reflected on what networking was like when he had a powerful job as a school principal with what it's like now as a precarious jobseeker:

> It's night and day. . . . When you're in a position of power, you can go there and shake hands and kiss babies all you want. And when you're in a position of non-power, it feels *fake*. It feels *transparent*. It's hard. It's really hard.

For Jeff and Steven and very many others, the challenge is not a personality that makes social interactions—or even networking in particular—difficult. Rather, it is the specific action of networking when unemployed that, over time, bruises even the most confident schmoozer.

MIT Alumni Help MIT Alumni Unless They Are Unemployed

The key factor shaping my interviewees' networking experiences and making them so universally difficult was also the key factor in their interactions with recruiters: stigma.

Sharon, who has been looking for work in finance for over 2 years, observes that while we typically think of stigma and bias as an issue affecting employers, it in fact "permeate[s] life." The ubiquity of this stigma is what makes long-term unemployment—including networking—so challenging. As Sharon puts it:

> We say employers have this bias. But at the end of the day, you're not dealing with the company or the organization. You're dealing with those people and those people just don't work at these companies, those people permeate life. It could be your neighbor, it could be the person that you buy coffee from. They could be your networking contacts. They could be your hairdresser, it's everybody.

To explore how the stigma of unemployment may inform the thoughts and actions of potential network contacts and to gain insights into what unemployed jobseekers experience when networking, I interviewed 15 alumni of the prestigious MIT Sloan School of Management, all of them with MBAs. I picked alumni of MIT Sloan because, from my experience working there, I knew that networking among alumni is routine and encouraged. A common slogan I had heard was "Sloanies help Sloanies." This culture is fostered by MIT Sloan, which, like other elite institutions, strongly encourages its graduates to make use of their alumni network for mutual support.

I began my conversations with the alumni by asking how, in general, they would respond to a fellow MIT Sloan alumnus with an MBA contacting them to network. I then explored how this response may or may not change if the alumnus had been unemployed for a year. This is, in fact, a very realistic scenario, as the alumni all reported that being reached out to by fellow alumni for networking purposes is a regular part of their professional life.

As expected, the MIT Sloan alumni uniformly expressed a strong desire to help a hypothetical fellow "Sloanie" who contacted them. Most took the slogan "Sloanies help Sloanies" quite seriously. Matt explained that he would be "happy" to help, simply because "it resonates when they are from MIT Sloan." Erica shared a similar sentiment: "I have an inclination toward helping a Sloanie in principle because they are a Sloanie."

Why do Sloanies help Sloanies? A common reason was a sense of comradery or loyalty. As Rick elaborated: "First and foremost, my own mentality is essentially one to help out the network as much as possible because I feel loyalty to the brand, to help out the brand." Other alumni discussed wanting to help because at different stages of their career they had received this kind of help and now they want to reciprocate. Sheila says: "I feel like I've previously gotten such great support. . . . The network has been very helpful for me, so I feel like I owe the network, or I should give back in some way."

But the strong inclination to help a fellow alumnus all but vanished when I added one detail to the hypothetical scenario. It was still an MIT Sloan MBA alumnus, with experience working at prestigious firms, but one who has been unemployed for the past year. As I uttered the word "unemployed," I could see the previously expressed enthusiasm instantly freeze into a wall of skepticism. The words and expressions used to describe this skepticism were strikingly similar to the way HR recruiters spoke about unemployed jobseekers. All the halo that comes from having graduated from such an elite institution, and all the camaraderie and desire to help a fellow "Sloanie," were unmistakably outweighed by the fact of unemployment. Matt, who had said he would be "happy" to help, expressed his skepticism this way: "If they're a Sloanie and they happen to have been out of work for a year, I don't know. My cynicism says that very few people who are really good get laid off—which is probably a bias that's unfair, but it's a bias I have." Matt is aware that his reaction is based on a "bias," suggesting that he is also aware that it may not be accurate, yet he sticks to it. He continues by explaining that he can't help but wonder, "Why are you in the situation that you're in?" Likewise, Erica, who had said she's inclined to help a Sloanie because they are a Sloanie, also changed her tune: "There is a little negativity there, just a connotation or something. It's unfortunate, but you wonder if there is something going on." Like Matt, Erica is a bit apologetic, noting that her response is "unfortunate," perhaps suggesting that her reactions may be unjustified, but then she likewise doubles down: "They'd have to have a pretty convincing reason for *why* they've got such a hole in their resume." In both Matt's and Erica's reactions we see the tendency to assume that unemployment reflects negative individual attributes. Any thought that the unemployment may be the result of larger economic forces or the result of a vicious cycle of stigma begetting more stigma is drowned out by this individualizing narrative. It is also noteworthy how Matt and Erica's reactions perfectly mirror those of recruiters in Chapter 2 who discussed the perception that "people who are out of work or laid off are not the top performers."

Some alumni's answers made clear their awareness that it is possible that the unemployment is the result of circumstances and not individual characteristics, but they emphasized that while *they* might be personally understanding, *others* will be skeptical. This means they would need to "defend" their actions and would therefore hesitate to help. This line of reasoning is identical to that of the recruiters in Chapter 2 who told me that even if they were understanding about the unemployment gap, they would hesitate to move a candidate forward because of questions they will be asked by the hiring manager. Here is my back-and-forth with Sara on this issue:

Sara: I would want to understand what the circumstances are and feel comfortable about the unemployment before I referred them, because I would most likely be asked that question and I would need to be able to defend my referral. I don't know what reason they would give me. Do you have some ideas?"

OS: Yes. They were laid off and it's a tough job market. They've been applying and it hasn't worked yet.

Sara: Yes, I think that would be a tough answer because it's actually a pretty good job market right now. So that would actually raise a flag for me in this kind of environment. If it was 5 or 6 years ago, then I think I would be open to that reasoning. But in this current climate, that would not fly.

At the time of the interview, the overall unemployment rate—the rate most often discussed in the media—was back to relatively low pre–Great-Recession levels. This is likely why Sara felt that it was a "pretty good" market. What was not clear to Sara was that the rate of long-term unemployment, particularly for mid-career and older workers, was at historically high levels. The obstacles facing older unemployed jobseekers were invisible to Sara, just as they had been to recruiters who, in both cases, noted that the topline unemployment rate was not particularly high and then used this fact to justify stigmatizing long-term unemployed jobseekers.

The Experience of Networking When Unemployed

A central challenge that unemployed jobseekers face in networking is enduring responses from others that convey stigma. Sharon refers to this kind of experience as "people being rude." She tells this story:

I had one gentleman who was sitting there and, literally, I felt like I was on trial the way he was interrogating me. He was just firing off one-off questions rapid-fire. I asked, "What is it you're trying to figure out?" He flat-out said, "Well, there's something that doesn't add up, so I'm trying to figure out what's wrong with you. . . . I'm just trying to get to the bottom of this because there's just something about you that just isn't right."

As a result of Sharon's experience of being interrogated and told that something is "wrong" with her, Sharon now enters every networking interaction braced for the possibility of a stigmatizing response and struggles to avoid coming across as defensive. She explains: "I'm also running through this list of 'What is going to be your reaction?' and I need to be *on guard* in case you're mean to me or in case you say something nasty or offensive or condescending or whatever." She recognizes that this defensive stance can undermine her ability to develop rapport and makes her seem anxious and inauthentic:

> I think this is something people pick up on. If you don't know what's going through my head, you can imagine how that reads, like "This person is unsure of themselves. This person is not authentic. This person is a little anxious. What's the problem? What are they hiding?"

While she knows that her guardedness may undermine her effectiveness, Sharon nonetheless remains vigilantly on the lookout for stigmatizing interactions because, as she says, "I need to move on before you start with the condescending remarks because, at this point, I can't handle it."[6]

Stigmatizing responses can arise during networking interactions regardless of whether the jobseeker is reaching out to a familiar former colleague or to a new person. Typically, the first step in networking is to reach out to former colleagues. These are perceived as the most promising contacts since they likely feel some sense of connection with the jobseeker and have direct knowledge of the jobseekers' skills. Steven explains the clear advantage of networking with former colleagues, as compared to new people:

> With the new person, I feel like they really don't know. I could say what I want about what I can do. But they have no way of knowing. Anybody can say what they can do. So with people who I don't know, they see this guy who can't get a job, who is saying all this stuff he can do but he really probably can't. With people that I know, I know they know what I can do.

Studies show that jobseekers' perceptions are accurate and that the network contacts that most likely lead to jobs are indeed former colleagues.[7]

Reaching out to former colleagues is relatively easy at first but becomes more difficult over time. As the period of unemployment lengthens, unemployed jobseekers need to repeatedly turn to the same finite pool of ex-colleagues for referrals or introductions. At a certain point, after some repeated attempts, it gets awkward. Joseph is a 60-year-old product manager in the tech industry. He explains: "It's sometimes embarrassing to keep asking the same friends to help me submit my resume over and over again. . . . After a while, at a certain point, you feel like maybe they're giving up on you. But anyway, that *could* be just my feeling." Joseph is not sure whether his former colleagues have in fact "given up on him," making it pointless to keep trying, or whether in his prior efforts they simply were not in a position to provide a referral. Kim, too, has a hard time deciding whether to continue reaching out:

> People are just busy. They just don't have time to devote to your problems. I feel like, for me, sometimes I don't know how far to push things. Should I follow up or should I not? Are these people not returning my calls because they are busy or because they don't want to help me? I don't know what to do, what my next move should be.

The ambiguity that both Kim and Joseph describe often results in jobseekers continuing to reach out until it becomes clear that no help is forthcoming. For this reason, networking with ex-colleagues often ends with painful bruises. Relationships, sometime built over many years, lead to *expectations* of support and thus also to vulnerability to feeling hurt. Tim explained:

> The people I worked with, they haven't helped me out at all. That's been a real disappointment, that people I worked with for 11 and a half years haven't been able to help me out. That's been one of the biggest disappointments for me. It's like, "Wow! Just nothing. Those are the people I was working with?" Really, *really hurts* you inside.

Jobseekers who expected support from ex-colleagues—particularly after working together for more than a decade—are often disappointed this way. The vulnerability to feeling hurt is even stronger if the prior work relationship was close. In such cases, a lack of responsiveness can feel like betrayal. This was the case for Steven after he reached out for support from a person he had closely mentored for many years:

The toughest thing I had to deal with in all the networking was reaching out to a former colleague whom I had hired and mentored and she has not really lifted a finger. *That kills.* We were close. She knew what a difficult place I was in and could have done something about it and she hasn't. . . . It was really painful. Unbelievable betrayal. Just the worst. Just the worst.

Such disappointment—or even betrayals—along with growing self-doubts make continuing to reach out to ex-colleagues emotionally loaded. Susan has been unemployed for a year. When she thinks of contacting a past colleague, she imagines them thinking, "She's *still* unemployed? What's wrong with her?" I just get the sense that people think we're damaged goods and that there's something wrong with us. "How come they're still unemployed?"

The experience of networking with former colleagues can often be tinged with a sting of humiliation because of the contrast between one's former position and one's current unemployed status. Remember how Steven explained the key advantages of reaching out to former colleagues who know his skills firsthand? Here's what he said next—after a pause and a deep breath: "But it evokes shame. A lot of people that I have known for a long time know me as boss or at least as a peer. And now I'm saying, 'Help me out. I'll take anything.'" For Steven, the very act of networking with former colleagues feels like a declaration of having professionally fallen: "Networking is brutal. You're going out there, you're shaking hands and everybody that I network with is used to seeing me in a very respected position. And now, in order to network, I feel like I am walking out and saying, 'Hi, good to see you,' and nobody wants me anymore." Underlying Steven's shame is the same unspoken assumption made by recruiters in the prior chapter and by MIT Sloan alumni earlier in this chapter: You're unemployed for a *reason*—lack of merit.

Feelings of shame and embarrassment mean that, over time, unemployed jobseekers become less likely to seek help from former colleagues. Sam, for example, is a 62-year-old unemployed pharmacist. After 2 years of unemployment and much financial pressure, he reluctantly began collecting Social Security benefits. Recently, he attended a professional event that provided him with a golden opportunity to reconnect with about 50 professional colleagues and seek referrals. But at the moment of truth, he could not do it:

I'm chatting with them and when I was asked what I'm currently doing, I'm like, "Yes, I've decided to retire basically." And some of these guys began saying, "Congratulations, Sam! I'm happy for you." They were all thrilled and I'm mentally thinking to myself, "Yes, I started to collect retirement, but I wouldn't mind working part-time or something like that." But I didn't want to press it at this point. I didn't want to sound too desperate.

With all his colleagues gathered, Sam turned down the opportunity to ask for help in finding a new job and instead characterized himself as voluntarily retired. By shifting his identity from unemployed to retired, Sam was able maintain his image as a successful person but at the cost of undermining any possibility of receiving much-needed help.[8]

Again, we see the workings of the stigma trap. Receiving a referral from a colleague may be the single most likely way to get hired, but the stigma of unemployment makes obtaining such a referral less and less likely—regardless of how much it is merited. While the experiences described above range from confusion about the lack of responsiveness to intense feelings of betrayal or shame, the overall effect is to erode the jobseekers' sense of self as respected and valued professionals in their fields, making networking with former colleagues more and more difficult.

Networking with New People and Developing a Connection

Given the finite pool of ex-colleagues and the growing difficulties of reaching out to them, most unemployed jobseekers eventually begin networking with new people.[9] In seeking new ties, jobseekers act on the assumption that a referral does not *require* a prior working relationship but can result from even a single positive interaction. Joseph explains how he imagines this works: "The person who refers you may not know you very well, but they just say, 'Hey, I just met this person at such-and-such event and they seemed to have some of the qualifications we're looking for. Why doesn't So-and-So take a look at it a little more deeply?'" Given recruiters' typical filtering practices, as described in Chapter 2, where long-term unemployed jobseekers stand little chance, Joseph's strategic reasoning appears sound. Even if the person making the referral knows nothing about the jobseeker, the referral may at least remove the application from the large pile of cold applications that will most likely be rapidly sorted using biased proxies for merit such as duration of unemployment. Richard had a personal experience that reinforced his sense that "a bare connection is much better than no connection at all." He recalls how earlier in his career he had reached out to someone "I had met years before, just once in passing," and this "bare" connection provided a referral that "got me a job." Richard's takeaway from this experience is that, regardless of the strength of the connection, "knowing somebody who knows the head of the group that's hiring will get my resume looked at and give me a much higher chance of being considered for the job." This form of networking is plausible because all that is ultimately asked for by the jobseeker is to have their resume directly passed on to a hiring manager to bypass the typical filtering, and this passing on of resumes need not include any form of endorsement or active recommendation.[10]

In seeking to create connections with new people, unemployed jobseekers face some built-in obstacles. Foremost, they are by definition excluded from the site where most professional interactions occur, and crucially the site where one can display professional skills in an organic and spontaneous manner—the workplace.[11] To meet new contacts, jobseekers typically seek introductions from people they know, reach out to college alumni, or attend professional conferences or association networking meetings and simply strike up conversations.

When reaching out, jobseekers use different strategies to create a connection. Some begin by trying to find things in common with networking targets. As Joseph explains:

> I've been working very hard at just breaking the ice with new people and focusing on finding something in common. It could be just about anything. I think you can strike up a conversation just talking about the weather or, you know, the fact that spring has now arrived and it's just a happy time of year—whatever. Then you can start getting into the subject matter a little more, about the event itself, and from there, just segue your way into making further connections.

To develop a connection, jobseekers also often attempt to keep the conversation focused on the other person. Kimberly, who is in her mid-50s and most recently worked in business management, explains: "I've learned that when you meet with people, it's all about them. It's not about you, how great you are, or what you can do." Kimberly recently had coffee with the president of a small company for an informal conversation: "I just let him talk and, honestly, he talked about himself the whole entire time. He just kept going. So I left and thought, 'He doesn't know one thing about me, really.'"

Nevertheless, Kimberly ended up getting some contract work[12] at this company. She believes her approach worked because

> we're all so egocentric. At the start of my job search, I thought I needed to communicate how great I am and these are all the good things I did, but my experience has taught me that people love to talk about themselves.

In addition to feeding their egos, keeping the conversation focused on the other person has other benefits. Charles, who worked in fundraising and is in his early 50s, struggles with a lack of self-confidence. He finds it helpful to remind himself "that in connecting with people, it seems like a lot of people like to be asked questions about themselves. It's this exercise in *applied flattery* in some ways." In formulating his questions for others, Charles asks himself, "What do they want to tell me? What do I think they want me to know about them?" Aside from having the other person feel good because they are flattered by being asked questions, this strategy is also helpful in uncovering potential commonalities: "The more that you ask them stuff and get things that you can relate to, the more you can connect yourself and find common ground." Another perk of keeping the focus on the networking target is that it helps deflect attention from the jobseeker's own stigmatized unemployed status. Instead of talking about their professional qualifications, about which they may not feel very confident, most are happy to keep the focus on the other person.[13]

Another common jobseeker strategy for building connection is to try to meet in person. Paul explains: "I think I can make a much stronger relationship meeting people face-to-face than just emailing them or talking to them on the phone." Julie also works hard to set up in-person meetings because "if I sit down with someone and have coffee, it's a lot easier to talk about the weather. . . . *And then everything else sort of flows out of that naturally.*"[14]

Is networking for a job starting to sound a lot like dating? Karen explicitly uses dating strategies in her networking:

> There's a book I read as a teenager, *How to Get a Teenage Boy and What to Do with Him Once You Get Him*, which is really about how to go up to a total stranger and have a conversation. And everything I learned in that book I apply every time I do networking. When you come up to someone and you have to start a conversation, say something that cannot be answered with yes or no. Or use a conversation starter. You say, "You look like . . ."—Fill in

the blank. You look like you've been here before. It's such a great icebreaker that starts a conversation. Also, putting yourself in the entry door. Because people coming in are full of energy, they're full of anticipation. They want to network.

Whatever the individual jobseeker's specific strategy to create connection, there is usually an implicit assumption that a social bond will motivate professional support. Sandra is clear on how she expects this process to work:

> Recently, after I had coffee dates, two different people said to me, "You're very likable!" [She laughs.] Honestly, I think that's how this is all going to work out. Somebody will like me and they'll go, "Oh, shouldn't So-and-So know about this person? Doesn't So-and-So have something?" Whatever.

Kimberly, quoted earlier about how she works to keep the conversation focused on the other person, is even more explicit about strategically cultivating a social connection to obtain a referral:

> My motivation inside was always to either find a job or make a connection. I would never come across that way, but inside, of course, that's what I'm doing when you make it about them and you ask them questions.

Whether they like it or not—and most jobseekers do not like it—the strategic cultivation of a social connection is perceived as a necessary part of networking. The MIT Sloan alumni whom I asked about how they would react to jobseekers seeking referrals made it clear that *how* a jobseeker approaches them matters; there was a uniform dislike of being directly asked for a referral or of any approach that seemed overly transactional. Instead, the alumni wished to be made to feel that the jobseeker wants to connect with them. For example, Matt explains that if someone approaches and just asks to be connected to a hiring manager, "that's very transactional, that's not really interesting to me." What Matt preferred was a more personalized approach:

> If you're reaching out, "Hey Matt, I'd love to connect and talk about what you guys are doing and just connect, right? Just spend time talking." Then I'm like, that's interesting. . . . It's like dating, I guess. . . . I don't want to be the guy sitting at the other side of the table because I was the one who took your call. *I need to feel like you want to be there.*

Matt's sentiment was widely shared among the MIT Sloan alumni. In fact, a number of them used the identical words to describe the kind of approach that won't work with them as "too transactional."[15] Paola, for example, told me that it feels "too transactional" if someone just asks, "Could you refer me?" She is more open when someone reaches out with, " 'I just want to learn how you got to where you are.' . . . So it's more of a conversation." She wants to feel that the person reaching out "has thought about this." Echoing the jobseekers' sense that, when networking, it is best to keep the focus on the other person, Carl openly admits that he is most likely to respond to a networking request email that starts with something about himself: "People like to hear about themselves. When someone mentioned something about my military experience, it made me want to put in additional effort. I don't want to sound like I'm egocentric or something, but I think people in general like to hear about themselves."

The strategic cultivation of a social connection may be necessary to increase one's chance of success, but it also exacts a significant personal cost.[16] Ultimately, it leads to two typical and distinctly difficult experiences associated with networking among the unemployed, captured by two metaphors: being a beggar and being a used-car salesman. We'll see next that both are deeply unsettling to a jobseeker's identity.

Feeling Like a Beggar

The networking strategies to establishing a connection—in particular, the comparisons to dating—may suggest an experience of playful social engagement. This is not the case. The core experience of both unemployment and networking is a series of rejections. We must not imagine exciting social adventures but instead how we might feel approaching others after hundreds of rebuffs.

Susan reports that networking "puts a pit in my stomach" due to fears of rejection: "I just can't help but wonder, what is this person going to think of me?" Charles's hesitation about continuing to network is rooted in his self-devaluating questions: "What interest might there be in me? What can I offer this person?" He explains that underlying these questions is the deeper question of "what kind of self-worth and self-esteem do I have?" He links his low self-esteem to his unemployment status which, in his words, generates "a sense of risk of being *exposed* in the [networking] interaction at any moment by the question of 'What do you do?' Then, it's 'Uh oh!' It's a challenge. No matter how much I practice it, it's a challenge."

A common experience described by jobseekers is feeling like a "beggar." This arises most frequently when jobseekers describe networking while feeling bereft of any value to offer, which makes the act of seeking support akin to seeking a handout. Karen describes how "there are times when I'm feeling very down about things, due to not seeing a lot of success." At those times, "networking is very hard to do" and feels like "standing there with a cup looking for a handout. You know?" Steven used the same metaphor of holding a "cup":

> The only way I'm likely to get a job is through personal connections. I have attended professional organizational meetings and functions, but *I feel almost like a beggar with my hat in my hand*. Having been very independent, having been self-sufficient, having been the coordinator, it's tough to say "Put a tin cup in your hand." I don't like the phrase and I don't do it that way. But internally, in my gut, I feel like I'm asking for something and I'm going to be perceived as not meriting it.

The experience of being a beggar is related to feeling needy and dependent. For Karen, the most frustrating aspect of networking is that, as a result of financial pressures, she feels she has "no choice but to reach out to people, to ask for help, which is not something I love to do. I would rather be able to do things myself. . . . I would prefer not to have to ask for so much help." As she speaks, Karen pauses and reflects with some irony and surprise at herself:

> I would happily help someone else. So it's not necessarily logical for me to not enjoy that part of it, but I don't enjoy that part of it. . . . It's putting yourself out there again and again. That's the hard part. But if you don't, then the financial pressures continue, so you kinda have no choice.

This asymmetry—happy to help others but unhappy at needing others' help—is not at all surprising if we remember that, in the United States, economic self-sufficiency is seen as a prerequisite for adulthood.[17] Thus, for long-term unemployed jobseekers, the experience of networking severely challenges their identities as self-sufficient adults. This is a challenge that we will revisit in Chapter 4.

Feeling Like a Used-Car Salesman

Networking is difficult not only because it challenges our desire to present ourselves as successful and self-sufficient, but also because it requires multiple layers of strategic masking. Among the things that may need to be masked in any given interaction are one's ongoing emotional turmoil, one's lack of confidence (including feeling like a beggar), one's motivations for interacting in the first place, the duration or in some cases the fact of one's unemployment, and one's financial desperation. These multiple masks often generate feelings of inauthenticity, which then itself must also be masked—and all along one is fearing that a mask will slip and one will be exposed and stigmatized.

Sandra made a comparison that I heard several times: "I sometimes feel like a used-car salesman." The beggar is desperate but transparent. Used-car salespersons, by contrast, are manipulative. They pretend to have a great product but in fact are hiding their internal doubts. Sandra is not feeling great about herself because, as she put it, "it's hard to lose a job without internalizing negativity. It's hard not to think, 'Maybe there's a damn good reason why I don't have a job now.'" Yet, while feeling negative about herself, she needs to act in a way that will lead her networking target to form a positive judgment. She compares her situation to that of the main character in the movie *The Music Man*: "The main character is a salesman and he's actually selling flim-flam and I feel a little like that. 'Is there substance behind that flam?'"

Masking Doubts, Anxiety, and Desperation

A key challenge of networking for the long-term unemployed is the need to project confidence at a time when one is feeling exactly the opposite. Jobseekers who feel like beggars must nonetheless outwardly project professional self-assurance. As Richard puts it, "It behooves you not to expose all of your doubts and fears to people."

The jobseeker's dilemma is that, on the one hand, for networking to succeed jobseekers believe they cannot reveal feelings of anxiety and must project confidence, but on the other hand, the very act of hiding their actual feelings can also undermine the success of their networking by coming across as inauthentic. Some unemployed jobseekers believe they are successful at masking. Kimberly, for example, claims that "I have a lot of anxiety but I guess I am pretty good at faking it. I consider myself sort of an actor at times." But many others, like Sharon, are anxious that their acting is not effective. Sharon explains the kinds of thoughts that run through her mind as she tries to fake her way through an interaction:

> There's only so much you can reveal about how the situation makes you feel and what's going through your head with people who are outside or not aware of long-term unemployment. You have to put on that happy face and you have to be confident. But inside, you're not always confident. You're not always happy. You have to pick and choose your words carefully, how you answer these questions. For people who aren't aware of this whole complex dialogue that's going through my head, it could read like, "What is she hiding?"

It is a difficult challenge for anyone, in any life situation, to navigate having one set of thoughts and feelings on the inside and yet needing to project a completely different set of thoughts on the outside. But long-term unemployment makes it even harder because those internal thoughts and feelings are not just a momentary emotional state but the product of a long series of rejections. Here is how Steven describes trying to communicate something very different from what he is actually feeling:

> You're trying to present the fact that you are one confident, capable human being. And inside, because of what you've been dealing with for so long, you feel the exact opposite. You feel like you must not have the capability because nobody wants to hire you. You must not be good. . . . I'm feeling all that because I'm unemployed and . . . processing it constantly, "Why is this? Why is this? Why is this?" And you go into a situation where you've gone from this [self-questioning] to a situation where you're dealing with somebody you're trying to impress and you're talking to somebody about what a great professional you are.

A part of the stigma trap is that the very act of trying to escape it—by covering one's negative feelings—can result in being perceived as fake, awkward, or inauthentic and result in the trap door being shut even tighter.[18]

Jobseekers must mask not only their self-doubt, but often their feelings of desperation. All the jobseekers in this study reported believing that if they ever revealed their actual level of desperation, it would destroy any chance they had of making an effective connection. As Gail put it: "If it looks like you're desperate, people are going to avoid you. . . . If I was coming across as a person who needed a job and felt kind of desperate, I think a lot of people would be scared of that and would go in the other direction."

As with so many other aspects of networking, the widely shared understanding that one must not appear desperate evokes comparisons to dating. Here is how Sandra discusses the issue of showing desperation for a job: "Sometimes in networking, I'm too aware that I'm really pretty desperate for a job." She pauses and reflects:

> It's amazing how similar this is to dating. If you're in a situation when you're dating—I remember this—I was always much more successful when I really didn't care! That always seemed much more successful than when, "Oh, I'm so lonely . . ." What doesn't work [in job seeking] doesn't work for the same reasons.

The need to hide one's desperation presents both a problem of self-presentation and a strategic dilemma: How assertive should one be in networking? Some level of assertiveness in approaching others and asking for referrals is surely necessary for mobilizing support, but if one over-reaches and is perceived as too assertive, it may backfire. For example, Sharon shares her belief that to succeed in networking she must be assertive, but "when you're being assertive, somehow that air of desperation comes out." She pauses and then says in an exasperated tone, "Because I *am* desperate. There's no masking that."

The fear of not effectively masking what must be masked generates yet another anxiety. For many jobseekers, the most uncomfortable question in networking is also the one hardest to avoid: "What do you do for a living?" Richard has a well-rehearsed and strategic response: "I would be less inclined to say I'd been having trouble finding work than I would be to say, 'I've been a stay-at-home dad.' Which is true, but it's not the whole story." While taking time out of the workforce for parenting has its own stigma, Richard believes that it is less severe than the stigma of long-term unemployment. But even with this well-rehearsed cover story, Richard fears that the emotional crisis he is experiencing due to his unemployment—and which is right under the surface—will show: "While people may not know exactly what it is that's underneath it, they can very frequently sense if you're being inauthentic." Of course, his sense that others can detect his actual feelings magnifies his anxiety. Steven likewise senses that his attempts to mask his negative feelings are not successful. As hard as he tries to appear confident, "it's obvious to people. It feels like the negativity—the feelings that you have inside—are leaking out your pores."

In a vicious cycle, unemployed jobseekers not only need to mask the anxiety rooted in their unemployment, but also the anxiety that arises from their fears that they are not effectively masking their unemployment anxieties.

Stalking for a Job and Masking One's Instrumental Motivation

Beyond masking your anxieties, diminished self-confidence, desperation, and emotional turmoil, it is also necessary to mask the very purpose of the interaction. The unemployed worker's internal motivation for the interaction is typically crystal clear: to obtain a referral to a job or, at least, an introduction to another person who might lead to a referral. Yet, as discussed earlier in the chapter, it is widely—and accurately—thought that directly asking for a referral is not effective and that one should instead focus on developing a social connection, seemingly for its own sake. Recall Kimberly's earlier quote explaining that that while her "motivation inside" is focused on getting a referral she is also clear that in networking "I would never come across that way." Or, as Sharon imagines, the people she is talking to are likely thinking "What doesn't she want me to know?" Sharon pauses and raises her arms in a sign of exasperation: "Well, I don't want you to know that I'm really desperate for a job and that I'm looking for you to give me a job lead."

In other words, unemployed jobseekers perceive that they cannot directly ask for the thing they most need: referrals. This is often borne out by their experience. Aaron, a business analyst in his early 50s, explains that he has learned from his own experience networking that "You don't ask for things. They volunteer things." Interactions that lead others to volunteer things are, in Aaron's words, "delicate" and require showing that "you're eager but without the impression that you have expectations." Along the same lines, Paul tells me that he handles this delicate aspect of the interaction by "asking, after small talk, 'Do you have any suggestions for my job search?' I leave it open to them as to what they might comment." The hesitation to directly ask for help sometimes directly stems from jobseekers' previous negative experiences.

Sam, for example, recalls that when asked directly for a referral, others have responded with awkwardness: "I've learned you don't want to approach it [directly] because you'll make people uncomfortable. You make them feel bad." Jobseekers like Sam are not simply imagining or projecting. What they sense is exactly what my interviewees at MIT Sloan emphasized about being turned off by any approach that seemed too direct or "too transactional."

To avoid appearing transactional, some jobseekers spend considerable time planning how to approach each interaction. Paul thinks he is effective at masking, but only with significant preparation work:

> I know I have to fake and I think I'm reasonably effective at faking it. I think I'm reasonably good at coming across as a normal business professional—despite the fact I've been unemployed for 5 years—and not showing the stress I feel I'm under. Keeping that carefully hidden when I'm networking with people. One way I deal with it is creating a detailed script in advance of the interaction. Thinking about how I'm going to break the ice with a total stranger. I usually sit there for a good 15 to 20 minutes just preparing and going over in my mind what I might want to say and frequently make some pencil notes.

Tom also does his homework, deciding whom to approach and how to approach them. But for him, this makes networking feel like stalking:

> I mean, here you are, looking for a job, and you don't want to come across as being somebody looking for a job. You don't want to just come out and say, "I need a job. Are there any jobs where you work?" People don't like that. It freaks them out. You want to build some kind of bridge, a genuine interest. But by the same token, you're trying to connect with them. . . . It's awkward to do. It's not easy. It's almost like *stalking for a job*.

When I ask Tom to elaborate on the "stalker" analogy, he refers to the process of deciding whom to target for networking. He studies people's social media profiles: "It's a little awkward. It feels like you're stalking. I did the online dating thing a long time ago and you know when you're going through it, you feel like, 'Oh yeah that one, not that one.' You know what I'm saying?" The experience is like a stalker watching their romantic interest from afar, waiting for the right moment, and then approaching with feigned spontaneity. The term *stalking* conveys the covert and asymmetrical aspects of the relationship: one person secretly following the other for their own purposes and strategizing about how to approach without revealing that it was all planned because a more spontaneous-seeming interaction stands a better chance.

The Challenge to Identity

The varied layers of masking typically involved in networking are in tension with jobseekers' identities as ethical beings. Jobseekers generally want to think of themselves as honest people who treat others with authenticity.[19] Yet the networking practices made necessary by prolonged unemployment pushes them in quite a different—and unwanted—direction. Daniel explains the challenge to his identity:

> I am a very open person and I love people and I love to talk to people. But I'm uncomfortable with networking. In networking, you want to sound very friendly because all I want is to get something from you. . . . My sense of identity. *I don't want to lose who I am just because I need a job and I need to ask.* I don't know. It's confusing.

The need to "sound very friendly" in order to "get something" is unsettling because it violates unspoken rules of ethical social behavior. In the world of dating, this might be called using someone—instrumentally creating a social connection as a way to achieve some other goal. It is striking that in the context of professional work, we lack the vocabulary to describe our discomfort for instrumentally creating a social connection as a means to achieving a career goal, but the feeling of shame is there even without the words to name it.[20] Daniel, for example, reports that after attempts to network with his friends, "I'll end up with a very bitter sense inside myself. 'You shouldn't have done that.' I tarnished my friendships just because, all of a sudden, I am like wicked desperate trying to find a job. People don't react very well to that, regardless of how close they may be."

Anthony, like Daniel, generally likes talking with people. As he puts it: "I'm completely comfortable talking to new faces." At his former job in sales, he deeply enjoyed "meeting people [and] explaining a new product, explaining the features of the product." "But," he pauses, "*networking is different.*" In work interactions the underlying purpose of the interaction—selling a product—is clear and transparent to all. Networking is different because the purpose of the interaction is selling oneself to obtain a referral but this purpose is masked. Moreover, the selling of oneself involves acting in socially connecting ways even when one does not feel socially connected. Anthony explains it this way:

> The key thing with networking is about building relationships and through those relationships, those people you meet are going to put in a good word for you or connect you to the right company and so forth. Well . . . *maybe I didn't like the people* I saw at that networking thing and don't want to go back to establish a deeper relationship. So that's the part of networking that—I do it, but I should probably do more of it. *It's just kind of against the grain of who I am.*

As these quotes reveal, both Daniel and Anthony struggle with acting in ways that are inconsistent with their identities. Daniel doesn't want to "lose who I am just because I need a job" and Anthony finds networking "against the grain of who I am."

One of the cruelest aspects of unemployment is that it pressures jobseekers to act in ways that threatens their sense of the self as an ethical person.[21] To network effectively—and remember that this, by all accounts, is the most likely way to escape the trap of unemployment—one must put on multiple masks and work to create a personal connection. Jobseekers cannot network effectively if they are overtly transactional in their dealings with others. Hence what must remain unspoken and hidden from view is that the path to escape the unemployment trap involves treating others in instrumental ways—that is, as useful tools. Sharon, for example, is painfully aware of how the pressure to find work has changed her perception of others; she finds herself seeing them less as people and more as potential network contacts:

> I'm starting to look at every interaction with every person as a business transaction. It's like, I wonder if this person can connect me? Over time, what happened is I get very few interviews and desperation has started to kick in. So now it's not just about meeting people. Honestly, it's like you shake the person's hand and it's like, running in the back of your head. It's like, "Are you going to introduce me to somebody? Do you have any leads?" *You stop seeing a person.*

The discomfort arising from the challenges to one's identity as an ethical person is rarely discussed in support settings or by job coaches, but it is an experience that eventually leads many unemployed jobseekers to reduce or cease their networking.[22] Strikingly, only two of my interviewees discussed networking efforts that felt consistent with their identities and these were, in fact, the exceptions that proved the rule. Mitch, one such exceptional case, explains: "When I first started networking after losing my job, I was probably not authentic because, prior to the networking interaction, I would try to anticipate, 'What are they gonna want me to be? Let me try to be that person.'" Yet, at a certain point, he decided to stop strategically presenting himself and to view networking as "a process of getting to know people. So I don't have to be impressing them with anything from my background." However, a key factor in Mitch's case, and in the one other case like his, was the rare absence of financial urgency, which allowed him to take a longer time to build relationships. These two exceptional cases suggest that building relationships without short-term instrumental goals may be a luxury that comes from financial cushioning—which very few unemployed American jobseekers have. And the longer they are unemployed, the less likely they are to have it.

The Networking Black Hole and Discouragement

Networking can lead to jobs. About half the jobseekers in this study ultimately found some kind of professional job, often with the aid of networking.[23] But even for those who ultimately succeed, any given networking interaction is likely to end in some sort of rejection—sometimes polite and apologetic—or more commonly in the form of no response at all. Lance describes a typical experience of the latter:

> The funny thing is that I talk about this sort of anonymous sending of your resume through these computer systems. But even when I try networking, I'm getting what I can't help but think is a similar treatment from people that I sort of know. I can think of twice recently when I identified a friend of mine at an organization that I have some interest in. I contacted them and had some initial positive response, saying, "Oh yes, I'll help you do whatever, find out who to talk with," or something along those lines. And then when I follow up, sending resumes or doing whatever, *total silence. Nothing.*

I realize people are busy, so I contact them again, trying to prod them in some way. Still nothing.

As in Lance's story many other jobseekers discussed the tendency of network contacts to initially respond with a promise of support and then do a disappearing act. Monica, who worked in church administration, put it this way: "People say they'll do everything for you . . . then you don't hear from them." How does this affect her? "It is just getting harder and harder for me to actually network."

Networking indeed becomes harder over time as one exhausts both one's external network and one's own resilience. Unemployed jobseekers who keep it up despite the difficulties do so because it remains the most viable path to a professional job. But often the negative experiences of feeling like a beggar or a used-car salesman, of having one's identity challenged, and of putting oneself forward and getting no response lead to a reduction in networking or even a complete withdrawal. Deborah, a technical writer in her early sixties, explains her decision to stop networking altogether: "I feel I don't have enough courage and self-esteem to ask for things from my friends or acquaintances or to branch out through them to other people."

* * *

Networking when unemployed is bruising. For unemployed jobseekers— and likely for others who may be working but are in positions of low power and high precarity—networking interactions may entail a direct hit on core bases of identity. Instead of feeling self-sufficient, many come to feel like beggars. Instead of feeling moral, many come to feel like the proverbially ethically challenged used-car salesman.

Unemployment—and, more generally, the increasingly precarious nature of work, even for those who have it—means that no matter the personal toll, no matter how exhausting and dispiriting it is, the instrumentalization of social relations is increasingly seen as a necessity for survival. Precarity effectively turns one's social ties into a safety net. Everyone you meet—and the people you already know—are potentially valuable tools. Yet, for all of its psychological costs, this safety net isn't even guaranteed to catch you when you fall.

Masking is not unique to networking and, for as long as we have any record, has been an important aspect of social relations. For example, in the analogy drawn by unemployed jobseekers themselves, used-car salespersons needing to sell an unreliable car may indeed mask their ambivalence and only highlight the car's strengths. But in the used-car dealership there is no ambiguity about the nature of the relationship and all parties understand that interactions are instrumentally motivated. By contrast, the networking interactions discussed in this chapter involve not only a masking of unenthusiastic feelings about oneself—a tricky feat—but also masking instrumentally driven actions as socially motivated.

By showing how and why networking while unemployed is difficult due to the jobseeker's precarious position rather than to any particular personality characteristic or to lack of will or effort, I hope to counteract the tendency among some workers and career coaches to *individualize* the challenge and to overstate the degree to which the trap of unemployment is easy to escape if jobseekers were *only willing* to get out there and network. The trap is difficult to escape because of the ubiquity of the unemployment stigma. We have seen how this stigma shows up in recruiters and network contacts, but it is not limited to them. As Chapters 4 and 5 will show, it also appears inside ourselves and in our closest relationships.

4

The Stigma Inside

Stigma is like the air all around us—invisible, ubiquitous, and something we can't help but breathe in. We have heard it in the way recruiters talk about unemployed applicants, and then saw it surface in strikingly similar ways in jobseekers' network contacts. Jobseekers are aware of the toxicity of this stigma and try not to internalize it, but they usually end up doing so anyway. We can see internalized stigma when unemployed jobseekers talk about the shame they feel about their unemployment and how their sense of identity is undermined.

As we will see in this chapter, unemployment and its related stigma is a multi-front assault on identity. It includes not only the bruising interactions in the labor market with employers and network contacts discussed in the prior chapters but also the challenges that arise from the growing financial crisis accompanying unemployment, including difficulties providing for one's children and keeping one's home and way of life intact.

Insidiously, internalized stigma also plunges jobseekers deeper into the trap of unemployment. Not only do feelings of shame and loss of identity make it difficult to continue the search, but—as we will hear from recruiters—jobseekers are routinely ruled out of consideration if they exhibit even a hint of negative emotions or appear less than fully confident.

The stigma trap comes full circle. Unemployed jobseekers are excluded and stigmatized. As any of us would, they experience negative feelings as a result of being excluded and stigmatized. And then those negative feelings become further reasons for exclusions and stigma. You're punished for no good reason, then punished again for not liking the punishment.

The Distorting Mirror: Identity, Shame, and the Internalized Stigma

Unemployment tends to gradually undermine the jobseeker's sense of self as a competent and valued worker. Losing one's professional identity is not simply the automatic and unavoidable result of losing one's job. Identities are socially constructed and deconstructed.[1] In sociology, identity is understood as the product of how we imagine others see us, which generates a "looking-glass self."[2] In the context of American unemployment, jobseekers see themselves reflected in a distorting mirror. Distorting mirrors can be fun in a carnival, but the mirror held up to unemployed jobseekers is warped by a deep and ubiquitous stigma.

As we have already seen, this stigma is evident in the reactions of recruiters and network colleagues; we will see in Chapter 5 that it also appears in interactions with friends, family, and spouses. The pervasiveness of the stigma leads many unemployed jobseekers to develop a distorted self-image of themselves as people with whom there is "something wrong." Here, for example, is how Craig, a manufacturing engineer in his mid-50s, puts it:

> Not doing work diminishes you. Some people say that you are identified with the work you do. Well, kind of. When you work, people know that you have ideas, that you can figure things out. It does identify you as the kind of person who has a specific skillset and when you're not doing that, people look at you like there must be something wrong with you.

Sharon describes perceptions similar to Craig's but also reveals how the distorted image of oneself that is reflected back from all directions can creep inside and shape one's own self-perception:

> The problem that most long-term unemployed people have is that because we are not working, there is a perception that there is something wrong with us. I think it does impact your self-confidence and your self-view.

The way stigma comes to shape one's view of oneself is also illustrated in Barbara's story. Barbara had been a very successful sales executive for over 2 decades. But, after 2 years of unemployment, her thoughts reveal that she is looking at herself through the same skeptical lens as recruiters and network contacts:

> Even though I think I'm good at selling, I haven't sold myself yet. I have self-flagellation. . . . This is a fairly major yardstick that we all put against ourselves, our employment. We define ourselves in part by what we do, not who we are. Right now, I've had the rug pulled out from under me in terms

of how I identify myself. I'm right back in high school and college, trying to find myself again.

Barbara's difficulty in maintaining her identity as a successful sales professional when she has not been able to "sell herself" is common to most unemployed workers, who ultimately internalize, to a greater or lesser extent, the ubiquitous stigmatizing perspective and interpret their inability to find work as a sign of questionable professional worthiness. As Daniel plainly puts it, as time passes without finding a job, "the thoughts go through your head that obviously you're not as good as you think you are."[3]

Unemployed jobseekers are aware of the risk of internalizing a distorted image of themselves and actively try to resist it. Their narratives are filled with descriptions of the struggle to maintain their old sense of self. Consider, for example, how Derrick, a sales manager in his mid-fifties, discusses his view of himself:

It's just really degrading to be unemployed. Yeah, the self-image, of course. Whether you were at the bottom of the ladder or the top of the ladder, you were doing something. And all of a sudden for that to be gone, one identifies oneself as being useless. We know otherwise and we know we have a lot to offer, but the world doesn't see us that way.

Derrick's quote reveals an inner tug-of-war. A part of him knows he has "a lot to offer," but this part is challenged by a recognition that "the world doesn't see us that way" and leads him to identify himself as "useless."

Ruby is in her early 50s and is a scientist with a PhD who lost her job in a research lab. She describes her struggle and effort to not internalize stigma but rather to see unemployment as a structural or even global issue:

I *try* not to take it personally. I *try* not to think it's because I'm not qualified and nobody wants me. I *try* not to think like that because that's like digging a hole that's not going to get me anywhere good. So I'd rather think about it as more of a global issue and I'm a part of this global issue. More like, "Yes, there aren't a lot of tenure-track positions. Nobody wants tenure-track positions because nobody wants to have full-time faculty because it costs more money because of health benefits. So there aren't positions. It's not that I'm not getting them, they're just not there to apply for."

Inner struggles like Ruby's and Derrick's tend to be losing battles, especially when one is isolated. Even jobseekers who intellectually understand that the obstacles they face are external and not a reflection of their professional worthiness often discuss how the experience nonetheless *feels* personal, and describe the immense power of such feelings even when they *know* the bigger picture. Here is how Christopher puts it: "I *feel* like it's my fault. I *know* it's not my fault. [My old company] is doing terrible and they're laying off people all the time. It still feels like, 'Gee, if I somehow had been doing my job better.'" Steven uses very similar language to describe how his feelings can overpower his thoughts. He knows the hard time he has had finding a job is "logical in terms of the reality of our job search. It's just logical. But it's the emotional part. *You don't feel it.* You still feel like, 'If I was good at what I was doing, I'd be hired now.'"[4]

Jobseekers' efforts to hold on to a structural perspective of their situation and to fend off the forces of internalization typically offer only temporary relief. Ronald, with a background in economics and public policy, describes the relentlessness of the "battle within myself":

> It didn't take long before my sense of self began to deteriorate. . . . I have battled internally with my own feelings of, "There's something wrong with me." And my reconciliation of all this is, "Well, I'm not as good as I think I am." That's kinda the gut-level–feeling response. But then I have this intellect and I have this education and I can put on my policy hat and say, "Yeah, but there have been some real, dramatic changes in the economy. Certainly since my father was in the work world. One job 40 years, same employer. That doesn't exist for most people anymore." I know that intellectually. I can make the intellectual arguments. With this sense of self, I do look at what's happened over the last several years and see the *battle within myself.* The battle between what I was feeling—"Oh, there's something wrong with me"—and then my intellect trying to come back and say, "Well, it's not you. Look at the state of things." Sometimes the intellect would win and I'd say, "Yeah, it's not me." And sometimes the feelings would win and I would get really down and say, "I don't know if I'm ever gonna be employed again."

It is striking that even Ronald, who has studied the very economy and policy changes that have shaped his career and is thus able to put on his "policy hat" and see the forces at work against him, nonetheless struggles with the feeling that something is "wrong" with him.[5]

The losing nature of the inner battle to maintain one's identity as a worthy professional—an identity so central to how American adults define themselves[6]—is revealed in the common experience of shame. Shame is the result of feeling that one has not lived up to the expectations one imagines are required to be accepted by others and to have a sense of belonging.[7]

As I did this research, I discovered that when I asked jobseekers to interview each other (and record the interview for me to include in the data), they were often able to open up about topics that are difficult to discuss, such as shame. In this excerpt from such a peer-to-peer interview, we can hear how Steven, the former school principal, and Liam, who previously worked in financial services, both worry about just being seen by neighbors or people in their community when at home or in the gym during work hours:

Steven: The loss of my work identity is pretty crippling psychologically. I have some difficulty going out of my house to the mailbox because you're going out there most of the time in the middle of the day and you're just not supposed to be home. . . .Going to the mailbox, *I am out there unemployed for all to see.*

Liam: Oh yeah, absolutely. In today's society, especially as guys, you identify with your job. People see you as your job.

Steven: Can I ask you, Liam—When you go to the gym, do you ever feel like people are saying, "Why is he in a gym at this time?"

Liam: Yep. . . . I do feel like people are looking around like, "Okay, why are you here?" Just that everyday stuff. It sucks. I feel old because half the people in there at that hour are either the moms who dropped their kids at school and run to the gym, or they're retired people.

Steven's feeling that he is "out there unemployed for all to see" reveals how the intense shame he feels about being unemployed makes him want to not even be visible to his neighbors.[8] Liam stresses that "especially as guys," people are defined by their work and indeed there was a pattern among men, in this study and in others, of feeling that their masculine identity is specifically undermined by unemployment.[9] Yet, as the many quotes from women in this book show, women are not exempt from this shame. In fact, in discussing her pain, Sandra observed that the very assumption that it is harder "for guys" is infuriating to her because she perceives it to downplay the intensity of her own pain:

It's a profound loss. A lot of people say, "It's worse for men. It's not an issue for women because women have other identities." But it was a huge part of my identity and a huge part of how people look at me. [She tears up.] It's hard not to feel like a throwaway.

In addition to shame, another common feeling is self-blame and the sense that unemployed people are at fault for their unemployment.[10] Some jobseekers constantly replay episodes of their job search with an eye to what they did wrong. Monica provides a good example: "Part of what makes it so difficult is hanging onto the frustration and reliving the experience of all the work you put into preparing [the job application] and replaying the conversations and shoulda, woulda, coulda done this and said this." Another form of self-blame focuses on one's actions in the period prior to job loss and criticizing oneself for not having the foresight to take steps earlier in one's career to somehow avoid being in the current trap.[11]

This questioning and blaming of one's past actions can be seen in Anthony's story, which also reveals how this kind of self-blame is linked to internalized stigma and the tendency to feel that something is wrong with oneself:

When you don't hear back anything . . . it makes you question yourself more because it makes you feel like your background, your experience is just not enough. It hits a lot of different buttons. It hits your self-esteem. If you don't hear anything, it leaves you with self-doubt. . . . It makes you question, "Oh, Jeez, I should have done this in the past and then I would have been better suited for that job." You start second-guessing your career, things you should have done in your career, that would have maybe set you up better for what this current condition is. I've done a lot of that.

When Anthony does not get positive responses from employers it leads him to question decisions he made earlier in his career. He experiences a "hit" on his self-esteem, and it challenges his identity as a worthy professional.[12]

In addition to the bruising of one's identity as a valued professional, extended unemployment also undermines jobseekers' identities by depriving them of engagement in work that contributes to others or to a larger whole. Job searching involves a lot of hard, draining work—finding opportunities, crafting cover letters, reaching out to networking targets—but with no sense of contributing to others or of being part of a larger effort. No one else benefits from all that work—usually, you don't either. Anthony, for example, explicitly links a sense of not contributing to the undermining of his self-esteem:

> The negative thing is that I went from a position where I was helping people every day, almost 24/7—helping customers, helping sales reps—to not doing that. There's something to be said about the satisfaction of knowing that you did something at work to help the company or to help a customer. And not getting any of that on a daily basis over this period of time is starting to wear on me. It definitely hurts your self-esteem and it also makes you question just how valuable you would be to your next employer if you haven't been hired yet. It does raise some questions about what is it about me that I'm not getting another job?

Here we can see a train of thought that starts with awareness of the pain of not contributing, continues to self-doubt and undermined self-esteem, and ultimately arrives at questions that perfectly mirror the skeptical queries we heard recruiters ask about unemployed workers in Chapter 2—"What is it about me that I'm not getting another job?" For Anthony and for so many others, the stigma-rooted questions about their value are not only all around them but are also *within*. Just as such questions can arise in any interaction, they can also arise at any given moment within one's thoughts.

Whereas traditional economics considers work as a "disutility," a negative experience that people seek to avoid and only endure because they desire wages, my interviews show the pain that comes from not working. Making a contribution through work is a source of esteem and generates feelings of being needed and included, while being unemployed leads to feeling unnecessary and excluded. The jobseekers' narratives show that, as social beings, we are fiercely attuned to others' perceptions of our contributions. These shape our status and identity, especially in a society like that of the United States, in which status is strongly tied to paid work.

Financial Crisis and Undermined Parenting Identities

Given the blow to one's identity as a professional, it might be tempting to try to shift one's basis of identity to another realm.[13] However, identities are the products of social forces and not simply individual choices. Some identities are more available than others.[14] Linda exemplifies the constrained choices: Although work does not *need* to be her primary source of identity, it nevertheless is:

> I've gotten into a bad state even though I tell myself, "Look, you're not going to be a different person if you get a job. You're not a better person if you get a job." But I don't have children, my job has had a lot to do with my self-identity. So for me, I guess it's huge.

Linda observes that her job is the focus of her identity because "I don't have children." Indeed, the most likely available and legitimate anchor of identity discussed by jobseekers who do have children is parenthood. Consider the case of Ed, an environmental researcher in his early 50s, and how he articulates an alternative identity focused on being a father:

> I feel like I'm a fraction of the guy I used to be. I see a lot of people, as soon as they retire, they go into a real downswing because they equated themselves with their jobs. I feel like I am now Ed, this guy who can still stop and smell the flowers and I can celebrate this extraordinary gift of a 7-year-old daughter who is just a delight. And fathering is my most important thing anyway, so that's still thriving. . . . Who I am is independent of what's on the business card or the payroll stub.

In this quote we can see how Ed consciously works to change his identity focus from the work realm where he is a "fraction of the guy I used to be" to a man who can "smell the flowers" and to appreciate himself as a "thriving" father. Later in the interview, Ed grieves the loss of his work identity and describes himself as in a "bog," having come down from the mountain peak of career success, but the alternative identity of fatherhood does provide him with a solid foundation for his sense of self. But in this regard, Ed is an exceptional case. His ability to re-anchor his identity in parenting is possible only because his wife makes enough to maintain their current standard of living. And even for Ed, this situation may not last long because, as I'll describe in Chapter 5, his marriage is in trouble. For most long-term unemployed jobseekers, including those with working spouses, extended unemployment ultimately brings about a financial crisis. As we'll see later in this chapter, that financial crisis combines with the constant rejection in the labor market to undermine *multiple core aspects* of one's identity, not only as a competent and contributing worker but also as a parent capable of providing for one's children and, in a few cases, even as an adult capable of providing food and shelter for oneself.

Jobseekers only rarely report silver linings to unemployment. The one exception—often mentioned by both mothers and fathers of school-aged children—is the opportunity to spend more time with their kids. And at the start of unemployment, with more time available for family, in a notable number of cases, a person's identity as a parent can receive a boost.

Coming from professional jobs that are notoriously "greedy institutions"[15] requiring long hours, the ability to be home when children return from school can be a welcome change. Liam, for example, appreciated being able to spend more time with his kids where "before, I was working 14- or 16-hour days." Anthony, who has a daughter in high school, says it feels good to "have not missed one of her varsity games because of work getting in the way." Also, he adds:

> I've been driving her to school every other day with a carpool thing. That's great because I get to spend time with my daughter. So yeah, there have been some benefits to me not working, I'm not under the gun with a 12-hour workday like I was doing before. So I have more time. That's a good thing.

Unfortunately, that silver lining does not usually last long. As unemployment lengthens and financial resources dwindle, the parenting experience can flip from "a good thing" to among the most emotionally bruising aspects of unemployment if one is not able to shield one's children from the financial fallout.

For the mostly upper-middle-class professional workers I interviewed, there is a lag between their job loss and the moment when financial pressures intensify to such a degree that the family is forced to make drastic changes. The first 6 months may be cushioned by unemployment insurance, savings, and a spouse's income. Although unemployment insurance typically only replaces a fraction of prior earnings, when it is combined with some cutbacks and rainy-day savings, many upper-middle-class families are initially able to make ends meet. But after unemployment insurance payments run out (typically after 6 months), the extent to which other financial cushions will suffice varies widely.[16] Married unemployed workers with working spouses have relatively more cushion, though spouses' incomes alone are rarely enough. Most families with a dual-earning couple rely on both incomes to pay for their expenses. Monica explains this typical situation:

My husband works, but our whole living situation is structured around two people bringing in significant incomes. . . . As time has gone on, I've had to withdraw money from my retirement to the point where it's down to practically nothing. It's been very, very difficult.

While those fortunate enough to have a working spouse and retirement savings are temporarily better able to maintain their lifestyle, it is usually only a matter of time before the savings run out. Even families with substantial savings, typically due to previously earning high incomes, run through such savings fairly quickly because high-income earners tend to have high costs of living, major components of which—such as housing and private schools— cannot be reduced without significant disruption.

The desire to keep life as normal as possible for the kids, combined with the hope that a new job is around the corner, leads families to run through their savings and retirement funds—sometimes even the kids' college funds—before making drastic changes that directly affect their children, like moving to a cheaper home or pulling them out of private school. The choice to spend down savings and retirement funds reflects parents' valiant effort to shield their children from hardships and, perhaps unconsciously, to protect their own identities as good parents. Sean, a 52-year-old software developer, is a good example:

I have a family to support. My wife absolutely works, but we have two children. One's in private school and the other is going into a private high school next year. So I'll do whatever I can to keep them there. If that means cashing out retirement savings, whatever I have to do to keep them there.

Another jobseeker, Paul, faced the agonizing choice of whether or not to stay in his current town with its expensive housing and keep his kids in their current schools with their childhood friends. The only way to do it would be by drawing on savings set aside to pay for college:

Our neighborhood is pretty expensive. . . . If it wasn't for the kids wanting to finish high school in the same town where they grew up, we'd probably move to a cheaper area. But we're staying here until the kids get out of high school. Right now, I'm supporting it out of my retirement savings and *the kids' college savings*. I've got to keep my fingers crossed that the kids can get some really good financial aid packages, because I have very little cash left for college.

At a certain point the savings, retirement funds, or college funds run out and children can no longer be shielded. This is when the financial crisis that almost invariably accompanies long-term unemployment launches a new assault on identity. When the financial resources are no longer available to maintain the lifestyle of children, unemployed workers often begin to feel like failures as parents.

Several interviewees who were single mothers, brought up as particularly painful not being able to afford Christmas gifts. Cheryl, who has college-aged kids, explains:

> This is a hard time of year. It's the holidays when you would really like to get them something to help them. Get them some nice new clothes so that they can go on an interview, or just give them a gas card that has a substantial amount of money so that they don't have to worry about that. There's no safety net for that kind of thing, that was so much a part of your life in the past. . . . You feel awful because you can't help your loved ones anymore.

She pauses, trying to find the right word for what she's feeling: "There's no word for it in our culture, but I would say 'emasculated' in a feminine form. I just feel like I'm . . . I don't know, there's no word for it for females, which is interesting." That she would feel the need for a female term of emasculation conveys just how deeply the inability to provide her children with gifts challenges her identity as a parent and provider.

Marcia, too, finds the holidays the hardest time of year: "Family holidays are just awful. We hate family holidays because we don't have any. I just have to pretend it's *not* a holiday. Christmas is the worst." Not participating in the ritual of gift-giving is painful because such rituals are symbolic of love and care. But, of course, the fact that Marcia has at times been unable to provide enough food for her two young children is also deeply scarring: "Even going to a food bank and getting free bread twice a week, it's really hard to make it through the month. The last week of the month is like starving time for us." In addition to the emotional blow of not being able to financially sustain ordinary life, unemployed workers also find it painful not being able to shield their children from the stress they as adults are experiencing. Marcia explains:

My children just don't want to hear about it anymore. They don't want to hear about the struggle, the job hunting, and not having enough money. They can't take it anymore. If it was just me . . . [In tears] . . . If it was just me alone in this, it wouldn't be as bad. . . . The kids don't want to go to food banks. They're starting to be teenagers and they want to be like everybody else and be positive about life.

Marcia's experience is not solely financial and driven by her difficulty in materially providing for her children; it is also importantly marked by the anguish of how her unemployment is emotionally dragging down her children and making it difficult for them to "be positive."

Kimberly talks about her efforts—not always successful—to protect her high-school–aged son:

It's very hard when he asks me for something and I say, "I can't buy that right now." One time I was outside crying and he came out and said, "What's wrong?" I just sat him down and I told him, "This is really stressful for me. I'd really like to be able to buy you things and do things. It's really hard finding that right job." He's seen different aspects of me he wouldn't normally see. You always try to protect your kids. You don't want them to see you fall apart. But I have, several times.

Parents want to be stable and supportive forces in their kids' lives and yet the crises they are enduring due to unemployment often render this untenable. Marcia's kids simply told her they do not want to hear about it. But in some cases, children respond to the financial and emotional stress at home by lashing out at their unemployed parents. Fred, for example, reports that when his son "gets really mad at me, he'll be like, 'Get a job.' He doesn't mean to hurt me, but it's just what he has in his back pocket. You don't want to hear that from your son." In such moments, children reveal that they too sometimes see their unemployed parent through a stigmatizing lens.

Sandra and her husband are both unemployed and their son is a college student who had applied for a prestigious internship. However, when he did not get the internship, he initially lied and told them he had. Sandra shares her son's explanation:

I said, "Why didn't you tell me the truth?" He said "Well, I was embarrassed. *I didn't want to be another failure in the family, like you and dad.*" And I was like, "I don't have a job, but I don't really think I'm a failure. And I don't think your dad's a failure. He just doesn't have a job. I'm really upset that you'd say that! Stop thinking that."

Stepping back, not being able to provide for one's children at previously taken-for-granted levels, and having children experience stress—and sometimes express their own stigma-informed view of their unemployed parent—all combine to challenge unemployed workers' identities as parents. Just at the time when their work-identities are clobbered in the job market, and thus the parental identity becomes an even more crucial anchor to their understandings of their roles and contributions, the financial crisis that accompanies unemployment can severely undermine this identity as well. And in fact, the challenge of not being able to shield one's children from the financial and emotional turbulence wrought by unemployment can be among the hardest aspects of prolonged unemployment.

"I Just Feel Like I'm a Little Kid Again"

It can get even worse. Unemployed workers may lose their homes, find themselves needing to move back in with parents, and turn to government assistance such as food stamps.[17] At this point, the assault on one's identity has reached all the way to one's sense of even being a grown-up at all.

When the savings are depleted and the bills keep coming, a typical last resort before losing one's home is to turn to your family for financial help. Jill, for example, waited to ask her family for help until she got to the point where "my electricity is scheduled for cutoff in a few days and my landlord's patience is approaching its end. I've run out of backup resources." It's a hard step because it feels like a reversion to childhood. And the degree to which parents can provide support varies greatly. Some were indeed able to save the day, but others were retired and facing financial difficulties of their own.

When Laura, a 55-year-old union organizer, lost her job she was living together with her husband and 15-year-old son in a house that they had bought after their son was born. Her story illustrates the typical way that hoping a new job is around the corner leads to spending down resources until one simply cannot pay the mortgage:

When I lost my paycheck, we lost the ability to cover [our mortgage]. And that was pretty devastating. We had hoped and prayed. . . And every time you get so close [in interviews for a job], you keep thinking, "Let's just wait and see this one play out. And then let's wait and see *this* one play out." . . . We sold the house the week before Christmas and lost $15,000 on it and had our-tree trimming party and tried to be happy at our last Christmas-tree–trimming party in the house we'd lived in for 15 years.

Laura and her family found an apartment to rent. Others were less lucky.

When the nightmare scenario occurs and you lose your home and can't find—that is, can't afford—anywhere else, the ultimate parental backstop is not money but housing. But moving in with one's parents, though a great source of comedy onscreen, is in real life a terrible blow to one's adult identity. Cheryl describes the shock of finding herself back in her childhood home with her parents after losing her housing:

I'm just having a lot of shock going from having a really solid home in a great community to being homeless. The first few months, I would wake up and I'm living in my childhood room, in my childhood home. I'm using my parents' car. Just putting on a smile though. I went through periods of literal shock where I would wake up at night and I would hear screaming and I would think, "Did someone leave the TV on?" And it was me! I would wake up in a fit, where I couldn't even catch my breath. So physically, besides these things, I lost 30 pounds within a year and just couldn't gain weight. I couldn't keep food in. I just felt traumatized and I started to have small anxiety attacks.

Like Cheryl, Susan found herself living with her parents, feeling a mix of shock and gratitude: "Thank God, because I very well could have been without a place to sleep. But on the other hand, sometimes I just feel like I'm a little kid again, stuck at home with mom and dad." As with Cheryl, the financial benefits of living at home came with a significant hit on Susan's sense of independence and adulthood:

I've been living by myself since I was 20. I paid for my undergrad and didn't take any money from my parents. And now, to have to come back home at the age of 51, I can't tell you how humiliating that was. Somebody once described me as someone who is fiercely independent and now to be in this position that I can't support myself. After 35 years on my own, I now can't support myself and it's just crushing. I should be taking care of my parents and instead they're trying to help me out. This isn't the way it's supposed to be. Okay, so that might be silly, but that's just the way I feel. They're in their 80s. They should be worried about other things than taking care of me. I've been living on my own since I was 20 and sometimes I just feel like, "Oh, you've got to be kidding me!"

The feeling of losing one's adult identity—so closely linked for Americans to financial self-sufficiency[18]—can also arise when turning to another last resort: the government. Cheryl, whose resources are completely depleted, reluctantly applied for SNAP (food stamps). Each time she uses her SNAP debit card to buy groceries, she feels that other shoppers are judging her and evaluating whether or not they approve her taxpayer-funded purchases:

Paying for something with a food stamp card is one of the worst things I've ever had to do. The first two times I had to do it, I just started crying in the supermarket. It was brutal because there's absolutely no way to have a grocery cart full of anything that people can't point at and make a comment about. I defy you, I defy anybody to make a full grocery cart full of unimpeachable things that no one would get upset with. It's impossible. But I've been working since I was 14 and I've been putting into the system, so it should be okay for the state to give me less than $200 a month.

Although a part of Cheryl thinks "it should be okay" for her to receive state support, the feelings that led her to cry in the supermarket also reveal other parts of her that don't agree. Heather, who likewise sought aid from the state when running out of resources, also felt her identity challenged: "It doesn't feel good to consider welfare. I know that technically I'm entitled to it. There's no shame in it, but there kind of is."

The experience of financial dependence on parents or on the state is challenging in a way that is similar to the experience of networking described in the previous chapter. In both cases, jobseekers must act in ways that undermine their identity as self-sufficient adults. In the case of networking with strangers, jobseekers used the metaphor of a beggar, whereas turning to parents or the state, the metaphor is a child.

Most jobseekers in my study did not end up losing their homes, but they all experienced a financial crisis that to some extent challenged their adult identities. A common sentiment was shock at being where they were at this stage in life. Stacy, for example, finds herself in more dire poverty than she experienced in childhood with immigrant and ill parents:

> My family has slipped out of the middle class and is quickly slipping into poverty. I am not able to provide any basic items for my son except food. I am living at a standard below where I was during childhood. My childhood wasn't easy. I am first-generation, had ill parents, and had a very difficult time financially. So the fact that I am worse off now says a lot.

For Sharon, an African American graduate of Harvard College, her unemployment upended a story of generational progress and her understanding of the rules of the game for success in American society, focusing on education and doing the "right things." She explains:

> It's just staggering to think about. And I don't know—we're from different generations, but I was brought up to get an education, work hard. My grandmother was uneducated, she didn't graduate from high school. My mother was the first in her generation to get a college degree. They instilled in me to get all this education and you'll be fine. My grandmother would say that she didn't want me to end up washing dishes like she did, get an education, be good in school, do the right things and you'll have a great life and you will go so much further than I did. I'm saying to myself, she didn't have much education and she washed dishes, but she had a job until she turned 65. I don't! And it's really hard to digest that. I feel I was brought up to do all the quote/unquote "right things" and I did the right things and here I am.

Long-term unemployment contradicts jobseekers' narratives of who they are and where they should be at this stage of their life. The intensity of the contradiction between circumstances and expectations is magnified by the fact that unemployment challenges multiple expectations at once. With the onslaught of stigma and financial disaster, it is nearly impossible to hold on to one's identities as a valued worker, a good parent, and—in some cases— even as a grown man or woman. As Chapter 5 will show, even spouses and close friends are often not a reliable source of support in the struggle to maintain one's identity as worthy and legitimate and, in fact, tensions in these relationships can become yet another force undermining those identities. This is why the struggle against stigmatization turns out to be most effective as a collective struggle—that is, the banding together of fellow unemployed jobseekers, which will be the subject of Chapter 6.

Ever-intensifying Anxiety

Decades of research show that unemployment undermines mental health and well-being.[19] This book takes a deep dive into some of the day-to-day experiences that lead to these results. We have seen how unemployment and the stigma it carries undermine multiple anchors of identity—an important mechanism by which unemployment upends well-being.[20] But that's not the only mechanism at work. In this section, I focus on how unemployment generates an ever-rising level of anxiety.

Among the most pressing challenges that emerge from interviews with unemployed jobseekers is their sense of constant and overwhelming anxiety.[21] They commonly report having difficulty thinking about anything else besides finding a job and navigating their financial challenges. Anthony explains: "I'm 14 months into it. I would say that looking for work and not having a job is in my thoughts the majority of the day. Some days it's almost completely 100% consuming my thoughts." Tom describes never being able to shake the feeling of "Did I miss something?"

> Is there something in my email that I didn't do? Do I need to improve this skill? I can't stop. It's like running a nonstop marathon. You run and you've got people beside you running along with you and they're looking for a job, too.

The anxious feeling that there is always more one can do, and the implicit fear in Tom's marathon analogy that those running alongside him are in fact doing more, is exacerbated by the fact that it is seldom clear *what* one should do and what one should prioritize. James articulates this layer of anxiety:

> One of the things that's hardest to deal with in the job search for me is that there are just so many things that you could or should be doing. There are so many people to talk to, so many groups to participate in, so many things you could learn. You can't do it all. So that can be very frustrating.

With no definable limits to the time and effort one could put into job seeking, it is often tempting to blame oneself for making the wrong decisions about how much time to spend and how to spend it. The interviews reveal that it is common for jobseekers to berate themselves for not doing enough. Aaron puts it this way:

> I put a lot of pressure on myself. I'm my own worst critic.... It always seems as if I can do more. So I get very self-critical when I realize, "Hey, I can do more. I have things on my list. I have a to-do list that's a page long." And you get upset when you don't accomplish everything on your list.

The ever-present anxiety and self-blame about the job search combines with similar feelings that arise from dealing with one's deteriorating finances. Just as job searching involves constant decision-making with no clarity on what one should be doing, long-term unemployment also requires daily spending decisions and strategizing about how to put off the day when you run out of money. This requires the taxing mental work of figuring out what to cut, what to pay, and what to try to postpone. Bruce discusses the nonstop task of dealing with the "list of the monthly bills and juggling them and how I'm going to pay this one and how far can I push this one out." Heather talks of the constant work of managing unpaid bills as a struggle to figure out "how can I pay at least something to everybody, but not pay full amounts, and not empty out and have a zero bank account, so that I am able to buy groceries." When Heather's father passed away a few months earlier, she faced a wrenching decision of whether to incur the out-of-state travel costs of going to his funeral at the risk of spending down money that may be needed for groceries: "Could I afford to go to my father's memorial service in Kentucky? How could I not go to my father's memorial service?" While that decision was unusually dramatic, the lives of unemployed workers are filled with less dramatic but cumulatively agonizing decisions about what they can afford and the juggling of paying for bare necessities, like food and gas.

Another source of anxiety for unemployed workers is that they are getting older and at some point will not be able to work, but meanwhile they are spending away their retirement savings. Retirement savings is a cushion that many Americans outside the upper-middle class do not have at all. Yet, the agonizing experience of having built up such savings—which usually involves years and or decades of careful planning and self-restraint—and then burning through them should not be minimized. Sharon explains: "I've liquidated about 85% of my 401(k) assets because that's what I've been living off. So I'm okay now, but what's going to happen when I turn 65 or 70?"[22]

The level of anxiety that comes with extended unemployment is not constant and steady; rather, it is constant and ever-intensifying. On the job search front, jobseekers are well aware that as their employment gap lengthens, which it does with each passing day, the stigma they face in the labor market becomes harsher. On the financial front, whatever one's resources, the passage of time means relentlessly moving toward a day when those resources will be depleted. Whatever resources unemployed jobseekers use to get by, whether unemployment insurance or retirement savings or support from family, they are feeling the clock—with each day bringing them closer to the day they run out of resources. Daniel describes the feeling shared by many: "I'm ok but not for too many months. Very few months."

One feels oneself heading toward a cliff. As the cliff approaches, unemployed jobseekers are increasingly likely to take what they call "survival jobs"—typically low-wage jobs in retail—which bring in some income. In most cases survival jobs do not pay enough to cover basic expenses, and they take time and energy away from the job search.

The ever-intensifying anxiety of long-term unemployment described in this section is reflected in jobseekers' feelings that during this period of being out of work—when they might at least have some extra free time—they are unable to accomplish non-work–related projects or even take time to just relax. For example, when Brian was first laid off, he thought that a possible silver lining would be getting things done around the house that he ordinarily does not have time to do. But this did not happen:

I thought, I'll have time and I can do these projects and things at the house and I'll build these shelves. But you just don't have the energy and desire to do that stuff because, at least for me, there's just this overwhelming feeling, an ever-present feeling, I should be working. I should have a job. My biggest worry is not getting another job.

Brian's experience of "ever-present" thoughts and anxieties about his unemployment preventing him from making positive use of the unemployment period was common. Kimberley put it this way:

Twenty-four-seven, you're thinking about the fact that you don't have a job. It never ends. People are saying, "Oh, it's so great that you had 2 years off."

It's funny. I was thinking about that yesterday. It is not great. It's not fun. I feel like I can never relax. I sleep a lot—part of the depression—but I never relax because I have absolutely no stability.

Unemployed jobseekers experiencing mounting anxiety and identity challenges often feel undermined by their own emotions, and as we will see in the next section some try to push back on such feelings.

The Struggle Against One's Own Feelings

The undermining of core aspects of one's identity and the ever-intensifying anxiety lead to yet another challenge—the effort to contain or safely compart-mentalize negative feelings. Almost all unemployed jobseekers I interviewed believe that the negative feelings they are experiencing are themselves a problem and must be contained.

Consider, for example, Tom's thoughts about the effect of his own anger on his continuing unemployment: "I can't get mad because that's wasting energy I could be using to find a job. Anger isn't going to get me anywhere. It's going to show when I go for an interview. I might smile, but they're going to know it. They'll hear it in my voice." While Tom sees negative emotions as a waste of energy and a liability in the job market, he is not able to fully contain such emotions, which intrude most disturbingly during his sleep:

I've had my days where I felt, except for the loss of my wife and those months after her passing, I was in the darkest places emotionally. I go to bed at night and I keep hoping that I wake up and I have to go to work. I've had dreams where I'm at work, I'm with some of my coworkers. I'm about ready to give a briefing and people will walk into the room and say, "We don't want to hear what you have to say." And I'll say, "I'm supposed to give a briefing." And they'll say, "You don't work here anymore. Didn't you get the memo?" I had a number of the same dreams over and over again. I've had my days where I've hit a kind of dark place. I can't function. I'm trying to stay focused and do the things that I think need to be done, but it just seems like I'm trying to jog through water.

Tom is the only one of my interviewees who reported recurring nightmares, but his experience of negative feelings that arise despite his best efforts to contain or ignore them is very common. Consider Eric's failed efforts to contain the pain from the experience of stigma, which have led him to think the unthinkable:

> I have considered taking my own life. Frankly, I am amazed I have survived this long, particularly with the negative judgments I receive from others, particularly the working world that sees me as damaged goods, and the unchangeable external forces that keep me out of the productive professional employment game. I am continuously stuck on the sidelines watching the parade go by. And there is nothing I can do about it. I don't know what the working world wants from me, I am never good enough for whatever reasons. I am so lost. I don't know who I am or what my purpose should be anymore. I'm trying to move forward, but the inner core of my being is a collapsing house of cards. My inner core is dying. I can only keep this problem covered up and "fake it 'til you make it" for so long. At times, the reality of my inner core has reared its ugly head at the surface and I have gone into bouts of major sadness, depression, and suicidal thoughts. The typical response I get from others is that it will all be fine, it will work out, don't worry, you'll get your chance. And when things inevitably fall apart, I get bashed, blamed, and criticized for my misfortunes, mistakes, and screw-ups.[23]

The advice that Eric typically gets for how to contend with his very difficult feelings resulting from being stigmatized and being perceived as "damaged goods" is "don't worry" and "it will work out." In other words, suck it up and bottle it all in. Eric's attempt to "fake it 'til you make it" means that he neither seeks nor receives emotional support and remains alone in his feelings. In addition, jobseekers like Eric often end up feeling bad about feeling bad and berating themselves for their inability to push away negative feelings.[24] In Chapter 6, I will discuss how the "fake it 'til you make it" approach is encouraged in some unemployment support settings but usually backfires. In that chapter, I will also explore an alternative and more sociological approach that facilitates the open sharing of feelings and experiences with others, which can offer relief and support and help combat internalized stigma.

The ability to share one's negative feelings in a supportive setting with people you can trust is critically important because there are other contexts, such as interviewing with employers, in which negative feelings do need to be safely compartmentalized. Doug describes his experience of feeling one way but presenting the opposite to employers as similar to being "Dr. Jekyll and Mr. Hyde:"

> Unemployment has challenged my thought of what value can I add. Have I been a failure in my career? It's been a real challenge. Like any jobseeker, I try to sell myself well and honestly and sincerely—you want to be everything good to every employer. But I also want to be myself and so I've got to put myself out there and really focus on the best things that I've done. That requires me to be—I don't know if it's Dr. Jekyll and Mr. Hyde—but to force myself to *present* self-esteem. Which is sometimes difficult.

While Doug reports that compartmentalizing his actual feelings is hard, Thomas, a health researcher in his late 40s, reports that it can make him feel like a "fraud:"

> Emotionally, it's been really tough. I've identified so closely with my career until recently. I mean I still identify with it, and yet I feel like a bit of a *fraud* because I haven't been working for several years. With strangers, I'll do a shorthand, "This is what I've done." But the deeper story is that it's been hard not to have something that I can contribute to. It's been tough and it takes its toll in terms of confidence, which is exactly what you don't want when you're going out trying to sell yourself to people for work.

These emotional challenges ricochet and build on each other, pulling jobseekers in multiple directions. Feeling like a "fraud" or like "Dr. Jekyll and Mr. Hyde" can undermine the confidence necessary for a job search. Sharon explains how the unemployment experience challenges her ability to effectively interact with potential employers: "I think I have begun to second-guess my every move to the point where I may come across as lacking confidence or not genuine or authentic."

The challenge facing Doug, Thomas, and Sharon is complicated due to contradictory forces. On the one hand, to effectively job search they must suppress and compartmentalize their negative emotions. This imperative will be clearly shown in the next section where I discuss recruiters' reactions to any expression of jobseekers' negative emotions. On the other hand, the broader culture valorizes and encourages authenticity and leaves these jobseekers feeling fraudulent, inauthentic, or like "Dr. Jekyll and Mr. Hyde" when hiding their negative feelings.[25] Feeling fraudulent or inauthentic in turn creates more negative feelings and constitutes one of the many feedback loops that make the experience of long-term unemployment particularly challenging.

Red Flags: How Negative Emotions Look to Recruiters

For all the reasons described in this chapter, the experience of unemployment is a powerful generator of negative emotions. As much as the unemployed jobseeker may wish to banish these energy-draining feelings, they nevertheless arise.[26] And if such feelings surface in interactions with employers, then they become a formidable obstacle to re-employment. The reason is simple: Employers' see negative emotions as disqualifying.

In my interviews with recruiters, it was clear that employers seek candidates who are "positive" and anything else raises a "red flag." As Erin, a recruiter, puts it:

> People who are older or feel discriminated against or lost their job due to an unfair boss, sometimes express that. That doesn't help to get a job. If you're not happy about your previous boss, it's a red flag at the interview. *They need to be positive.* Being upset with a past boss is a pretty bad thing.

Notably, Erin makes no attempt to discern whether the applicant may have a good reason to be upset with a past boss. Negative feelings—justified or not—are a deal breaker. Cindy, another recruiter, provides a more detailed explanation of why:

> Sometimes I think it's people's own attitudes and personalities that are keeping them out of work for as long as they are. You need to get beyond this negative feeling. If you don't, it's coming across to me. . . . Because it does come through that you're depressed or you're not feeling confident about yourself. When you go out and interview like that, it absolutely—I could see it the moment somebody walks in the door. I can hear it in their voice. You need to work through this before you go out and interview. Otherwise, you're kind of dead on arrival.

Cindy's pointing to "attitudes and personalities" as the cause of unemployed workers' difficulties is a powerful illustration of how stigma works. The stigmatized are shunned, they react negatively to being shunned, and then that reaction is held against them and becomes a further reason for shunning.[27]

Disqualification due to negative feelings or sharing emotional frustration with unemployment extends outside the context of job interviews. In Chapter 7 I will discuss how jobseekers speaking to the media about difficult unemployment experiences is also held against them, and the same holds true regarding sharing on social media. Bob, a recruiter, tells me that he follows potential candidates on Twitter to "see if they complain a lot."

Looking closely at recruiter Cindy's remarks quoted above, it is clear that not only must the jobseeker not be negative, he or she must project self-confidence, which Cindy, for one, claims she can determine "the moment somebody walks in the door." Ron, another recruiter, reacts the same way:

> Walking into an interview with those feelings [of lack of confidence], it comes through loud and clear. And they're not going to get anywhere feeling that way. You're not going to be able to convince someone that you can come in and do a job.

The requirement of self-confidence is a difficult obstacle because the experience of unemployment destroys self-confidence. It would require being superhuman for anyone to experience a long string of rejections from employers, on top of stigmatized reactions from colleagues, and yet, somehow, feel a strong sense of confidence. Confidence can surely rebound with positive experiences; research reveals that the most effective way to deal with the variety of distresses associated with unemployment is getting a new job.[28] But of course, this most direct way of rebuilding confidence is made difficult by the rigid hiring practices that make the lack of confidence a disqualification.

* * *

All told, we have a perfect vicious cycle, or what I call in this book the stigma trap. For whatever reason, you lose your job. Once you are unemployed you are treated with suspicion and stigma because of your unemployment, making it harder to find a job. The difficulties in finding work predictably lead to negative emotions and undermine confidence. And any hint of negative emotions or lack of confidence resulting from this stigma and job search difficulty lead to further suspicion, stigma, and exclusion from consideration.

This chapter has shown how prolonged unemployment undermines not one but several aspects of the unemployed jobseeker's identity. Not only that, but the different attacks on one's identity reinforce each other. Particularly powerful is the way that the labor market experiences of rejection and the subsequent destabilizing of one's identity as a valued and contributing professional is typically accompanied by a financial crisis that makes it hard to anchor oneself in other elements of one's identity, such as being a good parent. If the financial crisis gets bad enough, one may no longer even feel like a legitimate adult.

Meanwhile, unemployment also generates anxiety, and that anxiety gets worse over time. With each passing day, the resume gap grows longer, and the stigma grows stronger. At the same time, whatever savings you have are being used up and you're getting closer to going over the cliff. The anxiety is exacerbated by the constant and taxing mental work of figuring out how to stave off depleting one's resources and deciding what to cut and what to pay. This juggling act occurs simultaneously with various job search activities that also require constant decision-making for how best to spend one's time and energy.

The challenges to one's identity and financial well-being and the ever-intensifying anxiety all predicably generate negative emotions. These in turn become another formidable barrier to employment because recruiters rigidly exclude from consideration anyone exhibiting negative emotions.

To comprehend the complete picture of the emotional toll of unemployment we must also keep in mind other key aspects of the experience discussed in prior chapters, such as the repeated rejections from companies who seem to swallow applications like a black hole, and the often more painful personalized rejections from network contacts. While all these different experiences are presented here in separate chapters, one after the other, to fully appreciate the real-life experience of unemployment requires keeping in mind that unemployed jobseekers are enduring these labor market, financial, identity, and emotional challenges simultaneously.

And there is yet one more critical dimension of the unemployment experience that must be considered to complete the picture: the effect on close personal relationships. We may hope that in times of turmoil, most unemployed jobseekers would have spouses or close friends to lean on for support. But, as we will see in Chapter 5, these relationships can also be marred by stigma, producing tensions that exacerbate the crisis of unemployment.

5

Our Closest Relations

Marriages and Friendships

At their best, our closest relationships can be a crucial source of support. But when prolonged unemployment brings shame and self-doubt, and when one's identity is challenged on multiple fronts amid ongoing emotional and financial crises, the marriages and close friendships we thought we could rely on tend to become strained and either do not offer much support or, in some cases, even exacerbate the emotional hardship jobseekers are already experiencing.[1]

Spouses and friends generally do love and care, but like everyone else, they live and breathe the myth of meritocracy suffusing American society and can adopt the same stigmas that we have already seen in recruiters and network contacts, and that are internalized by jobseekers themselves. Yet, while stigma may be ubiquitous, encountering it in these closest of relationships can be among the most painful aspects of unemployment.

In marriage, the strains are often the result of the couple's lives being highly intertwined, which leads to mutual expectations and mutual disappointments. The spouse of the unemployed person often feels disappointed with the lack of financial and household contribution, while the unemployed spouse often feels disappointed at not being understood or receiving more empathy. Strikingly, the marriages that do well in such periods are those in which both partners have experienced prolonged unemployment, a shared experience that makes it less likely that the unemployed spouse will be seen through a stigmatizing lens.

Whereas marriages struggle because both spouses' lives are intertwined in the same rickety boat, friendships struggle because the friends now find themselves in such different boats and with powerful currents pulling them apart. Friends who previously worked together have less in common, and opportunities for socializing no longer spontaneously arise. Non-work friendships are strained by differences in financial resources—the unemployed friends can no longer afford to go out the way they used to—as well as by feelings of shame that lead to social withdrawal. Most painfully, some unemployed jobseekers experience stigma in their friends' reactions. Even in decades-long friendships, unemployed jobseekers report being seen through that same skeptical lens that we have seen come up everywhere.

What Happens to Marriages?

Marriages can make all the difference. In periods of unemployment, spouses become even more central in their partner's life and are often the only adult the unemployed jobseeker regularly sees and talks to. For some of my interviewees, the marital bonds were strengthened through this hardship and spouses were able to provide crucial emotional support. More often, however, unemployed workers reported increased marital tensions that exacerbated the multi-front crisis described in Chapter 4. I will first discuss the tensions that typically arise and then consider what makes the difference in the cases in which marriages provided effective support.[2]

At the top of the list of typical sources of marital tension is money. Simply put, the financial crisis frequently becomes a marriage crisis. Often, unemployment leads to spouses feeling disappointed, especially if they had strong expectations that their spouse would bring in a significant income. Among my interviewees, this marital tension arose most commonly for unemployed heterosexual married men, which fits with other recent research finding that men are still disproportionately expected—and expect themselves—to be the family's main breadwinner.[3]

Bruce, for example, is 58 years old and has worked at senior levels of corporate marketing. He has been married for 37 years. Bruce reports that "stresses at home on the financial side have been tough." When he first lost his job, his wife was encouraging and positive. But over time, tensions emerged, especially as it became clear that Bruce and his wife will need to sell their suburban house and move into a smaller townhouse. "I basically wiped out my entire retirement fund because I felt I needed to do whatever I had to do to support my family," he explains. "My middle child just started his last semester at college and I haven't yet paid the second-semester tuition." To pay tuition and other bills, Bruce and his wife were forced to sell the house in which they raised their kids, a move that has deeply destabilized their marriage: "My wife is very unhappy. As did I, she thought that our life would be in a different place at this point in time." Bruce's wife told him that, once they sell the house, "she's not really sure what we're going to do in terms of the marriage." At this point, Bruce gets quiet, gives me a pained look, and just says, "Obviously, that's very, very difficult."

Both Bruce and his wife are most certainly not where they expected to be at this stage in their life. They are both experiencing stress, uncertainty, and the hardship of downward mobility. But the fact that this leads Bruce's wife to question their marriage reveals that beyond the shared financial hardship, she is frustrated or disappointed not only with the situation but with Bruce himself. As Bruce explained in a follow-up interview: "We come from a generation of the husband being the breadwinner."

Ed finds himself in a similar situation and is more explicit in naming the role of breadwinner expectations in his marital tensions. Ed's wife works, but her salary is not enough to cover their expenses: "I have racked up credit card debt to try to cover some of the expenses of our household operations. We're reining back spending. We're living a whole lot more conservatively. Even so, it's tough. And it's put a huge, huge stress on our marriage." Ed explains:

> My relationship with my wife is really fraught with difficulty in this situation because I didn't realize how much she really wanted a breadwinner in the mix. I can also understand that completely. I'm not holding my own. . . . I don't want to let my loved ones down. So that's a huge thing.

In Ed's words we can hear that his struggle stems from both his wife's disappointment in his lack of breadwinning and his own internalized sense that he is letting his "loved ones" down. Derrick, too, feels that the well-being of his marriage is contingent on his breadwinning. At the time of our interview, Derrick's marriage was in better shape than Bruce's or Ed's, but this was only because he still had savings that allowed him to keep supporting his wife and daughter: "I haven't been condemned or anything because I'm still able to provide and so they're cutting me some slack. But they are wondering how I'm coming up with money, so I told them I had broken the piggy bank, and no one really knew how much I had in the piggy bank, so it's helping. But it's only for a very limited time, so money is definitely a concern daily." When I asked Derrick if his relationship with his wife has been affected by his unemployment, he answered: "No, because I've been able to provide. *Absolutely, if I wasn't able to provide, I probably wouldn't be married today.*" Ed feels like he is married on borrowed time, and with each day that his savings are depleted, he feels closer to the day when his marriage may collapse. Strikingly, in Ed's, Bruce's, and Derrick's narratives, there is pain but not anger at their spouses, suggesting that the breadwinner expectations are largely shared, internalized, and go unquestioned.

In an interesting twist, but one which further points to the gendered pattern where men are still commonly expected to be the breadwinners, Stacy describes how during her unemployment she has become resentful of her working but low-earning husband: "I have always been the primary breadwinner and it wasn't an issue when we first got together. It was okay with me and him that I was the highly paid career-charging workaholic and he would contribute much less than myself. Now, I really, really resent having made this partner choice." The arrangement of Stacy being the main breadwinner worked well as long as Stacy had a high-paying job. Now, when she is unemployed, she has difficulties accepting her husband's relatively low earnings. This was the only case in which disappointment with respect to a spouse's capacity for breadwinning was expressed by the unemployed jobseeker and not by their spouse, but it fits the larger pattern of breadwinning expectations falling disproportionately on men.

Intertwined Lives: "Everything That Happens to Me Happens to Her"

Marital disappointment can flow both ways. Whereas spouses of unemployed jobseekers can feel disappointment regarding their partner's failure at breadwinning, the unemployed person often feels disappointment at their spouse's lack of understanding, inability to relate, or incapacity to empathize with their experience of unemployment. Of all relationships, marriage comes with the strongest expectations of understanding and emotional support; yet this was often lacking. For example, this is how Michelle describes her husband's response to her unemployment:

> It's not a really strong, supportive relationship. He is somebody who doesn't particularly like his job. He would love to not have his job. He doesn't get why I'm sitting around complaining all the time about not having a job. Why aren't I enjoying not having a job? Why aren't I going out and doing fun things and making the most of this? So for him, he wants to quit his job. So I feel like he doesn't get me, doesn't understand what I'm going through.

Echoing Michelle's experience, Brian told me that his wife "knows what I'm going through, but personally she doesn't really understand it." The interviews suggest that the challenge of not only knowing, but—as Brian put it—"really understanding" what the unemployed partner is experiencing stems from the complicated ways in which married couple's financial, emotional, and domestic lives are intertwined. When trying to think about the factors that make it difficult to talk about unemployment with his wife and to receive emotional support, Doug insightfully observes that whereas his friends "can more just sympathize and there's no strain there from a financial relationship," for his wife, "there's the financial thing . . . and everything *that happens to me happens to her.*"[4]

Doug's observation crystallizes how a spouse's own significant personal stake in the outcome, direction, and intensity of their spouse's job search makes it hard for the spouse to assume the role of a purely supportive and empathetic partner. The intertwined lives of jobseekers and their spouses and their shared stakes in the outcome often lead the spouses into the fraught territory of getting involved in the job search and advocating certain strategies or directions, which jobseekers can experience as pressure, judgment, and even criticism—certainly not empathy. For example, a difficult strategic decision my unemployed interviewees need to make is whether and when to take a nonprofessional survival job just to help pay the bills. Such a job does earn some money and it can reduce isolation and feel rewarding, but it takes time and energy away from the search for a professional job, and it can also undermine one's identity as a professional and become a trap. Ideally, jobseekers would get support from their spouses in making this tough decision, but too often this is instead a loaded conversation that just increases the pressure.

Cynthia, for example, had been the director of a nonprofit organization and is now applying for jobs in nonprofits. Her husband, however, finds it hard to simply empathize with her job search difficulties and pressures her to take a survival job in retail:

> He keeps saying, "Why don't you go get a job at Trader Joe's?" . . . I'm trying to find that sweet middle ground. It might not be my dream job. I'm just looking for a job that I can find satisfying enough. The most challenging thing is just trying to figure it out. And continue. My husband said to me, "How long are you going to keep at this? When are you going to give up?" I don't know what to say when he says that to me.

As Cynthia tries to persevere in her job search and make strategic decisions, her husband's suggestions and questions are not only unhelpful but become yet one more source of stress and anguish.

Tim's wife is also actively involved in his job search, but in this case pushing in the opposite direction. Tim figures his best course of action is to aim for a lower-level job and work his way back up, but his wife is against it:

> She's like, "Oh my god, that's so low." She doesn't want me to take it. She's thinking we're going nowhere with me taking a lower-paying one. I feel like I have a longer-range view of things than her. I think she's got more a real short-term thing and she's just looking for how much are they going to pay me right now. And I'm looking at how much I'm going to end up getting after 5 or 10 years.

Spouses of unemployed workers are not only invested in the kinds of jobs their spouses apply for but also in the equally fraught topic of how hard they're looking. Emotional support is complicated by the frustration spouses may feel about their unemployed partners' negative emotions, which can result in a decline in the intensity of their job hunting.[5] Sandra and her husband are both long-term unemployed, but Sandra perceives herself as the one trying harder to find a new job and this leads to considerable marital strife: "I think I'm more of a fighter than he is, so it's hard to watch somebody not fighting, giving up. Hard for me to be patient with that. . . . I've had a lot of anger with my husband because he has just given up. He didn't show any inner fortitude in this and sometimes in my home I feel alone." Such difficulties in fully understanding and empathizing with the other person's struggle are common—Sandra was hardly the only unemployed jobseeker feeling *alone* in her marriage.

"Having Me Not Work . . . Works for Her"

Married couples are intertwined not only financially but also in the realm of household labor—and this can become another obstacle to empathetic support. Richard has been searching for work for 2 years. Rejections and fruitless networking have taken the predictable emotional toll, so that, as he readily acknowledges, "even being at home, I haven't been so productive. Frequently I just feel too low to get moving or get the car fixed or refinish the furniture or whatever it is that needs to be done. There's a tension there from that." His marriage has become an additional source of tension due to his wife's resentment that he is not doing more household tasks. A similar tension undermines Sandra's marriage. She and her husband are both long-term unemployed, but she feels resentful that she is "struggling to hold the fort" in terms of housework and her husband "isn't volunteering and I can't get him to help with the housework." Sandra is particularly upset because "all the time I spend on housework is time I'm not spending looking for a job."[6] It may seem reasonable to expect that an unemployed spouse who is not bringing in money at least contribute more household labor. But from the unemployed person's point of view this expectation can feel like a lack of understanding of the draining effects of job searching and the emotional toll of unemployment. Ryan discusses his wife's expectation that he do more around the house:

> She might think I'm not doing anything, but looking for a job is more than 40 hours. You always have to be on—that's a stress. There's a lot of pressure if you're in a family. From a financial perspective, it puts on a lot of pressure that you have to deal with. My wife says, "You're not doing enough." What the hell? I can only do so much. It hurts.

The issue of the division of household labor can also play out in other ways. An unemployed spouse who does take on a large share of the housework can come to fear that the working spouse is becoming invested in this new division of labor and therefore less interested in—and supportive of—the unemployed person actually finding a job. Alicia reports that her financial situation is "not bad because my husband is a programmer in a financial organization" and makes a good salary. Given the lack of financial pressure, Alicia has noticed that her husband seems to rather like having her unemployed: "Of course he likes when I'm at home not working because I usually spend my time cooking, decorating, and making the house cozy." Ronald's wife also seems to be enjoying having him unemployed and doing more around the house, even though they are financially strapped:

> I have had a lot of free time to be the househusband. To take care of so many things for [my wife]. I do the shopping, the cooking, the cleaning. I get our daughter to and from school. I take care of all that and I think there is some degree of fear on her part: "Well, if Ronald gets a full-time job and

has to work, I'll have to do some of those things that I don't have to do now."
I know she often feels that her full-time job taps her out. . . . She doesn't
like the challenge and the emotions that unemployment created for me. But
I think also for her, having me not work is a good thing. It works for her.

Stepping back, listening to my interviewees, we hear that whether they are
doing a little or a lot of housework, the deep intertwining of their lives with
their spouse means that it is often difficult for the spouse to assume to role of
a support person whose primary agenda is to hear, understand, and empathize with their partner's multi-layered emotional crises and experiences of
stigma as discussed in prior chapters.

Ironically, receiving effective emotional support from a spouse can also
be tricky because the spouses' deep emotional investment in the unemployed jobseeker's well-being can make hearing about their pain difficult
to bear. Nathan has experienced the sadly all too common emotional turmoil of crushed hopes throughout his search process: "I had a number of
positions that I really wanted, that I thought I was very qualified for, that
I went through several interviews for, only to be the second choice and to not
get it. And those would be followed by a period of depression, where I would
get down." Unfortunately, his spouse could not provide emotional support in
those hardest moments:

> My wife would always have a sort of problem-solving mode. "Oh, just do
> this. Just do that." To resolve that, as opposed to being able to enter into the
> hurt of that rejection and say, "Well, that's natural. That's OK. You should
> be disappointed." Her inability to really enter into that in a way that was
> supportive to me, is definitely a challenge for our relationship. She doesn't
> want to see me feeling in pain because it causes her pain. And so she is just,
> "What can we do to stop Nathan's pain as quickly as possible?" And that's
> not necessarily what I need at that point. I need to just kind of feel my way
> through that and say, "Yeah, this is disappointing."

Nathan contrasted his disappointing experience with his wife to the experience of being interviewed for this book: "You and I are talking about this
differently. You're asking and you're just listening. The emotional content can
be whatever the emotional content is. And you're not jumping in and telling
me, 'You should do this, you should do that.' " Much easier, of course, for me
to stay calm and listen than for his wife.

"We Have Been Able to Face the Terror Together"

Despite all the obstacles, some marriages are a strong source of support. What makes these different? The most striking factor was that both spouses had at some point experienced long-term unemployment.

Aaron's case is typical for marriages that provide strong support. Aaron's husband had also been through prolonged unemployment earlier in his career, as Aaron explains: "My husband is very sympathetic. He went through the same process about 10 years ago himself. He was in a greater financial bind. He has understood what I am going through since I first lost my job." It also helps that Aaron's husband is frustrated with his current job and looking for another, so they're both job hunting: "I understand what he's going through now with his frustrations with his job. So we can truly sympathize with each other. I'm giving him advice about job-searching and how to deal with his resume and he gives me the motivation I need to continue what I'm doing as well."

The commonality of experience helped marriages by allowing the spouse of the unemployed worker to better understand the challenges at hand. In some cases these common experiences also helped the unemployed jobseeker retrospectively better understand the past struggles of their spouse. For example, Brenda describes her marriage as remarkably supportive: "We have been able to face the terror together and, in so doing, built a bond that is amazingly durable. . . . That together we have been able to endure outrageous assaults on every front is a tremendous balm." Brenda explains that her marital bond has been strengthened by the fact that her own struggles with unemployment have allowed her to better understand her husband's past struggles and responses:

> I've been married for almost 30 years and there were tensions in my marriage before I lost my job. Most of them relate to differences in ambition and effort. I am ambitious and act on my ambitions. My husband has plenty of dreams and ambitions, but doesn't work at it like I do. Ironically, with my job loss, things have gotten better between us. One of the reasons is that I now know what it's like to want to work—to know you're good— and to be overlooked, underestimated, and ultimately never hired. This is what happened to him and it's been happening since he was in his 40s. He's African American, an early adopter, and a geek—but he's older, he doesn't look like anyone else, and he can't get a job in his field to save his life.

Brenda's current experiences with unemployment are allowing her to see her husband's past struggles in a new light, less about a lack of "ambition and effort" and more about external obstacles due to his age and race. This recognition brings them closer together. Another variation on this theme can be heard in Laura's story. She, too, receives strong support from her spouse and finds that her unemployment "somehow brought us closer together." In this case, there was repair of past tensions stemming from breadwinning expectations that Laura's husband had imposed on himself and internalized. Laura explains:

> Having to go through this unemployment together and losing the house and losing the retirement, *we sort of came together*. We worked it through together. We problem-solved together, we cried together. In some ways it was good for my husband because I've always been the primary breadwinner in the family. He stayed home for 18 years raising our kids. And he works now in [a hospital]. He only brings home like $450 a week, which is not a lot of money. But we are living on that money and it is good for him to feel like his contribution is essential.

In the positive cases where marriages got stronger during unemployment, spouses often expressed feelings of appreciation for their partner's contributions. The previously discussed tensions around breadwinning and household work boil down to a core concern of married couples that each person make a contribution, or at least be understood as doing their best. While for most couples, the contributions are tangible, in one unique case the contribution was simply one's presence. Steven's wife made it clear to him that even though he is not bringing in money, he is still contributing to her happiness and well-being simply by spending time with her—an understanding that allowed Steven to have the exceptional experience of seeing his own value independent of breadwinning or housework:

> My wife has been unbelievably supportive. I mean beyond reason. When I do nothing during the day, I'm killing myself because I haven't been functional. My wife says, "You do what you can do. It's okay. You don't have to be perfect or functional every single day." She lets me know that I enhance her life, which I didn't know 3 years ago. I'm contributing something. I'm not working. I'm doing nothing. But I feel better being able to see that now,

so I don't feel as guilty. She's happy when she comes home and she sees me. That's offering something in a relationship.

Steven's articulation of a sense of contribution that is not related to paid work, housework, or caring for children—but simply to spending time with his wife—is inspiring, and rare. Most marriages are challenged by long-term unemployment and, for many jobseekers, their marriage is not a source of support but one more aggravating factor that increases the emotional toll of unemployment.

Exceptional cases are often helpful for understanding the typical forces at play that determine whether a couple ends up "facing the terror together" or not. These exceptional cases suggest that an important factor is the extent to which the long-term unemployment is viewed through a lens that highlights external barriers or a lens that blames and stigmatizes the unemployed spouse. In the encouraging cases above, we saw how a spouse's past experience with prolonged unemployment helped reduce stigma and enhance empathy and understanding. But even if a spouse has not directly endured a similar experience in the past, it can help to know someone else—besides one's own spouse—who is also in this position. For example, Paul reports that his wife "accuses me of being too particular" in his job search and is "frustrated by having to live on an austerity budget." Nonetheless, Paul explains that it helps that his wife knows another person who is long-term unemployed:

It helps to have a distant family friend who lost his job like a year and a half ago. It helps support my position that he's been out a year and a half. She can see that it's not just me. Plus we have another friend of mine and he's been struggling. He lost his job a year and a half before I lost mine and he's been struggling for just as long as I have, and he's 10 years younger than me. That further supports the fact that it's not just me.

Paul's story reveals the importance of a spouse's understandings and assumptions about the causes of unemployment and—implicitly—how much blame he or she attaches to the individual for their unemployment. Unfortunately, many couples do not personally know others who are long-term unemployed. A more typical case is Ryan, who feels undermined by the fact that his wife was recently unemployed but very quickly found a new job:

What happened was she was laid off for four weeks and she was able to get a job in four weeks. So that was good news and that was bad news. Meaning that she never got to go through this. . . . My wife doesn't understand it.

Let's leave the subject of marriages for now. What about friendships? They presumably aren't as intertwined and fraught as a marriage, so are they perhaps a better source of support and empathy?

What Happens to Friendships?

Compared to spouses, friends appear to be well-positioned to be strong sources of support. Friends care, but unlike spouses, they are not directly affected by their friend's unemployment. For unemployed workers who are single and who are not close to their families, friends may be the only source of potential support. And for some interviewees, friendships are indeed deeply supportive and in some unusual cases even become closer during the unemployment period. When this happens it is due to spending more time together and to the emotional support strengthening their bond. Unfortunately, it is far more common for friendships to weaken during periods of long-term unemployment.

Why do friendships generally not live up to their promise? My interviews reveal that just when unemployed workers feel isolated and most in need of social support, a set of predictable forces—themselves tied to being unemployed—leads them to paradoxically withdraw from their friendships. At the same time, the forces of stigma—that we have repeatedly seen in this book—also lead their friends to withdraw from them.

The Predictable Forces Pulling Friendships Apart

The loss of a job not only entails the loss of income and a challenge to core identities—as if that were not enough. It also brings the loss of work friends and other social connections that are built into one's work. As Tom, a widower, put it: "One of the hardest things for me is missing my immediate coworkers. I miss their voices. I miss the 10 minutes we'd take to go get coffee in the morning. It's tough. I miss their friendship." Tom, like many others in their 50s, has a very meager friendship circle outside work.[7] Even those who had many friends when they were younger typically find themselves in their 50s and 60s with a circle of friends that is much smaller and—critically—is more centered at work. Damon explains how this typically comes about:

> Since I got married, the only friends we really talk to are my wife's high school friend and her husband. I've kept in touch with a couple friends, but for the most part, people get married and the people you grew up with, you send Christmas cards to each other, and you stay out of touch.

Damon would like to get back in touch with old friends, but given his current unemployment, he feels that "it would be kind of difficult to tell them what I'm going through."

Many interviewees describe how, after their job loss, work friendships evaporated more quickly than they expected. Ruby observed that until she lost her job, she "didn't really appreciate how much of my social contacts were work-oriented." To her surprise, work friends were just "no longer a part of my life." She explained how those friendships faded, despite good intentions, because they were rooted in work-based commonalities:

> When you leave, people all say, "Stay in touch." But in the real world, people don't generally stay in touch because you can't talk about your boss anymore and you can't talk about what you did—that day-to-day of the job. So generally, people don't stay in touch. Even if [they] have good intentions. Even though I may have a Christmas card from people or maybe get together for a drink now or then. But it never really happens.

There are numerous predictable forces that undermine continued friendship with former work colleagues, even if everyone has "good intentions." One key factor is the absence of unplanned interactions. Friendships that were previously constantly renewed and developed in everyday work interactions or during brief breaks now require deliberate effort and planning. With American professionals typically working long hours,[8] many find it difficult to connect with their old work friends, who seem to always be, as Mary put it, "overwhelmed and very tired."

An additional force pulling friends apart is that unemployed people and their old work friends have much less in common. As Ruby said, "You can't talk about your boss anymore." This was often noted by interviewees who now realized how much work friendships depend on bonding through gossiping or complaining *at work and about work,* and how quickly those friendships faded without that common grounding. Elizabeth pointed to the fact that this happens even to close relationships:

> When you're not working any more, even colleagues that you had close relationships with, you have less and less in common with. And so even those that were really such great friends, you don't have much in common. So if you go out for a drink, there's no more gossip. There are friends that I really miss, but we are just not in touch anymore. People are busy and our friendship was based on work, even though we talked about family and other stuff.

The loss of spontaneous interactions and work-based commonalities are only two of the predictable factors undermining work-based friendships. Another key factor that threatens to undermine all friendships, work-based or not, is money.

Money, Money, Money

As we saw when talking about marriages, money is a key source of tension because spouses are financially intertwined. Friends do not typically rely on each other financially, but the lack of money nonetheless plays a critical role in undermining friendships because friends tend to meet outside the home, most typically going out for dinner or drinks or other activities, which requires spending the discretionary money that unemployed workers no longer feel they have. Having friends over to one's home is possible, but many formerly work-based relationships aren't up to that level of intimacy, and spending time at home may not provide an opportunity for one-on-one connecting if one has a spouse or partner, children, or roommates or is living with parents.

Lack of money leads unemployed workers to pull away from friends. Elizabeth explains that she avoids friends in order to avoid uncomfortable interactions:

> I don't have the money to go out for dinner. If somebody says, "Let's have dinner," I don't. I can't. So that's sometimes a little uncomfortable. I don't

want to say, "Because I don't have the money." And sometimes people say, "Oh, I'll buy." And I don't want them to say that either.

Anthony did go out to eat with friends, but he's not likely to do it again:

> We're at a restaurant or something and I'll be thinking to myself about, "Gee, I hope this bill isn't too big." Whereas they're working and they're probably not thinking twice about it, like I didn't used to think twice about it.

Elizabeth not wanting her friends to buy her dinner and Anthony's thinking to himself about the size of the bill but not openly talking about it with his friends suggest that the issue of money is about more than just money, or being able to afford going out with friends.[9] It's a matter of identity—an identity one can no longer project. For example, the lack of money leaves Sandra unable to keep up her social identity as a generous person who treats others: "I've always enjoyed being generous and I can't be generous anymore." The lack of money also undermines the sense of similarity and commonality underlying friendships. Nicole's group of friends enjoys traveling together. Nicole can't afford to do that with them anymore, but even worse, she finds it difficult to get together with her friends locally because "they're talking about places they've been and I haven't." Even if most of the time Nicole's friends are not engaged in unaffordable activities, her inability to participate in group trips means that she misses out on key bonding moments and comes to feel like an outsider. It marks her as different. Or, as Daniel put it, not being able to spend money like his friends makes him "weird":

> You are watching every penny and so you reach a point where, indirectly, a lot of other things have started to happen. You feel a little bit isolated and like a *very weird creature*. It's not a good feeling. Where you are not making a living and you're having a very hard time surviving, it becomes a very, very ugly situation with the abundance in the wider society. A lot of standards are so well in place that when you fall below those standards, maybe you feel like, "Huh, *I'm odd* in the way that I don't want to be."

Well before you can't afford basic necessities, you find yourself unable to afford to be the kind of person you want to be with other people. Daniel's quote illustrates how beyond the material level of the financial struggle—paying your basic bills—there is another level to the struggle which is about falling below what he refers to as the expected "standards" of spending that is necessary for maintaining sense of social belonging and not feeling "odd."

Stepping back, the lack of money needed for social belonging is just another way that prolonged unemployment undermines commonalities among friends. Whereas shared experiences like having the same irritating boss or going out to dinner and traveling together can lead to bonding, the typical unemployment experiences—which involve financial and emotional distress—are not shared with one's friends and as such open an experiential chasm that even formerly close friendships often cannot bridge. The way many long-term unemployed interviewees discussed this growing divide is simply observing that their friends cannot "relate," and that they come to feel different from their friends, in Daniel's words, like "a very weird creature."[10]

Unemployed jobseekers feel they have become not only *different from* but also *less than* their old friends. Socializing can lead to comparing one's situation to that of friends, and given the financial, emotional, and often marital crises unemployed workers are experiencing, comparisons usually leave them feeling bad about themselves. Joseph puts it this way: "I've certainly cut back on socializing. You feel uncomfortable about where you are in your life versus where your friends are. Some of these folks have jobs ranging from vice presidents to directors to doctors. So you tend to not socialize as much."[11] As we saw in the previous chapter, important elements of identity are rooted in perceived professional success, and socializing makes differences in career success painfully clear. Steven puts it this way:

> I've withdrawn from a lot of people. I don't feel like going out and socializing as an unemployed guy. I don't get together with people. I've actually let relationships go. It all has to do with the change in my status. I was very proud of what I did. Not very proud of this state that I'm in right now. It's hard. It's just not an easy, comfortable thing to go out and have interactions and relations in the outside world when, for the most part, they're working, functioning people, and you're not. I have to own a lot of this close friendships being dropped. A lot of it's on me.

We can hear the internalized stigma. It is Steven, not some job recruiter, who describes himself as *not* being a "functioning" person, and how this in turn leads him to socially withdraw. Similarly, Doug explains that he has not been "great at maintaining my friendships" because "I kind of feel like I'm bereft of a position and I often feel like, 'Okay, what do I have to talk about?'" Doug's misgivings, and his uncertainty about what he could "talk about," suggest the great extent to which he relies on his worker identity when presenting himself to others. This same loss of identity—and the shame associated with it—led Deborah to go to the extreme measure of not even letting her friends know she was still unemployed:

> Virtually no one knows I'm living a lie. My writing job is volunteer and my resume and LinkedIn profile are set up to gloss over that fact. It is a great strain. I never thought I would end up like this. I went to a competitive school, got a master's degree at another great school, had a great job and now am living in near-poverty, accepting help from my mother and the government. My college and graduate school friends and acquaintances have all far surpassed me. Part of me feels too unworthy to be. It is a great huge strain, virtually all of the time. It is ego-taxing and ego-draining. It makes me not want to have relationships because I feel "less than."

I spoke with many others who felt the same pain of internalized stigma and of feeling "less than," that led Deborah to hide her unemployment status from her friends, and cut back on relationships. But there is also a powerful external force that undermines friendships just when we need them most. It's that force that comes up in every chapter of this book: stigma.

Stigma Among Friends

Unemployment stigma is ubiquitous. It can be spotted in any situation when the unemployed person is seen as potentially flawed or otherwise solely to blame for being unemployed. We've seen stigma arise in the reactions of recruiters, network contacts, and spouses and in how one sees oneself. Not surprisingly, many interviewees also experienced being stigmatized by their friends. In a few exceptional cases this was explicit and said out loud. Brenda was called a "loser" by a friend who dropped her. But much more commonly, stigma is communicated indirectly through friends' awkward questions, unsolicited advice, silences, and subtle withdrawals that, over time, undermine the friendship connection.

Why do friends stigmatize their friends? In addition to the widely held belief in the United States in the myth of meritocracy and relatedly that unemployment is a personal failing, when someone who is considered similar to oneself becomes unemployed, it likely provokes fears about one's own job security. To quell such fears, it might seem helpful to imagine how one would not get caught in long-term unemployment oneself or how one would find a way out of it. The problem with this approach—imagining how you would avoid or overcome such a disaster—is that it implicitly paints the unemployed person as "other" and "inferior."[12] It is tempting to think that whatever you would have done, obviously this person has not done—but should have. This implicit belief in the culpability of the unemployed person undermines relating and connecting. Sharon describes her experience of a close friend simply disappearing:

> I have been surprised at how little support I receive from friends, especially one who I considered my closest friend. When I was first laid off, she was a little bit helpful. But less than 6 months after I got laid off, she just fell off the planet. She and I were friends for years and we had a relationship beyond work. We used to talk all the time. It just seems like just when I need a friend the most, she disappeared. I don't know whether she couldn't deal with my situation.

When I probed Sharon about *why* she thinks her friend disappeared, she shared a hunch based on interactions with other friends:

> Among my friends, there is some attitude of, "Well, you went to Harvard, so I don't know what your problem is. But I'm over hearing about it." With my friends *it's almost like a contagion.* They don't want to hear about it because *it might spread to them*, like they may be next to lose their job. They feel like, "Well, if I talk to you, somehow this is going to spread to me."

Sharon's description of being treated as "contagious" is a classic hallmark of stigma.[13] The idea that one might "catch" unemployment, as if it were a disease, clearly suggests something wrong with the unemployed person— something that is in fact scary and transmissible and best to stay away from. Like Sharon, Sandra also perceives a fear among her friends of "catching" whatever is wrong with her:

> People who have been long-term friends, they haven't been through it. They don't have an understanding and it's threatening. I've heard people say who have gotten divorced, whose marriages have failed, that people often drop them because it's almost like it might be *catching*. So I think there's a little of that, "There must be something wrong with her." . . . I think people who

have jobs think you're not working hard enough to get a job or there must
be something wrong with you. I think it's threatening.

The assumption that something is wrong with the unemployed person can
be revealed through friends' skeptical questions. I asked Cheryl whether she
talks openly with her friends about her difficult experiences:

> I really don't. That's something that is hard for me. My friends I've had for
> most of my life have not really gone through those things. They really can't
> understand it. So when I say I've applied for over 100 jobs in a year, they'll
> say, "Really?" And they find it hard to believe. . . . There's an elephant in the
> room and the elephant is, "Why don't you have a job? We don't understand.
> You're college educated. You have this great background. We've had our
> jobs for 20–30 years. We can't understand why you can't get another job."
> I've had *people who have known me since I was 4 years old say that.* "You've
> always been able to get jobs. What's wrong with now? Maybe you're really
> not working hard enough. We know that sometimes you felt sad and do you
> get out every day?" And I say, "Yes, I do!" And you try to take a breath and
> say, "Okay, they really do not understand."

Sharon's and Cheryl's friends seem desperately to want to hold on to the
myth that if one goes to college, especially a "good" college, one should be
able to find a good job. In the face of clear evidence that this is not the case,
as seen in the story of their close friends—and in Cheryl's case someone
they have known since they were 4 years old—we see the tendency to stigmatize and to explain the unemployment as a personal failing of their unemployed friend.

Friends' negative judgments make their advice fraught. Nicole describes
it this way: "At times I get 'tough love' or get suggestions that show they don't
realize it's what I'm already doing or trying to do." Sharon shares a similar
frustration of having friends say things like " 'Well, if I were laid off, I would
do this.' Or, 'If I were you, I would do that.' And it's like, 'I've tried that and it
didn't work." Friends' advice often conveys the implicit assumption that the
problem is the unemployed person and their actions, or lack thereof, and not
larger forces such as employer stigma and the shrinking availability of good
stable jobs in America's precarious capitalism.

It may be comforting to the friend to imagine that if they were unemployed deploying this or that strategy would offer a way out, but with this sort

of advice the unemployed worker is left feeling belittled and judged. Larry discusses this challenge:

> At a party, they're telling me, "You should do that." Like, "Please, leave me alone." To the point that even holidays are something I dread. I don't want the third degree. Does that make sense? It's always, "You should . . ." Or, "You're doing this wrong. . . ." The suggestion is that you don't know what you're doing. You don't know what to do to find a job. And it just gets really tiresome. It's pointless. Drives you insane. If someone came up with, "You know, I have a colleague who works at this company and I'll put you in touch," that's completely different. But no one has *ever* said anything like that.

Larry's quote captures the experience of many interviewees who received advice from friends, which essentially communicated that their unemployment is their own fault for not searching correctly.

When friends are not able to relate and empathize, the friendship can become a source of pain. This is the case whether friends ask questions and give unsolicited advice or whether they just keep quiet about the unemployment elephant in the room. Silence is the flipside of the coin of unsolicited advice. While advice pretends that if the unemployed jobseeker only did this or that the problem would go away, silence pretends there is no problem. Here is how Lance, who is 54 years and who most recently worked as a university administrator, and Sam, a 62-year-old pharmacist, discussed their interactions with friends in a peer-to-peer interview:

Lance: I think [friends] pretty much keep it to themselves. Every now and again they might ask what's happening or something like that, but that's about it.

Sam: I actually went out with a friend from up the street. We went to a hockey game. He didn't even ask me if I'd been working. I think he's too polite and he's not going to get into it.

But that silence is often interpreted as a negative judgment. As Sam puts it, "There is that gnawing thought that by not mentioning my employment situation, they are commenting on it. So I find myself avoiding them somewhat."

In short, whether expressed through unwanted advice or awkward silences unemployed jobseekers perceive their friends' judgment or unease with their unemployment, which in turn makes the connection difficult. Janis puts it succinctly: "People don't know how to react around me and I feel there's the elephant in the room."

Ultimately, friends' uneasy and stigmatizing reactions to unemployment create distance, and the friendships fade. From the point of view of the friend, it is undoubtedly difficult to know when to ask about the job search and when to stay quiet, when to suggest fun activities or when to create a space for the sharing of dark feelings. There are no scripts or readily available models for how to talk to an unemployed friend.

In some of the cases discussed above, friends withdraw. In other cases, the experience of stigma and awkwardness leads the unemployed worker to be the one to withdraw by either no longer talking with friends about their unemployment or ceasing contact altogether. As Kimberley explains, "I just don't feel comfortable with others, for whatever reason. I don't know, there's just something." In the past, Kimberley found support and comfort with her Bible study group. But fearing negative judgment, she stopped talking with them about her hardships:

> After a while, I just couldn't share any more. After 2 years, you start feeling pretty bad about yourself. I literally stopped all discussion about looking for a job. And no one asked me. All of them have jobs except for one person who has her own business. They're all pretty successful. I got to the point where I felt really uncomfortable [discussing it].

Susan has completely stopped seeing friends: "I can't explain what that is. Just that I'd rather go for a walk by myself. I just don't want to deal with anybody else because I don't want them to ask me what's going on."

Feeling judged and stigmatized, many unemployed jobseekers' friendship bonds weaken just at the time when they are most isolated and need friends. Digging deeper into this dynamic I discover that in some cases, on top of all the other factors that lead to the decline in friendships, another key contributor is the very notion of what a friendship is.

The Meaning of Friendship

Unemployed jobseekers overwhelmingly expect steadfast emotional support from their spouse, but not all of them have this expectation of their friends.

Some of my interviewees expressed an understanding that friends are people with whom you have fun, and therefore engaging with friends requires a certain level of energy that can be in short supply during long-term unemployment. For example, Sharon wishes she had more of a social life, but laments that "I just don't have the mental energy to do it." Kimberley feels the same way:

> I don't have much energy anymore. At times, I feel like I'm barely keeping it together. Taking care of my son and finances and our house. Sometimes I just don't feel like talking. I have met some new friends through the job search, so I connect with them because we have something in common. But there are quite a few people that I don't. Some old friends I just really don't see any more, they don't understand. Certain people have never been out of work or they've never struggled. It doesn't feel comfortable. There's almost no point.

Kimberley can't find the energy to stay connected with old friends who do not understand her situation, but she does have energy to connect with fellow jobseekers who do understand. This suggests that not all friendships are energy-draining. Friends who understand and provide support may in fact boost one's energy. Unfortunately, most friendships are commonly seen as requiring energy that unemployed jobseekers no longer have to spare.

But why are friendships often seen as draining—as *work*? Digging beneath the surface we hear the implicit expectation that interacting with friends necessitates a positive self-presentation. Steven makes this clear:

Steven: When you go out, you can't tell people where your head's at. You're socializing. . . . When people socialize, for the most part, they're putting on their best face. *This is up time.* And you don't feel like being up, especially on demand. Do you know what I mean?

OS: I do. That's why I'm asking about close friends. You feel like in your close friendships there would be a negative reaction if you fully shared where your head's at?

Steven: I think any time you share where your head's at, when it's so consistently negative, I think in any relationship it would be negative.

But Steven also notes an exception to his experience that social interactions require being in "up time" mode. When he attended a support event aimed at unemployed workers "who were all in the same boat," the situation was different: "That was almost liberating in a way because there was no phoniness." Chapter 6 will explore the extraordinary level of support and connection unemployed jobseekers find with others who are in the same boat if they are fortunate enough to meet such others in a setting that encourages and facilitates supportive connection.

Indeed, a shared assumption—especially noticeable among some of my male interviewees[14]—was that friends are for sharing "up time" and are not able or willing to support unemployed workers through their unpleasant feelings—at least not for a prolonged period of time.[15] Men expressing this view talked about how sharing hard feelings would violate the unspoken boundaries of friendships. Here is my back-and-forth with Larry:

Larry: I try not to talk to friends that much.
OS: What do you think holds you back with good friends, to share what's fully going on?
Larry: That might be a layer of what's acceptable to share with friends. I think with friends, it's kinda like there is this line you don't cross. You don't go into emotional issues. Maybe there is something that feels like it's taboo to talk about problems with friends.

Interviewees also report perceiving their friendships as fading when they themselves are not being interesting or fun. Richard observed that "people are just less inclined to schedule a lunch with you if you're not doing anything interesting." Sandra likewise reports that a friend whom she has known for 10 years "more or less terminated the relationship because I didn't have a lot of positive things to share. I wasn't a *fun* friend."

Given the negative emotions that many unemployed workers are experiencing, the expectation that social interactions should be "fun" or "interesting" means either withdrawing from the friendship or having superficial interactions and burying the negative feelings, which requires an output of energy that jobseekers like Kimberley and Sharon, discussed above, reported not having. Others, like Sandra and Richard, decide to limit what they share with friends. Sandra explains that, having lost a close friendship, "I've become very careful about what I say to people because nobody wants to hear it. . . . I mean, people are very sympathetic at first, but after a year, it's a drag." Richard likewise explains that he does not talk openly with friends because, as he puts it, "it's no fun to be telling a dismal story." In Richard's case, this also extends to his wife. He is trying to present a more upbeat mood to her because his marriage is "at times a strain" and an important cause of that, he believes, is that "feelings of inadequacy are not attractive . . . and expressing my frustration, my feelings, it's not always such a welcome topic for either of us." Thus, for Sandra and Richard, relationships are maintained but at the cost of limiting what one shares and thereby limiting the possibility of receiving support.

For unemployed jobseekers who are single and without family nearby, their friends can be their sole social contacts. Daniel, an immigrant and single, sees the maintenance of his few friendships as vital. But it's only possible, he feels, if he holds back from talking about his difficult unemployment experiences, even if his friends invite him to share:

Daniel: My unemployment cannot get in the way of my friendship. You see, if you start to run around like a persecuted cat, trying to find a way out, it's not going to make you look better. It's going to make you look worse. And the end result is that people, whether they like it or not, whether they are good by nature or not, people like to be happy and see nice things. People don't like to be unhappy and see not-so-nice things. When you present them with things which are not very nice, whether or not they like it or whether they tell you, "Oh it is okay," deep in their hearts, they just don't want to deal with it. Everybody has their own little shit in their life. It's a bit of a catch-22 because you isolate yourself. But then again, you'd rather be isolated and trying to resolve it yourself than to lose another friendship because you overwhelm the situation. It's a tight line that you have to walk every day. Therefore, I like just to have a good time whenever we are together.

OS: It sounds like with your closest friends, that even there you don't ever really directly talk about some of the things we've been talking about today.

Daniel: No. No. I don't. Unemployment is a very ugly subject. And people could look at you with pity and condescending. I don't know, it's a tricky business.

Based on his experience, Daniel believes that friends need to only be shown "happy" and "nice" things, even if this leaves him emotionally isolated. Whether one withdraws from friends or continues to see them but without talking about the most pressing issue in one's life at the moment, the upshot is the same: At a time when they are enduring professional, financial and emotional upheavals, they do not receive support from their friends, not even the close ones.

Unemployed jobseekers often accept these boundaries on their friendships and believe that they should be providing their own support for themselves. Monica, for example, explains that "I don't look to my friends to be counselors or to lift my spirits or anything like that. I don't depend on people to do that because I think it's too burdensome. I try to do that for myself." That ethic of self-reliance we hear from Monica, or as Daniel put it in the quote above— "you'd rather be isolated and trying to resolve it yourself"—may preserve the friendship, such as it is, but it leaves the jobseekers alone in their experience.

Some of my interviewees had similar experiences with their own extended families (that is, outside their spouses and children). Sharon's case provides a good illustration of how this plays out in family relations, where she perceives an aversion to talking about the hard emotions that come with unemployment. Sharon explains this in our back-and-forth:

Sharon: My family, they don't want to talk about it at all, so we have these boring conversations about the weather or whatever, and then they're like "Oh, I'm glad you're doing okay, I'll hang up now," because they don't want to hear the bad stuff. . . . They just don't like to talk about the problem. They want to pretend like it doesn't exist. If they call me or I see them and I'm down or depressed, they want me to just snap out of it and move on.

OS: Why do you think the family is not more available to emotionally support you through this incredibly hard period?

Sharon: I think it's just the way they are. You've got that problem? Suck it up. Press on. It will work itself out.

OS: Is it a belief that if you just ignore the negative emotion, things will get better?

Sharon: Yes. It was kind of summed up in one of my grandmother's favorite phrases: "You've just gotta roll with the punches and pray." Okay, Grandma, that's really not helping me because rolling with the punches means I'm going to run out of money.

Like friendships, extended family relations can come with the expectation of a cheery presentation.

As we have seen, friendships during prolonged unemployment tend to weaken due to having less in common, having financial constraints, feeling social comparisons, sensing stigma, and in some cases honoring the expectation that friendships should be fun and cheery. The overall result is that friendships seldom provide consistent emotional support for long-term unemployed jobseekers.

Feedback Loops and Isolation

To understand the long-term unemployment experience in a holistic way, we must consider the various feedback loops that make it so difficult to escape. The relationship struggles with spouses and friends described in this chapter have two important implications. The first is that jobseekers are often not receiving the support they need. The second is that crises in marriages and friendships often exacerbate the already severe emotional turmoil described in the prior chapters, which in turn makes it harder to overcome the very real obstacles to finding a job—especially given the stigma that employers attach to being unemployed, and the further stigma attached to being unhappy or unnerved by it.[16]

William's story brings out the mutually reinforcing nature of difficulties in relationships and the challenge of negative emotions in the job search. For William, the unemployment crisis and his marital crisis are "closely re-lated." His wife had brought up divorce for many years, but William's job loss brought the issue to the forefront. Early in his job search, William received an invitation to an interview for a high-level job at a large company:

> It's around 11 at night and the next morning, I have a job interview with the chief information officer at [a large company]. It is a *Fortune* 10 company and I'm going in to talk to one of their C-level guys first thing in the morning. So I'm there, I'm fully prepared, I've done all of the preliminary stuff. I'm just relaxing at 11 at night. My wife comes down and just flies into me: "We're gonna get a divorce and that's it. It's over." The next morning, driving down to [the interview]. I'm having a hard time focusing. I did not get that job. As a matter of fact, that interview did not go very well at all. . . . The divorce proceeds, I move out, and I'm completely depressed because I'm very attached to my kids and they seem to feel the same way. So it is dif-ficult. I'm sitting here in my apartment alone.

The upshot is that many unemployed workers—whether married or single— are experiencing a crisis in isolation. Brian, for example, finds it difficult to talk about his extreme stress with his wife and he no longer sees friends. He sums it up this way: "I don't have a go-to confidant." Lisa, who is single, also feels very isolated:

> I've been disappointed in the response from my friends and family. My friends and family have no understanding of the stress that I've been under these past months. They feel I should be able to find a job relatively easily. They do not offer any type of support or encouragement. It's been really difficult to realize *I have no one supporting me. I'm on my own.* I feel it's negatively impacted my physical and emotional health. . . . I really don't feel like I have anybody in my inner circle. I really feel the weight of this is on myself. It's really emotionally devastating to feel that sort of isolation.

Whether married or single, a common sentiment is succinctly voiced by Susan: "It's almost impossible to find someone who gets me and my life. I don't know. It's just so hard."

In a time of emotional, financial, marital, and career crises, getting support is crucial. But what kind of support is effective and where can it be found? These questions are the focus of Chapter 6.

6

Sociological Coaching and Countering
Internalized Stigma

Read any chapter of this book you like: You'll find no place to hide from the stigma of unemployment. It's there in interactions with recruiters, network contacts, friends, spouses, and even within yourself. These are all people we hope would be supportive. Yet we find stigma even with those whose *job* it is to be supportive. I begin this chapter by briefly explaining how well-intended providers of jobseeker support often unwittingly convey and perpetuate the unemployment stigma. I then introduce an alternative and more sociological approach to support, which aims to address some of the specific challenges we've been seeing all through this book. We will see that a sociological approach to support—what I will call sociological coaching—can mitigate some of the most difficult challenges of prolonged unemployment, including the internalization of stigma, and social and emotional isolation.

Support That Stigmatizes

The support provided to unemployed workers—whether in nonprofit networking groups, state-run career centers, for-profit outplacement services, private coaching, or best-selling books—typically follows the same self-help model. This model presents the unemployment challenge as primarily a matter of strategy and attitude. It views the main task of support as helping jobseekers improve their job-searching skills, such as resume writing and networking, and emphasizes the importance of maintaining a positive attitude. In this approach, any negative feelings that arise from unemployment are distractions to be avoided. Open expression of such negative feelings is understood as unhelpful self-pity and a poor attitude.[1]

While researching my previous book, *Flawed System/Flawed Self*—which compared job searching experiences in the United States and Israel—I spent a year at a support organization in California that used this self-help model of support. Week after week, coaches and motivational speakers presented different versions of the same message: You are in control of your career. For example, one speaker stood in front of the group of unemployed jobseekers and offered the following advice about how they should think about their situation: "We are all *free agents*. What if *that* was your perspective? It's *up to you. You get to choose.*"[2] Over and over, I heard from jobseekers how this support was initially motivating—leading them to believe that if they could only push away negative feelings and learn the strategies of perfecting their resumes, they would find a good job—but that over time, this message turned into yet another echo of the stigmatizing voices all around them, essentially blaming them for their own unemployment.

The self-help approach to support indeed adheres to the key assumption underlying the myth of meritocracy—that outcomes reflect skills and effort—which implies (whether it is said openly or not) that failure to find work is the fault of the jobseeker.[3] The unemployed jobseekers I interviewed for this book who had experiences with this form of support certainly felt the blame. Consider, for example, Sharon's experience:

> [Workshop leaders] just want to get up there and give you this generic talk where "You should do this, and you should get on Twitter, and you should do that." But when you say that stuff doesn't work, then they tell you you're not doing it right. . . . It's just: give the generic advice and if the generic advice doesn't work for you, then there must be something wrong with you. . . . They accused me of being negative.

The workshop also kept Sharon isolated in her feelings and undermined any chance she might have had to connect to others going through a similar experience:

> A big barrier to connecting with other [jobseekers] is that facilitators don't want you to talk about the negative feelings and experiences in this process. Anytime you say how bad you feel or how bad your situation is, you get shushed. They think they are helping by only talking about the happy stuff. However, in some ways they are making it worse. It helps to know you are not alone.

Sharon's experience was common. Eric described how self-help support took him on an emotional roller-coaster ride: "They charge up your emotions with unobtainable pie-in-the-sky promises, only to have them come crashing down after the reality of no job success and the financial and family pressures set in. And then comes the inevitable criticism from the job placement personnel that leaves you even more devastated."

Hearing how self-help support backfires made me wonder how practitioners of this model of support understand their own approach—surely it isn't their goal to kick people when they're down. This curiosity led to me to interview Dick Bolles, the author of the best-known self-help guide for job-searching ever: *What Color Is Your Parachute?* This book has sold over 10 million copies, has been published in 49 editions, and is widely recognized as the "most popular career advice book ever published."[4] In some self-help settings I have heard it referred to as the jobseeker's "Bible." The core strategy of the book is for jobseekers to first do a self-inventory exercise to determine what kinds of jobs they feel most passionate about. The next step is to network and convey their passions to potential employers.

In my interview, I told Bolles about the findings presented so far in this book—including the stigma that unemployed jobseekers face when job-searching and networking—and asked what advice he could offer. He responded by focusing on self-reflection and attitude: "If they have done a self-inventory first, they don't have the kinds of problems that you find in your interviews. . . . Surely, the reasons people can't find jobs is not some immutable framework to the whole job market and the whole job hunt. It's because of differences in job-hunting behaviors."[5] When I pushed back by bringing up research showing that from the standpoint of any individual jobseeker there is indeed "some immutable framework to the whole job market"—forces such as the stigma against anyone already unemployed—Bolles acknowledged that jobseekers have only partial control:

You look for what is in your control. Maybe your degree of control is only 2 percent—work on that. . . . If I find out what parts are within my control and try to change that, then sometimes you get the butterfly effect, little things can cause huge alterations in personal success.

At the end of the interview, I asked Bolles if there is anything he wished to add. He reasserted his original emphasis of jobseeker control and considered any discussion of external obstacles to be "complaints" and self-defeating:

I've spent so many years listening to the same kinds of complaints as you have. I spent so many years listening to them and I know there has to be some way around the problems. If we decide we are going to create excuses for why our life is not working, then that becomes its own defeat. We defeat ourselves. . . . It makes every difference in the world whether we are determined to conquer our obstacles and challenges in life or we are determined to find excuses.

The exchange with Bolles is illuminating. Pressed about the reality of external, systemic obstacles—things over which no individual has any control—he concedes that jobseekers have only partial control, maybe even as little as "2 percent." But then he re-asserts the premise of jobseeker control—not as an empirical claim but as what he seems to believe is a helpful fiction. Focusing on the obstacles, he says, is making "excuses" and does not motivate us to "conquer our obstacles." This belief that exaggerating individual control is a helpful fiction is in fact a widely shared view in American culture and transcends left-right political divides.[6] It can be heard in presidential addresses and in the everyday encouragement that parents, teachers, and coaches give their children: "You can do it."[7] Whether or not the kid really can do it seems not to matter; the assumption is that asserting with certainty that they "can" will boost their confidence and motivation.[8]

Can one "do it"? It's true that there are situations in which you never know until you try, so that kind of encouragement—"You can do it!"—might well be productive. But in the situation at hand—long-term unemployment—the exaggeration of jobseekers' individual control only distorts empirical reality and overlooks real obstacles. It is a *harmful fiction* because it reinforces stigmatization. When in support settings Sharon feels accused of being "negative," and Eric describes the blows of the "inevitable criticism," they are referring to interactions with career coaches who mirror Bolles's view of jobseekers as offering "complaints" and "excuses." The exaggeration of control may be a common cultural norm but it is harmful in contexts like unemployment and similar other situations, because it leads to a blaming of the victim and can intensify the tendency to internalize stigma.[9] Robert Sapolsky, a leading biologist and neurologist, finds that "when the stressor is truly awful, an artificial sense of control is damaging because it induces self-blame."[10] In discussing research on supporting people diagnosed with cancer, Sapolsky emphasizes that "leading patients and their families to believe that there is more control over outcomes than exists is "simply teaching the victims of cancer and their families that the disease is their own fault."[11] Self-help does the same thing to unemployed jobseekers.

The fiction of control is at the heart of the myth of meritocracy discussed throughout this book. It is this assumption of individual control that makes plausible the belief that individual outcomes simply reflect effort and merit and thus—as we have seen in the reactions of employers, network contacts, friends, and spouses—sooner or later leads to the stigmatizing conclusion that unemployment is the fault of the unemployed. Recognizing the harms of this myth led me to wonder what support might look like if it did not exaggerate jobseeker control and openly acknowledged the stigmas and obstacles discussed in this book. This is where I turn next.

Sociological Support

To explore whether and how it is possible to provide jobseeker support that incorporates a sociological understanding of the stigmas and obstacles that generate long-term unemployment, I collaborated with a group of 63 career coaches and counselors who agreed to provide free support to unemployed workers under the umbrella of a nonprofit organization, which I co-created, called the Institute for Career Transitions (ICT). The story of how the ICT was started is detailed in the appendix at the end of this book.

The support provided by the ICT is distinct from the self-help model in two ways. First, it openly discusses the stigmas and obstacles unemployed jobseekers face and makes sure not to exaggerate their degree of control. In my initial meetings with the volunteer coaches, I discussed the harms of the self-help approach of emphasizing the fiction of complete jobseeker control, and proposed that the ICT's approach would instead be to candidly acknowledge external barriers. In addition, at various ICT support gatherings for jobseekers, I directly discussed research findings—my own and others'— about the typical obstacles facing the long-term unemployed. This included sharing rather sobering research results like the *much* lower callback rates for jobseekers who have been out of work for more than 6 months than for otherwise identical jobseekers.[12] I explained to jobseekers that while these research findings may be upsetting, it is important for jobseekers to know what they're up against and to understand how the barriers they face have nothing to do with them as individuals. At such gatherings I frequently said that the only thing worse than hearing about employer stigma was not hearing about it and thinking that you must be doing something wrong or that something must be wrong with you.

The second distinct aspect of ICT support is openly discussing how unemployment almost invariably generates difficult negative emotions and encouraging jobseekers to share those emotions with their coaches and—very important—with each other. I discussed with the volunteer coaches and directly with jobseekers my own prior research and other studies showing that prolonged unemployment is typically accompanied by emotional turmoil, and that the usual self-help support approach of asking jobseekers to suppress such emotions in support settings reinforces stigmatization and isolation. Specifically, in every ICT support gathering, time is set aside for jobseekers to share and discuss with peers the emotional roller-coaster of unemployment.

The support provided by the ICT has come in different forms, including small weekly groups facilitated by a coach, intensive one- or two-day "rebootcamps" which bring together 50 to 100 unemployed jobseekers, one-on-one coaching, and an intensive 3-month group program called the "Collaboratory," in which participants meet three times a week. All these varied forms of support included meetings in which I directly discussed research about unemployment, stigmas, obstacles, and negative emotions with the participants. One hundred four jobseekers who received ICT support were then interviewed about this experience. In the rest of this chapter, we'll see what I learned from these interviews and how the sociological support offered at the ICT helped unemployed jobseekers push back against internalized stigma and isolation.

"When in a Group You Realize . . . Nothing Is Wrong with You."

Let me start with the biggest takeaway from providing sociologically informed support through the ICT: The most potent force countering the tendency to internalize stigma is the experience of openly sharing with other jobseekers whom one comes to recognize as being "in the same boat"—a phrase that was used by more than half the interviewees. Lionel explains his sense of relief when the open sharing in his group allowed him to gain some critical distance from his own situation:

When in a group, you realize it's not you. Nothing is wrong with you. Everyone is in the same situation. It's amazing how supportive it is to recognize that others are going through the same thing. It's helpful just being with other people who are in a similar situation and just realizing that everyone has their issues, everyone has their strengths and weaknesses. Being with a group of people who are in the same boat, it's very—what's the word? It makes you feel less strange. Because when you're unemployed, you tend to feel like there's something wrong with you, even though there isn't.

Many of my interviewees offered some version of this experience of realizing that "it's not you" and "nothing is wrong with you." Michelle, for example, is very clear in describing how the experience of being with others in the same boat led her to reduce her self-blame:

The ICT [gathering] really lifted me up and confirmed for me that I'm not alone, and helped me to reframe my point of view that I made a poor career choice that got me here. For the first time, I stopped beating myself up over not having completed my education, as there were so many intelligent people who were also in transition.

Being with similar others who are also struggling gave Michelle a new perspective on her situation, which allowed her to stop focusing on her own perceived mistakes and halt "beating" herself up.[13]

It is important to emphasize that this "same boat" experience that helps counteract internalized stigma does not just happen spontaneously once you bring people together. It requires explicit permission and encouragement to openly share. As prior chapters showed, the ubiquitous stigma of unemployment means that jobseekers are hesitant to bring up hardships even with close friends and loved ones. It may be assumed that in a support setting, knowing that they are with others who are also unemployed, jobseekers would automatically feel comfortable sharing. But this is not the case. The unemployment stigma—and more generally the American stigma attached to sharing negative feelings—is extremely strong. Recall that the dominant self-help support approach views any sharing of negative experiences as complaining and self-pity. That's what most ICT participants—including my interviewees—were used to. In the gatherings, networking events, and self-help workshops they had previously attended, participants were encouraged to share only positive emotions.[14] To avoid being perceived, as Dick Bolles had put it to me, as making "excuses," the default mode was to keep their painful experiences of stigma, isolation, and discouragement to themselves. They'd long since learned that no one wants to hear it.

For unemployed jobseekers to feel permitted and encouraged to openly discuss their full experiences, the support must be designed to validate these experiences as legitimate and as important topics of discussion. A key step in the support process, therefore, is having the facilitator openly acknowledge that unemployed jobseekers frequently come to feel shame or otherwise that something is wrong with them, and that the taboo against sharing these feelings can create the false—and very counterproductive—impression that one is all alone in having such feelings.

Having put this on the table, the next step is for the jobseekers to discuss their unvarnished unemployment experiences in small groups. To get a sense of how big a step this can be, recall how Steven, in Chapter 4, was so humiliated by his continued unemployment that he didn't even want to fetch the mail during work hours lest he be spotted by his neighbors not at work in the middle of the day, or in his words *"out there unemployed for all to see."* The first time Steven discussed this shame was not in my interview with him but at an ICT gathering:

> The ICT put shame on the table. I remember talking to Barry [peer participant], who looked like the most together person in the place because he had the suit. And him talking about shame and people talking about that. It was like, "Wait a minute. *I don't know if I've talked about that much with anybody."* The feelings that they were going through, like how we are not seen as valid human beings. That spoke something to me. So a lot of that sort of thing just felt like, "I feel hungry. Tell me more. Tell me more about how it feels." I'm pretty good at articulating how things feel, but it was helpful to have it come from the outside. *It made my feelings respect-worthy.* Because you're always willing to give the other person the benefit of the doubt that you're not willing to give yourself.

Because the ICT's open discussion of shame made Steven's feelings, in his words, "respect-worthy," it allowed him to speak about his experience of shame with others. Once Steven talked openly, following Barry's lead, he came to realize the harm caused by his internalized stigma and shared with his small group his determination to push back on such feelings of "guilt":

Take the pedal off the guilt so that you can more effectively deal with this rigged system. All the guilt does is it keeps you stuck in your place. Take the guilt away and it may still be the same rigged system, but at least you're functioning better in that system.

Stepping back, what exactly was it about the open sharing among peers and the sociologically oriented support at the ICT that helped people recognize their internalized stigma and start to push back on it? The first important aspect of Steven's experience is the break from isolation. Talking about feelings of shame—something he does not think he had previously discussed with *anybody*—is crucial for the recognition of the *shared* nature of the experience. That, in turn, opens the door to supportive mutual connections.

Recall the isolation described in Chapter 4 by many of the unemployed jobseekers? Charles, like Steven, explains that before joining ICT, he was isolated in his experience both as a result of others withdrawing from him and not wanting to hear about his situation, and because of his withdrawal from others to avoid the pain of stigmatizing comments:

> I spend a lot of time by myself and that's a bad thing. Because unless you're in this situation, people don't want to know about it, or only know what they've read, or just throw out stupid comments, like "Just get any job." These really unbelievable, horrific comments. So you just basically shut yourself off.

The effect of the ICT support has, he says, "made me feel like I'm attached to others. . . . It's taken me out of my own head or being isolated, which is really, really bad for unemployed people." Daniel, quoted in the prior chapter as feeling like a "very weird creature" among his friends, said that prior to the ICT, "I wouldn't have *dared* to talk about anything about my unemployment situation with anybody. . . . The [ICT gathering] gives me people that I can let that part of myself out once in a while." The fact that prior to the ICT Daniel would not "dare" share "anything" about his unemployment reveals the intensity with which he perceived the stigma of being unemployed and the relief of letting that part "out."

Beyond lessening the isolation that comes from sharing one's previously hidden experiences, a second critical aspect of the support experience was jobseekers' realization that they are not the only ones feeling the way they do. Barbara describes her relief in realizing that everybody feels very blue. I had no idea. I thought I was the only one and when somebody brought it up, then we started talking and it sounded like everybody was pretty much feeling like they were circling the drain. . . . In some ways, it felt better that I wasn't alone, that I wasn't isolated in the discouragement. Others were discouraged, too.

It is difficult to feel blue and discouraged, but it is much *more* difficult to experience these feelings in isolation. Janis put it this way: "It was good to be around other people who understand the struggle, not feeling like I'm on Neptune."

Not feeling like you are "the only one," or like an alien from another planet, and recognizing that others are having a similar experience, greatly helps in the struggle against shame and internalized stigma. Research on shame shows that the reason this feeling is so powerful—called by some the "master emotion"—is that it signals a threat to our social bond with others.[15] Shame usually occurs when we feel exposed as flawed, and therefore unworthy of connection. The recognition that others are having these same feelings is a strong antidote to shame. It normalizes these feelings by helping the individual realize that it is not something specifically about them, but something about the situation that tends to generate this difficult internal experience in everyone.[16]

In combating their internalized stigma it also helped jobseekers to learn that some very accomplished and qualified people were among those in the same boat. This particular recognition is powerful because it challenges the assumption underlying all the stigmatization—including the self-stigmatization—that if someone is unemployed, there must be something wrong with them. Lionel explains how his realization in an ICT session that *"Nothing is wrong with you"* had a lot to do with who else he found was in the same boat:

> When you're with this group of people and you realize there's two lawyers, there's a marketing professional, there's all these *people with all these skills* and they're also having trouble finding stuff for whatever reason. It just helps you feel better about yourself.

Lionel is feeling "better" about himself because he no longer necessarily equates someone being unemployed with a lack of skill or some other individual deficiency. Being in a group that includes "people with all these skills" and who are "also having trouble finding" work means that perhaps skills are not the issue. This in turn creates an opening for re-examining assumptions that Lionel has made about himself. We can see a similar process in how Becky describes her experience of support:

> I *try* not to let [unemployment] have an impact on my self-esteem and confidence, but I wouldn't be completely honest if I said it had no impact.... Jane [another group member] is doing everything she can and she's not getting anywhere either, although she gets a bunch of interviews. There's another woman who I think is incredibly thoughtful and very, very—I would hire her in a heartbeat if I had a job to give her.... It's nice to be among people you think are very competent and just unfortunate in that situation.

Becky's experience is much like Lionel's. In Becky's struggle to avoid internalizing stigma and to view herself as someone with valuable skills, it is very helpful to be in a group with others who are unemployed and struggling despite putting great effort in their search ("doing everything") and being the kind of worker Becky herself would want to hire. This recognition allows Becky and others to consider that perhaps they too are also competent and hardworking and "just unfortunate in that situation."

The connection between recognizing that all kinds of people are in the same boat with you and the ability to push back on internalized stigma comes through loud and clear in Sharon's recollection of how she came to see that "it truly is not me":

> I found it helpful to be in a room full of people who were going through the same thing I am going through, experiencing the same thing, and to see the level of talent in that room. You have people with all kinds of crazy, ridiculous degrees. I was at a table with a gentleman who holds two patents and he can't find a job. So it was kind of comforting to know that *it truly is not me* and that it is hitting a cross-section of people, so it's not like if I had more education or less education, I wouldn't be in this predicament, because again, it is hitting a lot of people and a wide array of people. Job searches can be kind of brutal on your self-confidence, but it was bolstering to be in a room full of people that you knew were as educated, as talented, or even more talented or educated than you were and still having the same problem. So I take that as "*It's not just me, it's not something I'm doing wrong.*" If it is, it's something we're collectively doing wrong. Even then, I don't think so.

The wide range of people in Sharon's group who are encountering the same obstacles that she is made it tangibly clear that unemployment is not a matter of talent or education, or for that matter any other individual factor, and it is not about doing something wrong. This clarity creates an opening for thinking about the sociology of unemployment and for considering the larger forces that may be at play.[17]

Sociology and Critical Consciousness

When for the first time I stood up in front of over 100 unemployed jobseekers at an ICT support event and saw in their eyes the hope for some helpful advice, it was not easy to let them down with sociological studies revealing how employers stigmatize and exclude them from consideration. The typical support message of "you can do it," which inflates jobseekers' sense of control, is not helpful but it is tempting. While the sociology of unemployment is not an easy message to deliver or hear, it did help jobseekers make sense of their realities. Yes, something was really wrong in what was happening to them. But there is nothing wrong with them. The sociological research helped jobseekers see the link between their shared experience and the larger social and economic context. Here is how Steven put it:

> You couldn't have said anything more important to me than sharing about the research showing the obstacles unemployed workers face. That was perfect in my mind because no matter what anyone tells you, people are thinking that it's not outside things, it's inside you. When you have a [self-help] coach tell you, "You can do it if you just stay positive in your thinking," my feeling is this absolutely misses the boat. [But] basically you're saying, "Look outside yourself instead of taking it out on yourself." As far as I'm concerned, that is *the* most important message you can give unemployed people.

The discussion of research about external obstacles was even helpful to Laura, the one unemployed jobseeker that I least expected it would affect. Laura's previous job was as a union organizer, making her well-aware of employer practices and external obstacles. Yet even Laura tended to blame herself for her continuing unemployment, and she benefited from the sociological approach to support:

It set my experience in a broader socio-political context. . . . That I'm not alone in experiencing what I'm experiencing. That there's some politics involved and that just helps with perspective. . . . It was a relief to think about *we* and *us* and systems. It was a helpful relief.

As we also saw in Chapter 4, even jobseekers who intellectually understand the external and systemic obstacles arrayed against them nonetheless tend to internalize the stigma and feel that their unemployment is their fault. This is where the ICT's explicit message was helpful. It reinforced awareness of the broader context, which took the focus away from individual fault and self-blame.

The ICT's sociological support can be understood as facilitating jobseekers' "critical consciousness," the capacity to reflect on how the obstacles one is encountering are rooted in larger social conditions rather than in individual shortcomings.[18] Being in a group with others who are openly sharing their struggles in the job market—struggles much like your own—and then hearing about research that explains this shared struggle disrupts the habit of assuming that your failure to get hired is a personal failure. Brene Brown compellingly explains the usefulness of critical consciousness by using an analogy to a camera lens.[19] When we are zooming in, we only see ourselves as an individual person and tend to focus on our own perceived flaws and shortcomings. But if we can zoom out a bit—that is, by sharing in a group— we can see that others are facing the same challenges. Zoom out a little more, using sociology, and we can gain the critical consciousness to recognize that others are facing similar challenges because of systematic forces like stigma. This critical consciousness serves as a shield against internalized stigma.[20]

Sociological Coaching

An important aspect of the ICT support was clarifying the inner workings of institutional processes such as hiring. Because sociology is the academic discipline most focused on the workings of social institutions, I call this kind of support "sociological coaching." Its aim is to contextualize unemployed workers' personal experiences. One of the strengths of sociology is that its empirical and research-based approach avoids both selling illusions of exaggerated jobseeker control that backfire when labor market obstacles persist, and at the same time mitigates against discouragement and hopelessness.

A specific analysis of the workings of institutions allows jobseekers not only to see the nature of the barriers but also the space of possibilities.

To most jobseekers, hiring institutions are a black box. Opening up this box through sociological coaching doesn't stop a rejection from being a rejection, but it does depersonalize the rejection. That's important because it makes it easier to keep trying. Jennifer recalls what it was like before the ICT support she received:

> You're really working blind. Unless you've got oodles of self-confidence, it's very difficult to work blind. You need somebody who had been on the other side. I've never had anybody like that. I felt like I was given encouragement that it isn't really going to a black hole, or it doesn't always go to a black hole. But more than that, really, was the fact that it's a numbers game. Every time there's a job that seems to line up with my ability and experience—apply for it.

Beyond framing the outcome—hired or rejected—as a depersonalized "numbers game," clarifying the inner workings of hiring can also suggest particular strategies. For example, jobseekers often have the misconception that employers take the time to carefully read their resumes and cover letters. Learning that application materials are actually filtered very rapidly has important strategic implications. Doug, for example, came to realize that "given how busy people are, and [that] their attention span is somewhere between 6 and 30 seconds," it is important to develop "short accounts, phrases, key words, sound bites that will convince employers of how I would add value."

A related misconception is that, as Lily put it, "my resume should speak for itself. I've got good job experience. I'm competent." This is a very reasonable way of thinking about how the labor market *should* work, but unfortunately it confuses what ought to be with what is. A resume that at best receives a quick glance is not doing much speaking. Sociological research shows the advantages to jobseekers of a network contact who can do the speaking for the resume. That means that finding a job often requires not only a good resume, but also active self-marketing and—most of all—networking.

The encouragement of networking is not in and of itself a unique feature of the support discussed in this chapter, and it is in fact the most common advice in job searching workshops and coaching. What is unique is the refraining from any suggestion or implication that effective networking is only a matter of individual effort and willpower. Support that merely advises jobseekers to network exacerbates the feelings of self-blame and the sense that one's difficulties are due to internal shortcomings and barriers.[21] The approach to support discussed in this chapter, by contrast, is open with jobseekers about the practical, social, and emotional challenges of networking for anyone who is unemployed (as discussed in Chapter 3) as a way of countering discouragement and debilitating self-blame. The open sharing with peers on this issue aims to help jobseekers appreciate that networking is both helpful and extremely difficult and therefore to brace themselves for the challenges ahead and not interpret obstacles as internal shortcomings.

Support that offers search strategies such as networking is transmitting what is often tacit knowledge about the rules of a complex game. Since tacit knowledge is an important resource and is not evenly distributed among jobseekers, this dimension of support may reduce inequalities of know-how in navigating the labor market.[22] For example, Aaron reported how useful it was to receive networking advice from his coach on "how to approach, what to ask, getting people to notice and respond. Framing your emails in a certain way. Asking the right questions."[23]

When such hands-on strategies are discussed within a broader sociological framework that recognizes external barriers, it changes the focus. It avoids the trap of the self-help approach with its assumptions of meritocracy and exaggerated individual control and its heavy, even if unintended, dose of blame. Jobseekers are not presented at the ICT with any formulas for guaranteed success, but they are given strategies that may increase the probability of jumping through what are acknowledged to be difficult and biased hoops.

Networking Revisited and Practical Support

Networking in the context of the sociological support of the ICT is a strikingly different experience from the usual networking we examined in Chapter 3. Instead of feeling like a "beggar" or "used-car salesman," jobseekers described networking with fellow ICT jobseekers as the giving and receiving of practical and caring support. Daniel, for example—who in Chapter 3 described his disgust with the pressure to "use" his friends and to act fake when networking—felt entirely different about networking within ICT: "It was probably the first time I've been in a group of people, that was good, real networking. It's much more natural. You have a lot of people there who have the same purpose." When you are with others in the same boat and with whom you are openly sharing your experience, there is no need to engage in the layers of masking that networking typically requires.

In a complete flip, the ICT context transforms networking from a dreaded activity with a high emotional toll to a source of emotional support and replenishment. Angela explains that when fellow unemployed jobseekers share contacts, it is not only practically helpful but also "keeps us motivated, knowing that somebody is thinking of us and looking out for us." In a similar vein, Doug reports that when he receives an introduction, "It's just showing that people are out there thinking of you as well. And that's reinforcing. There's a little strength in that." In the ICT context, networking helps foster a sense of having a supportive community for job search activities that are otherwise a lonely pursuit.

In fact, the practical and emotional dimensions of support are linked. In the context of an emotionally supportive community, jobseekers felt better able to openly discuss their search strategies and receive feedback. This was particularly true in the case of the Collaboratory, where jobseekers spent 15 hours a week together for a 3-month period. As Nicole explained, conversations about strategy happened "because we were open to each other, not judging each other." Steven noted a similar relationship between the emotional and practical aspects of the support: "The group—everyone understands what you're going through. It's interaction with people that you know *care about you* and want to see each other succeed." Feeling cared about by their peers, jobseekers were able to both share their fears, hopes, and plans and to receive suggestions and advice. Unlike advice coming from friends or spouses, which, as we saw in Chapter 5, often conveyed negative judgments and stigma, advice from fellow unemployed peers, who fully understand the complexity and difficulty of the situation, went down a lot more comfortably.

The practical and emotional dimensions of support are also linked and mutually reinforcing because the act of offering practical support to others in and of itself provides an important emotional boost to the giver. Recall from Chapter 4 that one of the hidden injuries of unemployment is the painful loss of a sense of contribution to others. The opportunity to support fellow jobseekers mitigates this injury. For example, Marcia met Larry at an ICT event and then introduced him to a key person she happened to know in his industry who turned out to be very helpful. When Larry asked what he could do in return, Marcia replied: "Look, letting me help you gives me a feeling that I'm not a total loser. I have some ability to be useful, and that's huge." Ryan likewise describes how good it made him feel to help fellow unemployed workers:

> I'll try to help people out. I want to say that I've helped people get jobs at least 10 times. Whatever I can do to help them out, that's a pay-it-forward. So at the end of the day you say, "Okay, I didn't get a job but I helped somebody else do it." So you feel good.

Ryan also felt that he regained some of the camaraderie that had been taken away with his job: "That's something I need. I'd be going crazy if I didn't have that." Recall the way unemployed jobseekers in Chapter 5 discussed missing their work friends and community. We can see in Ryan's comments that support, when done well, can restore this sense of belonging to a community of colleagues.

The peer community of support is a powerful force. It breaks through the isolation, it facilitates recognition that it's not "you," and it provides practical support and a boost from knowing you're helping others. Coaches are critical to facilitating this peer support and helping it take form, but coaches also play important roles in their one-on-one support practices, which is what I discuss next.

Coaching and Destigmatization

This chapter has thus far focused on how gathering with other unemployed jobseekers who are encouraged to share openly their experiences powerfully counteracts the tendency to internalize stigma. While the interviews suggest that facilitated peer interactions were critically helpful in counteracting stigma, the work of individual coaches and counselors can also be decisive.

Coaches help counteract internalized stigma by reminding jobseekers of their past achievements. Craig describes what typically happens to one's sense of self and why this form of support is important:

> It didn't take long before my sense of self began to deteriorate. The unemployment and underemployment and constant rejection for positions really pushed me down for a large part of that period. So the lack of work definitely shaped my sense of self.

Given the hit to his sense of self, Craig explains: "I think one of the crucial roles of the coach for me was to rebuild a sense of confidence." His coach helped him stay aware of the fact that, as he puts it, "I've done a lot of different things. There's so much to what I could be offering a potential employer. So there was a lot of rebuilding to get me to really embrace that I am a prize. I am somebody that should be desired by an employer for the variety of things that I could do for them." An effective coach brings an external perspective, not distorted stigma, and therefore is well-positioned to notice and point out the various things the jobseeker had achieved in the past, achievements that tend to get erased from one's self-concept in the stigmatizing context of unemployment.[24]

Jennifer had become discouraged and had even given up looking.[25] The support, she explains, was "critical to motivating me to continue searching." Key to the support was how her coach "reaffirmed my confidence in my abilities." As she put it:

> We've talked a lot about what did I do, how did I work with people, and he's made me realize that I have a lot of skills that never go away. They're still valid. I really needed that kind of feedback. I guess that's it. You don't get any feedback when you're looking for a job. You get either nothing, or you just get a rejection. . . . Now that I know that I'm still eminently employable, I just have to keep working at it.

Prior chapters discussed how the ubiquitous stigma of unemployment creates a distorting mirror reflecting an image of someone with nothing of value to offer. The sociological support experience holds up a different mirror—a destigmatizing mirror that reflects the professional value one really does have, but without falling into the self-help trap of inflating the jobseekers' degree of control or ignoring larger obstacles. Any kind of success is likely to involve merit and luck; it's very helpful to be reassured of the merit without being falsely promised the luck.

Another way coaches help counteract internalized stigma is to mirror to jobseekers their accomplishments *as jobseekers*, which otherwise would leave no visible traces. Job searching can be usefully thought of as a form of work that involves challenging daily tasks. As in all forms of work which do not result in immediate tangible results, feedback and recognition of efforts and small accomplishments along the way are crucial. For example, Bruce's search for work has not yet yielded a job offer. Yet, he feels boosted by his coach because "he has been very impressed with my networking and with the things I have accomplished in terms of phone interviews or follow-ups or all of that." In providing this kind of feedback to unemployed jobseekers, coaching fills a feedback vacuum—resulting from the black hole into which one's applications disappear—that otherwise often enough fills up with thoughts informed by internalized stigma.

One might imagine that offering this kind of recognition for the work of job searching would be the province of family and close friends. Yet, as we saw in the previous chapter, for those trapped in long-term unemployment, informal sources of support are not reliably available. Family and friends may harbor stigmas, they may be too implicated and invested in the outcomes and therefore deeply anxious themselves, or the unemployed jobseeker may be uncomfortable asking them for support in a culture that valorizes self-sufficiency. In addition, encouraging words from friends and family may be discounted. Jennifer, for example, reflects on how supportive words coming from her family would not have the same effect as the same words from her coach:

> [My coach] is telling me that I'm going in the right direction, I'm doing the right things. And he's a professional. Versus my family members who are not professionals. Of course, they're going to tell you you're doing the right thing. But you need somebody who doesn't have a stake in it, who doesn't have an emotional tie, to give you support. It's not going to affect them if you do or don't get a job. They're not going to have to face you on a daily basis for the rest of whatever. So that was really helpful. I felt that he had the professional knowledge and background to tell me if I was doing anything right or wrong.

Two factors seem important: The coach is perceived to have the professional *capacity* to assess accurately, and his or her feedback can be trusted because it is free of relationship pressures and considerations. A coach does not have to say "good job" simply for the sake of the relationship. Here is how Cynthia described the boost she received:

> When people are out of work for a long time, you start doubting yourself. [In tears.] Just to have someone else *who is a professional* look at it and say, "No! You should be able to find something." It is amazing emotional support.

Cynthia's words brought me back to a moment when as a young sociology graduate student, beginning my way in a new field, my advisor—a very successful academic—looked me in the eyes and said, "You are a good writer." The same words from my mother or a non-academic friend would certainly not have carried the same weight.

Combating Isolation and Discouragement

Among the benefits of the kind of support discussed in this chapter is that it leads to important social connections. I previously discussed how the sociological approach to support breaks the isolation of jobseekers by encouraging open discussion with peers about their experiences. When this level of sharing occurs, connections may be formed that turn into close friendships—some of which continue outside the support context. In Chapter 5, we heard jobseekers discuss the tendency of friendships to become distant during unemployment, but the one exception to this general rule that some interviewees brought up—without any prompting from me— focused on friendships formed with fellow unemployed jobseekers. Sharon, for example, explained how the ICT gathering yielded social connections that have been supportive ever since:

> Actually being among people like me and being able to discuss my feelings and experiences openly. . . . At the [ICT gathering], I felt like we had the space and freedom to discuss what we really felt and are going through. Not only was this good for my well-being in the short term, I was able to connect with people who I think will help me in the long term. A lot of us can't turn to our friends and family. Making new friends is tough during this period because the general population for the most part doesn't understand us and our situations. Being able to build new friendships with people who understand what I'm going through is helpful.

A number of other interviewees reported developing relationships in the ICT support context that became close friendships. Jill explained that "ironically, my situation has actually brought important newfound friendships into my life. I made several close connections. These are supportive relationships that never would have developed if I hadn't become unemployed." Because unemployment is generally associated with the loss of friendships and isolation, the social dimension of the support discussed in this chapter is particularly important. Laura, for example, found that "surprisingly, people I knew [from before unemployment] were the least responsive," but with those "in the same boat professionally—fellow long-term unemployed jobseekers—I've made some really good friends."

The fact that friendships and supportive relationships are forged in the ICT support context is not a coincidence. Rather, it happens precisely because when individuals interact with openness and vulnerability and recognize they are "in the same boat," that leads to feelings of trust and connection. Melissa, a 57-year-old digital content creator, explained it this way:

> I met wonderful, fantastic people and everybody seemed very willing to help each other. I found that people who probably wouldn't have opened up were really opening up. You just felt very safe there, very open. I think there were people there who probably came out of their shell who never had before. You could see it. It's just felt very comfortable there.

While the typical self-help form of support focuses on honing job-search skills such as writing resumes and maintaining a positive attitude, we have seen how a more sociological approach addresses some of the deeper crises engendered by prolonged unemployment, including internalized stigma and isolation. By addressing these deeper layers of distress, this form of support may also be more helpful at the practical level. As we saw in earlier chapters the negative feelings generated by extended unemployment become their own significant barriers to re-employment, creating a vicious cycle. To the extent the support discussed in this chapter reduces isolation and provides a shield against internalized stigma, it enhances the chances of success in the job market.

A striking and tangible benefit of the support was the increased search activity. A large number of interviewees reported having been discouraged and finding it difficult to continue actively searching, but as a result of the ICT support they were re-energized in their search. Ed, for example, was among the most discouraged unemployed jobseekers I interviewed. He had completely given up looking for work and described himself as stuck in a "bog." A few months later, when I asked him about any effects from the sociologically informed support he received, his first words were: "We're all in the bog." Learning that mattered more than anything he had heard from me or any of the coaches:

> It had more impact hearing about [the emotional strains] from a fellow bog resident. The feeling that you're not alone. Being cheek by jowl with people who are slaying similar dragons boosts your feeling of coming out of the woods and into a clearing.

Realizing he was not alone in the "bog" helped Ed resume his search. Joe, too, had been discouraged and felt isolated: "I would close off and I wouldn't talk to anybody. And of course, I stopped applying for many jobs and then I didn't get any callbacks, which just fed my belief that I wasn't very employable." But, he explains, "the sense of community [at ICT] makes a huge difference in this process. Like, all right, this is difficult. They're having similar challenges and it is really helpful to know that other people are going through the same experience." The support helped Joe boost his search activity because it "gives you the confidence you need to go to the next level of connecting with people." At a purely practical level, Ed and Joe are both more likely to find a job simply because they have increased their search intensity. Searching does not guarantee landing a job, but ceasing to search does guarantee continued unemployment.

Stepping back, the interview data I have been discussing in this chapter suggest that sociologically informed support does indeed help long-term unemployed jobseekers in their job search and their well-being. The search is practically helped by countering discouragement which leads to more search intensity, and well-being is helped by reduced isolation, recognizing that many others are in the "same boat," recognizing that "it's not me," and ultimately by pushing back on internalized stigma with a more accurate and less-distorted view of oneself.[26] In addition to the interview data, during the first year of the ICT we also collected survey data from jobseekers who received ICT support and a from small group who did not receive support but who were otherwise similar. The differences between the supported and unsupported jobseekers were consistent with the interview data in suggesting that the ICT support both helped increase the odds of finding work and led to a reduction in internalized stigma.[27]

Sociological Support and the Destigmatizing Mirror

How you see yourself has a lot to do with how you imagine others see you. As I pointed out in Chapter 4, this is what sociologists call the "looking-glass self."[28] The stigma of unemployment surrounds the jobseeker with a distorting mirror and reflects an image warped by outright rejections from employers and the skepticism and judgment of networking contacts, friends, spouses, and self-help coaches. This warped image is then internalized and sparks a fear that there is something wrong with oneself.

Sociologically informed support can counteract the distorting mirror by holding up a destigmatizing mirror. The sociological approach to support can help unemployed jobseekers see themselves in a more accurate light and push away the distorted, stigmatized image. This happens when jobseekers are encouraged to share openly with others in the same predicament and break their isolation. The open sharing leads to a realization that the reason they are all experiencing difficulties is not that something is wrong with all of them as individuals. Hearing about sociological research on employer stigmas and hiring biases makes visible the shared nature of the obstacles and difficulties, and creates the possibility of seeing oneself in a new and destigmatized light.

My interviews with unemployed jobseekers who received sociologically informed support at the ICT suggest that this form of support not only improved their well-being by counteracting internalized stigma but also had directly practical benefits. Many reported that before the support they had felt discouraged about their search and that this support motivated them to re-engage. They also reported networking productively with others in the support context and, in some cases, developing new and supportive friendships that extended beyond the ICT gatherings.

More research is necessary on the effects of a sociological and holistic approach to support. Fortunately, as of this writing this approach to support is spreading and being evaluated. The Work Intervention Network (WIN)[29] program's team of scholars and practitioners, of which I am a part, is providing trainings for trainers and teaching workforce professionals around the United States how to most effectively support unemployed jobseekers with a focus on fostering critical consciousness and countering the internalization of stigma. The effects of this form of support are being closely researched by WIN's team of scholars, and initial findings point to the benefits of this approach.[30]

But there's something important I haven't brought up yet and which may be obvious: Any form of individual or group support can only go so far because it does nothing to change the underlying root causes of long-term unemployment. Effective support can aid in countering the internalization of stigma but it does not reduce that stigma. That requires collective and political action that brings about changes in institutions. American unemployed workers, as a group, have been almost entirely absent from the public political sphere for several decades.[31] Ultimately, the most important effect of sociological support may be that beyond countering the internalization of stigma in individuals, it may also engender insights into shared structural conditions and foster a sense of solidarity with others necessary to spark the political action needed to contest the institutions underlying stigma. It is striking that for a sizable minority of participants, the sociological support of the ICT led to engagement in collective action and the creation of a participant-driven advocacy group focused on policies affecting long-term unemployed jobseekers. This advocacy effort will be discussed in the next and final chapter.

7

Moving Beyond Stigma and the Myth of Meritocracy

Anyone reading this book may be one layoff away from falling into the stigma trap. And once trapped, escape is difficult. The pervasive myth of meritocracy at the heart of American capitalism means that unemployed workers are often viewed with stigma and suspicion by potential employers, network contacts, coaches, friends, and spouses. With stigma reflected back from all directions unemployed workers tend to internalize the stigma[1] and their core identities are challenged, which predictably instigates emotional turmoil. This in turn makes escaping the trap even more difficult as the unemployed workers' reactions to being stigmatized serve as further reason for exclusion and stigma. As we have seen, employers quickly reject any applicant whose words or actions even hint at any feelings besides positive and cheery confidence.

The stigma trap is cruel and circular. You are stigmatized for being unemployed and then stigmatized again for your reaction to the stigma. The circularity of the trap captures the essence of Goffman's observation that one's response to stigma, such as feelings of shame or loss of confidence, are perceived by others as a "direct expression of [their] defect."[2]

In times of emotional turmoil we turn to friends and family for support. Yet, the stigma of unemployment means that we may become tainted even in the eyes of our closest relationships. As we have seen, in some cases long-time friends may distance themselves from the unemployed person as if to protect themselves from catching a contagious disease.[3] The taint of stigma may also show up in the reactions of spouses, creating a feedback loop that predictably leads to further emotional distress and more relationship tensions.[4] Again, the experiences of the unemployed jobseekers discussed in this book correspond with Goffman's classic observation about the workings of stigma that "whether we interact with strangers or intimates we will find that the finger tips of society have reached bluntly into the contact, even here putting us in place."[5]

Goffman's insights help us comprehend the micro workings of stigma but do not have much to say about the nature of a society whose "finger tips" put anyone who is unemployed "in place." To understand why in the United States unemployment elicits the ubiquitous stigma we have seen in this book we must consider the common thread that connects all these varied manifestations of stigma. Whether the stigma is coming from recruiters, network contacts, coaches, friends or spouses, we see an unrelenting suspicion that unemployment, in and of itself, means something is wrong with the unemployed person. This common thread points to centrality of the myth of meritocracy: Position reflects merit.[6] This myth at the heart of American neoliberal capitalism, which sanctifies the market as the institution that verifies the societal value of anything or anyone,[7] taints anyone unemployed as suspect in every realm of life.

Stigma not only shows up in the private lives of unemployed individuals, but also informs our society's policy response to unemployment. As will be discussed later in this chapter, unemployment compensation in the United States at best offers only meager support to unemployed workers for the first 6 months. And for the unemployed workers discussed in this book, who are unemployed longer than 6 months, the United States offers absolutely no support.[8] Essentially, as a society, we are saying to those who are long-term unemployment: Too bad. You are on your own. Stigma normalizes what would otherwise be clearly seen as absurd. If we suspend stigmatized thinking for a minute, and take seriously the idea that unemployment is not caused by individual shortcomings but arises from how we as a society organize work and hiring, it would be very difficult to explain why long-term unemployed workers are offered zero support. Imagine a preschool with six children but only five chores and a rule that any child without a chore does not get lunch. If your child's preschool had such a rule, you would undoubtedly demand that this rule be changed so that all kids would get lunch. So why do we allow this to occur at a societal level? We collectively allow this because the myth of meritocracy lulls us into imagining that unemployment is not a societal issue, not something that could happen to any of us, but only something that happens to those other people, and we are not so sure what is going on with them.

As we consider institutional changes later in this chapter it is important to consciously push back on that part in each of us that is drawn to believe the comforting myth of meritocracy, which places long-term unemployed workers in some other category of people. Any of us can become a long-term unemployed worker, and the stigma trap is not limited to long-term unemployment. It implicates every American worker. Long-term unemployment is an extreme case of precarity, but extreme cases can be useful for bringing to light the vulnerabilities, fears, and shames that everyone feels—to varying extents and at different moments. The unemployed workers discussed in this book provide a window to the pressures facing all workers in the context of American capitalism, and its myth of meritocracy, which renders all of us vulnerable to stigma. Any career fall or step back can be seen as reflecting on one's merit and worthiness, and may lead to a cascade of stigmatizing reactions and reinforcing cycles.[9] Unemployment only highlights the kinds of stigmas that neoliberal capitalism breeds, which demand more attention and critical scrutiny from scholars,[10] and ultimately requires collective action to dismantle.

Confronting Stigma: Activism and Policy

The sociological support discussed in Chapter 6 can help unemployed jobseekers counteract the tendency to internalize stigma—and this has significant benefits. But it does nothing to address the root source of the problem: the ubiquitous stigma itself. Ultimately, if we want to live in a society in which people are treated fairly when evaluated for jobs, are generously supported when they do not have a job, and are not blamed or judged by those around them for what is at core a social problem with social causes, the stigma of unemployment must be addressed head on.

Addressing social problems requires sustained collective action that brings an issue to public awareness and, over time, generates social and political pressure to address it. What are the prospects of unemployed workers engaging in collective action to raise awareness of the unemployment stigma and advocate for institutional changes? The next part of this chapter will look at the efforts of one group of activist unemployed jobseekers that emerged from the ICT.

Changing the Game Committee

In the spring of 2015, the ICT held its largest event: a weekend-long "rebootcamp" attended by 100 long-term unemployed jobseekers. After two days

of programming on the various challenges of prolonged unemployment—
with a heavy focus on the emotional, social, and financial toll—came the
closing session. When I scheduled this session, I gave it the rather vague title,
"Changing the Game," because I still had only a vague sense of what I had in
mind. Here is what I ended up saying:

> This weekend we have largely focused on how best to play the game. But
> another question is, do we need to change the rules? Or the context? This
> question takes us beyond what's possible for any one individual, and asks
> what a collective voice can advocate for as part of a process of social change.
>
> We probably have lots of ideas about what change is needed, but even the
> best ideas will not have a chance unless there is also advocacy that creates
> pressures on policymakers and employers. It's very tough, scary, over-
> whelming for any one jobseeker to raise their voice on these issues alone.
> But this is where more than a 100 of us, working together, and bringing
> on board some of the other people we know, can create a collective voice
> that will be heard. I recently went to see the movie, *Selma*. It was aston-
> ishing to see that the first march from Selma—a march that led to events
> that changed America—had just 600 marchers. Imagine if each of us just
> brought our family and a couple of close friends to an event—we'd easily
> have more than 600 people.
>
> I think we all agree there is a long-term unemployment crisis. I think we
> can all agree that not much is being done to change the root causes. I don't
> presume to know what aspect of this issue should be given most attention
> or how to organize ourselves and others to create pressure. But I have a lot
> of faith in the collective wisdom in this room today. Here is what I pro-
> pose. Let's discuss as a group how the game may be changed and the best
> way to work together to achieve this change. Then let's ask the people most
> energized to take on leadership on this issue to write their names on the
> whiteboard under "Changing the Game Committee." This committee can
> meet after the re-bootcamp and brainstorm the next steps to organize those
> of us here who are open to being organized on these issues.

At the end of the session, 25 of the 100 unemployed workers in the room
stood in a line to put their name on the board. Steven was one of them:

> I joined the whole Changing the Game because it was like a rallying cry
> and people were saying, "Yeah, let's do it." And the idea in my mind was,

let's call attention. We need to call attention to this. I'm looking around this room and I'm saying, "I'm shocked at all the education and experience in this room. Somebody has got to know." I think I would have marched on Washington that day, you know? . . . I had to do something. It was an opportunity to do something assertive. You're so passive in this position. You take it, you take it and you take it. Somebody gives you the opportunity to go and say, "Hey, enough is enough." I knew it wouldn't be easy, but I had to do it. It gave me an opportunity to stand up and yell.

Susan described the moment this way: "Hearing so many different people talking about 'What if, what if, what if.' I wanted to be the first one up at the board to write my name, but I wasn't! It gave me some kind of renewed hope that maybe something could be done." Sharon likewise explained her sense of hope as she joined: "Whereas the job search is an area with limited control, this is something I can do. I can be involved and even if I don't change my situation, I can change somebody else's situation."

Although American workers have been suffering from unemployment for decades, they have only rarely in that time engaged in collective action. What accounts for the burst of collective energy on that Sunday afternoon? One important factor is the understanding and solidarity that developed over the weekend leading up to it. The mutual sharing of difficult experiences helped forge bonds of trust among the participants. Moreover, from early Saturday morning the ICT re-bootcamp helped jobseekers understand the larger context of their shared struggle. By contrast to the more typical self-help support focusing on search skills and a positive attitude—which tends to exaggerate jobseeker control, take for granted the myth of meritocracy, and implicitly blame the unemployed—the ICT's sociological approach centers on research that challenges the assumptions of meritocracy. As Brenda put it:

The ICT reminded me of something: There is nothing wrong with me. However, there is a lot wrong with employers. Much of the problem lies with employers. . . . *They should be called out for it.*

In a similar vein, Marcia explained that at the ICT she learned some "disturbing statistics" about unemployment but that she now wants "to use it as a catalyst to pray for new beginnings for us all, and to speak up about it." The desire to "speak up" and "call out" was mentioned by numerous other interviewees. And it seems likely that the sociological nature of the support, with its focus on explaining the larger systemic forces underlying unemployment, played a key role in galvanizing interest in becoming engaged in collective action.

Seeking Visibility

Following the re-bootcamp, 22 unemployed jobseekers formed the Changing the Game (CTG) committee and began to meet regularly. When I asked committee members why they had decided to become active, the most common answer was a desire to bring visibility to their plight, to raise public awareness, and to lessen the stigma associated with unemployment. Sharon put it this way: "My goal is to increase awareness among people—not just employers, but everyday people—as to what our situation is. And more to the point, get people to start to think how they can change their behavior to help us." The same theme of increasing "awareness" was also echoed by Susan:

> Just get the word out to the public: "See? There's nothing wrong with me." Or, "It's not just me, it's other people too." . . . I think we're all looking for, first of all, something to do to get rid of society's impression of us, maybe to get some kind of legislative action. . . . Or just to have people listen to us. For some of us, I think, it's more, I want my voice heard. I want my day in court.

I asked Susan if she had her "day in court," what would she say to America? She chuckled at the thought and replied: "First of all, that potential employers shouldn't be so reluctant to give us a chance. Just because we're not working doesn't mean that we're stupid or that we've lost all our knowledge. I just want America to realize, 'You know what? Just because somebody has run out of luck, doesn't mean that we should help them stay out of luck.' "

In sum, a key motivation to become active was the desire to make the reality of long-term unemployment visible to society, with the hope that this will help diminish the stigma. As Paul explained, the more knowledge about the scale of the problem the more the public would be aware that "there are lots of people out there who are in this situation, and it's *really not their fault.*"

After a series of brainstorming sessions, the group decided to organize a "Day of Advocacy" at the Massachusetts State House, where a number of unemployed jobseekers would speak about their struggles and the unfair barriers they face to an audience of lawmakers and reporters. Susan agreed to emcee the event, despite being, by her own account, an introvert afraid of public speaking. "I got a call from Laura, who said, 'Would you do it?' My heart stopped for a second, to be honest with you. But I'm like, 'Yeah, this is too important. Somebody needs to do it.' So I just stood up and did it. Honestly, I looked out into the audience, but I didn't look at anybody because I've learned from public speaking, it's like you look over their heads. It looks like you're looking at them, but you're really not. So I just got up, I said my thing, and I sat down." Beyond her fear of public speaking, Susan also feared going public about her job market struggles, but "I decided that I needed to get over it. I feel like I've got nothing to lose and I'm just going to go for it." A number of unemployed workers spoke, each telling their story of going to college or even to graduate school, working for decades, losing their job, and then being shut out of the market.

In conjunction with the Day of Advocacy the CTG also released a short report based on the testimonials of the CTG members. The report, entitled "Understanding Long-Term Unemployed Professionals: Massachusetts Residents Speak Out," discusses how long-term unemployed professionals' struggles are "hidden" and "invisible." Quoting various CTG members the report touches on many of the themes of this book, including the barriers long-term unemployed workers face such as "misconceptions about older workers," and the fact that if you "haven't worked for a period of time," the "implication" is that "there MUST be something wrong with you." It also discusses unemployed workers losing their homes, living in constant financial fear and anguish, enduring strained relationships, and feeling "stigmatized" and "being treated like 'lepers.'"

The report ends with a loud collective plea pushing back on the stigma: "We are not broken. We are not damaged goods. We are not lazy or incapable or unmotivated. WE WANT TO WORK."

There is also one explicit demand from the state for improved support services: "Most find that the state resources are not equipped to help Long-Term Unemployed Professionals" and "do not offer programming, career counseling, or training opportunities that would beneficial."

To follow up on the demand that the state provide better support services, after the Day of Advocacy several CTG members attended a series of town hall meetings held by the Commonwealth of Massachusetts' Taskforce on Chronic Unemployment. While the college-educated professionals of the CTG were not technically within the purview of this taskforce because they were not *chronically* unemployed (having worked for most of their adult lives), they went anyway to make the issue of their long-term unemployment visible. A year later the Commonwealth of Massachusetts implemented a new program which, for the first time, specifically aimed at supporting long-term unemployed workers. In advertising the program, it mentioned that long-term unemployed jobseekers include those with college degrees. This was not a large-scale change, but it was a sign that the state was listening and feeling enough pressure to take a first step.

How Stigma Makes It Difficult to Struggle Against Stigma

The states' policy changes were tangible positive results but they did not live up to the CTG's participants' initial hopes of bringing wide visibility to the stigma trap that makes unemployment such a difficult challenge.

Stigma makes it difficult to struggle against stigma. Determined as the CTG was to bring visibility to the challenges of unemployment and its associated stigma, because of this very stigma these same jobseekers did not want to bring too much visibility to themselves as individuals. Visibility may intensify the stigma. Steven, for example, was among the most fired-up members of the CTG and often frustrated with the group's reluctance to "upset people." His view was: "Let's be dynamic. Let's do exciting. Let's do this. Let's bring in the press. Let's do anything." He spoke at the State House Day of Advocacy—but only introduced himself by his first name. After the event he was approached by a National Public Radio reporter:

> Some guy asked me if I wanted to be on the radio. Right at the end of the event he came right over after I spoke and says, "Can you tell me your name." And I asked not to have that public. And he said, "Well, I can't put you on the radio then." Took me five minutes to say, "Yeah, put it down. If that's what would do it, I'm gonna give my name." But he was gone and I couldn't find him.

Steven later explained his hesitation: "I wanted to keep my name out because I don't want people googling me and finding, 'Oh that's the guy who can't get hired.'" Steven was ultimately willing to take the risk of visibility, but it was too late. Most others, for very understandable reasons, were generally not willing. Sharon was among the most dedicated members of the CTG, yet she tried "to remain anonymous" and did not speak at the Day of Advocacy. CTG members understand that media coverage is essential to their advocacy cause, but feel that they have to weigh furthering this cause against the great personal risk of using their names.

The CTG's own report, discussed above, is very explicit about how stigma hindered the extent to which CTG members were willing to come out publicly on the Day of Advocacy, or even to write anonymously about their experiences in the report. Here is how the CTG report's authors, who themselves were anonymous, explained the way stigma affected their activism:

> The stigma of being long-term unemployed is real; it impacts how you are viewed both personally and professionally. Many people who submitted testimonials did so under pseudonyms. Many opted not to have the details of their stories shared even using a pseudonym for fear that they would somehow be revealed to the general public. We also had a hard time finding people to speak at the Advocacy Day event for the same reason. The authors of this [report] are Long-Term Unemployed Professionals. They chose not to be credited because they share the same concerns as their cohorts. *No one wants to be further stigmatized in their communities or by prospective employers because they had the misfortune of losing their job.*

As the most visible face of the ICT, I was repeatedly contacted by national media outlets who wanted to write about unemployment and asked for introductions to long-term unemployed workers to interview for a story. Yet, the media's insistence on using real names generally led even the activists to decline. When I asked the unemployed jobseekers in this study if they would talk to particular reporters, I generally got a response like Sandra's: "I am dedicated to being ungooglable, and especially would never want 'I'm super old and was out of work once' to be the first 10 hits. But I'm glad someone is working on a story about this. Wish I could help."

Jobseekers' concerns about individual visibility, and specifically having their names appear in media stories that later appear in Google searches are unfortunately reasonable. Bruce's story illustrates the double-edged nature of having one's name used in a story about long-term unemployment. Bruce agreed to be interviewed for a story that appeared in a national newspaper in which he described how he went from having a high-level position in a big company to being long-term unemployed. Here is what followed:

> Within a week, I had 1200 LinkedIn profile views and 400 emails from people commiserating with me, people commending me for putting myself out there and some people asking if they could help in some way. . . . And out of that actually came a good job.

Bruce found it gratifying that by sharing his story he was helping others realize they are not alone, and was of course thrilled that one of his new contacts led to a job, even if it was a temporary contract position.

But, there is another side to this story. Alongside the appreciative and helpful responses to the newspaper article there was also a highly visible blogger who was irked by it and opined to his readers that someone who is "truly" as experienced and accomplished as Bruce would not have a problem finding work. In a clear articulation of the myth of meritocracy this blogger then claimed to his large audience that there must be some other unspoken "real issues" behind Bruce's unemployment. Based on nothing but stigma this blogger publicly questioned Bruce's integrity. But the worst was yet to come. Bruce's contract position ended after six months. After two more years of unemployment and job searching Bruce was finally on the cusp of receiving an offer for a senior-level position at a good company. But then, he explains, "someone on the team Googled my name and saw the article." The job offer never came. Bruce was later told that the newspaper article derailed his candidacy. Bruce recalls thinking "Why is this happening to me?" Four years later he had still not found a full-time professional job.

Bruce's story reveals an important dimension of the stigma trap. To collectively resist the stigma of unemployment and bring about change requires speaking out about it, and calling public attention to the harms of this stigma. By speaking to a national newspaper Bruce certainly brought much-needed attention to this issue and helped thousands of readers learn they are not alone. But, the very same action that helped call attention to the unemployment stigma also called attention to Bruce as an individual and led to an intensification of the stigma specifically directed at him. One reason the stigma trap endures is the risk of further stigmatization that individuals face when attempting to engage in public resistance to this stigma.[11]

The Challenge of Leadership

This book has detailed the multiple overlapping crises—financial, social, and emotional—that accompany prolonged unemployment. In the midst of such crises, it is difficult enough to navigate daily life, let alone take the lead on challenging societal institutions and the root causes of the unemployment stigma. Even a person with excellent leadership skills and experience will struggle to put these into action when faced with the challenges of unemployment. At the CTG, leadership was initially taken on by Laura, who had experience in leading social change efforts as a union organizer. Yet, from the very start, Laura's own unemployment status also created difficulties. At the time of the CTG's formation, she was about to lose her house:

> The way I led this group is not the way I would typically lead a group. Typically, when I lead a group, I spend a lot of time getting to know people. So I would do individual meetings with everybody and get to know them and their stories and let them get to know me and my stories. And that would form a kind of a bond, that would allow me to lead a lot more effectively than I was able to lead this group. But I just couldn't get my head and my priorities all the way there because of where I was in my life at that moment. Just being so preoccupied with myself and my family.

When Laura stepped down from the leadership position, Steven reluctantly stepped in only because he feared that unless he did so, "nothing was gonna happen." Steven was determined to "pull every bit of energy I have." Yet, he found himself struggling as much as Laura had: "It's all you can do to just live. You're really spending all your energy, and the group needed constant energy, optimism, fight to it." Steven came to believe that "it's unrealistic to have the unemployed people leading."

The leadership dilemma is that only someone who is long-term unemployed can speak about it from direct current experience, and yet having leadership come from someone who is himself or herself long-term unemployed means this person is struggling and preoccupied with the financial and emotional crises of unemployment, not to mention probably—and justifiably—reluctant to be visible in the media. From the outset I took it for granted that effective leadership can only come from someone unemployed who has a first-hand understanding of the experience, and insisted that I would not take a leadership role despite the fact that it was my monologue at the re-bootcamp, quoted at the start of this chapter, that initially catalyzed the formation of the CTG. In retrospect, I think it was a mistake to assume that the person or people involved in setting the advocacy agenda—who should include individuals directly experiencing unemployment—must also be the ones carrying out the day-to-day work of practical and logistical leadership.

Although taking a leadership role in advocacy while simultaneously navigating unemployment is a lot—maybe too much—my interviews suggest that participating in an advocacy group is beneficial above and beyond any social change victories. Other benefits include camaraderie, a sense of community, and the satisfaction of using one's skills. By the time Sharon joined the CTG, she felt "beat up" by her job search and unemployment. Joining CTG helped her in several ways:

> It allows me to tap into the things that I felt good about in the context of my jobs, like working as a team and being a part of something. Being on the Changing the Game Committee, it's almost like having a job because you have meetings, and we have tasks, and we're working to do something. But I'm also among people who understand my situation. Getting involved in that whole Advocacy Day, now I have something to do, and I am tapping into certain skills that I would have used at my job and working with other people who are not necessarily doing the same thing as you. We're all working toward a goal. We can start to think strategically and plan and be in charge of this thing. It's a lot like working, but then you also have this added benefit that you feel like you are trying to make some sort of difference in your situation and people like you.

An organization aiming to support unemployed jobseekers that also encourages and facilitates advocacy sends an important message to jobseekers. It communicates that the organization recognizes that the challenge facing them is not only a matter of improving their individual search skills or even their well-being, but requires social change. To Karen, "advocacy is important because it means that people are taking it seriously and they're not just throwing it under the rug. That helps my spirits." Karen had experiences with other support organizations that "shied away from anything that seemed to talk about mobilization of people or acknowledging the unfairness because they seem to be more about getting us these very low-paying jobs."

For all these reasons, providing a venue for advocacy and collective action should be seen as an important part of jobseeker support.

Stigma and the Policy Challenge

Effective advocacy usually requires clear policy demands. With respect to the challenges facing long-term unemployed workers, there are at least two kinds of policy solutions: policies that lead to changes in hiring practices and policies that de-link income from employment through extended and enhanced unemployment insurance or other government cash support. It is striking that in my interviews with unemployed jobseekers about the policies they would like to see enacted, almost no one spoke about unemployment insurance or cash support. I suspect they felt this would stigmatize them even more—not just as unable to find work but also as seeking an undeserved handout—as I will discuss below. Instead, unemployed jobseekers focused on policies to address discriminatory employer hiring practices, although most had their doubts that anything could solve the core issue of employer discrimination against older long-term unemployed workers.

Older unemployed jobseekers face discrimination based on their age and the duration of their unemployment. Earlier in this book I discussed studies that show that as workers get older and as they remain unemployed for longer durations, they become much less likely to be interviewed compared to similarly qualified candidates who are younger or are currently employed. But what can be done about it? Even Laura, the former union organizer who initially led the CTG, felt that "the whole age discrimination thing is very difficult—very, very difficult. People see the amount of experience I have and translate that into 'too old.' I really don't know how you set policy around that." Similar attitudes were expressed about discrimination based on length of unemployment. Paul explained the challenge this way:

> I don't know how you deal with the mindset that people just assume if you've been unemployed for more than two years that there must be something wrong with you. I think there's some discussion about passing laws to make that illegal, but I don't think it would have any effect. People just find some way around it and come up with some other reason why they passed on you. If they have a stack of 100 resumes, how are you going to prove why they threw out your resume? How are you even going to know?

Given that the "stick" option of current anti-discrimination laws, most notably existing laws against age discrimination, appear largely ineffective when it comes to the long-term unemployed, many jobseekers saw more promise in offering "carrots," such as tax incentives for companies to hire older long-term unemployed workers. Even Steven, the one who wanted to "make waves," ultimately suggested a policy of tax breaks:

OS: If you could speak directly to the governor or to the president, what kind of policies do you think would make a difference?

Steven: They need to make it financially worthwhile to businesses and places to hire people. Meaning some sort of tax break for hiring long-term unemployed older folks. Some sort of sharing of salary for a period of time. The only thing I think that's gonna get anybody's attention is financial. It's all about the bottom line.

But it's hard to see a demand for employer incentives galvanizing a social movement. I can't see a march on Washington or a state capital with placards calling for "Tax breaks to companies."

It is also not clear that the carrot approach would be effective. In 2012, the Obama administration attempted to incentivize companies to hire long-term unemployed workers by rewarding them with good public relations. Specifically, they attempted to cajole large American companies by having them sign a "pledge." At a formal event in the East Room of the White House, in front of leaders of nonprofit organizations and scholars focused on this issue, including the ICT, President Obama announced that 300 large companies signed a "pledge" to stop discriminating against long-term unemployed workers. At the event President Obama implored: "They just need that chance, somebody who will look past that stretch of unemployment."[12] The companies signing the pledge were listed on a fancy brochure with much fanfare. Back in Boston, unemployed jobseekers at ICT events became momentarily hopeful that companies were about to change their ways. They didn't. At a Department of Labor meeting which I attended 2 years after the "pledge," I asked members of the administration about follow-up to their efforts. Two small companies had instituted changes, but for the most part, the "pledge" proved to be a bust. Ultimately, the Obama administration initiative dashed hopes and created more disillusionment. Brenda put it this way: "I keep remembering Obama's speeches—at the White House, to Congress, and all around the country—along with the phony pledges on the part of the government and corporations, that somehow they will make this right. They haven't."

Is there any reason to hope that activism like CTG's, if undertaken on a much larger scale, can change employer behavior? The record on reducing other forms of employer discrimination—such as by gender, race, or age—has been mixed. On the one hand, there is wide consensus in the United States that employers should not discriminate in hiring, which makes it at least politically imaginable that anti-discrimination laws could be expanded to cover more categories of workers. On the other hand, the laws have been there for decades and we still have the rampant age discrimination described in Chapter 2. So without giving up on anti-discrimination legislation *with strong enforcement provisions*, it is worthwhile to also consider policies such as expanded unemployment insurance or even universal basic income, which have the advantage of not depending on immediate changes in employer behavior, and which can mitigate the financial crisis—if not the social and emotional crises—associated with long-term unemployment.

Expanding Unemployment Benefits and a Universal Basic Income

The stigma of unemployment is everywhere. And, yes, it is here too, in American public policy. The United States is particularly stingy when it comes to unemployment benefits.[13] Compared to other advanced economies, unemployment insurance benefits in the United States generally cover a relatively short period of time, typically 6 months, and at best only replace about half of one's salary, compared to countries like Denmark where benefits are provided for 2 years and replace 70% of the prior earnings of an average worker's wages.[14] It is likely that one important factor underlying this policy stinginess is the myth of meritocracy—much more pervasive and powerful in the United States than in Europe—and its associated stigma, which deems anyone unemployed for more than a few months is no longer deserving of support.[15]

A generous expansion of unemployment benefits in terms of both the duration and the portion of lost wages replaced could greatly diminish the financial crisis associated with long-term unemployment.[16] In addition, expanding and extending unemployment benefits might send a powerful destigmatizing message, signaling to all that unemployment is a social issue with social and economic roots and not a matter of individual fault.

Given the benefits of an extended and enhanced unemployment insurance system and given that, for over a century, unemployment insurance has been the most common policy approach taken by governments to support unemployed workers, why was this policy only rarely brought up by the unemployed jobseekers I interviewed?

The absence of a discussion of unemployment benefits as a potential policy likely reflects the power of stigma. Unemployed jobseekers may feel that demanding more generous benefits is akin to asking for an undeserved handout—playing the "beggar" role discussed in Chapter 3. Recall, too, the shame and humiliation discussed in Chapter 4 by jobseekers who received food stamps or other forms of welfare.

My suspicion that stigma plays a role in jobseekers' limited discussion of unemployment benefits is supported by analyzing *how* the few who did bring it up talked about it. Notice the preemptive defensiveness in Doug's answer to my broad question:

OS: What policies might be helpful to the long-term unemployed?
Doug: The view that the more you give people unemployment [benefits], the longer they'll let the job search go on and on—I think that's kind of puritanical and stereotypical and just prejudiced. Often said, I think, by people who have never been unemployed themselves. So I think that that's a very sad thing because at the end of it all, you're talking about people and in some cases their children, who could be literally suffering because of lack of government aid, when they're bailing out banks and things of this sort.

The few others who raised the issue of extending or enlarging unemployment benefits did not advocate for a universal increase of such benefits to all unemployed workers but rather raised it in a way that clearly marked themselves as particularly deserving, due to uniquely strong needs or to having worked for a long time before being unemployed. For example, Kimberley argued for a benefit policy sensitive to one's level of need:

There should be some other kind of relief based on your situation. Not everybody who is unemployed is a single mom supporting their son and getting no money from their ex-spouse. I feel pretty alone as a single mom.

I have nobody to depend on. It's all me. When you're married and you have somebody working, you still have an income.

Kimberley also offered another way to justify getting more benefits based on her having worked for many years and, in the process, drew explicit boundaries between herself as deserving and other less-deserving workers:

> I have been working since I was 16 and I'm 58. I found it insulting to only be paid unemployment benefits for a certain period of time. I think they should base getting unemployment benefits on how long you've actually worked and contributed to our country, not based on a set number. There needs to be some help for people who have really worked a lot and contributed a lot of money. I think there are people getting unemployment who haven't worked a lot and they're still getting the same amount of money. I think that's wrong. It was pretty upsetting to me. I thought, "All this time that I have always worked, like for 40-some years, and I'm getting the same amount of weeks as someone else." That kind of bothered me.

It is understandable that under the duress of ubiquitous stigma and the financial, emotional, and relational crises described in this book, unemployed jobseekers may be tempted to undercut each other by advocating financial support to "deserving" jobseekers like themselves. Yet, a more politically hopeful and impactful policy response would aim to expand, rather than narrow, the available support to a broader range of precarious workers. Advocacy for policy responses that expand the generosity and reach of support can more likely gain allies among other precarious workers and potentially mobilize a much larger coalition of political support. Unemployed workers are in fact the tip of a precarity iceberg that includes millions of others working on a short-term contingent basis, gig-economy workers, workers involuntarily working part-time with uncertain schedules, or those working at jobs that don't pay a living wage and thus create perpetual economic anxiety.

The sociologically informed support discussed in the prior chapter, which helps raise awareness of the shared external forces outside individual control that shape our economic fates, may lead to a rise in advocacy for policies that address unemployment and precarity. In support settings that adopt a sociological approach *and* bring together a variety of unemployed and precarious workers, participants may come to see that the challenges they face cut across class lines and other social divisions.[17]

What If Policies Were Stigma-free? Lessons from the Covid-19 Response

If policy solutions were considered in a way that was not informed by stigma or the myth of meritocracy, the proposed solutions would likely be much more generous and broad-based. The legislative response to the Covid-19 recession is instructive. For a brief historic moment, in the early stages of the pandemic, the stigma of unemployment was temporarily lifted and those without work were seen without distortion as people without work *through no fault of their own*. With the stigma lifted, the policy response was rapid and bipartisan in providing unemployment benefits that were substantially more generous than usual, and which covered typically excluded workers in the gig economy.

An even more ambitious, broad-based, and comprehensive policy response to address the precarity of most American workers would be a universal basic income (UBI). As a focus for advocacy, UBI holds the potential to generate wide political support because it speaks to the economic anxieties and insecurities not only of unemployed workers but of a great many other precarious workers.[18] As with expanded unemployment benefits, the early legislative response to the Covid-19 pandemic, which included unconditional cash payments—essentially a temporary UBI to all Americans, suggests that this kind of policy may be feasible in a context of reduced stigma. More broadly, the Covid-19–era legislation reveals how a society like the United States reacts when it is widely understood that economic precarity is not the fault of individuals but results from a force outside their control. A sociological understanding of precarity therefore holds the promise that, just as we did when Covid-19 hit in the spring of 2020, we will come to see through the myth of meritocracy and observe how American capitalism imposes economic insecurity beyond the control of most individuals.

Finally, a policy like UBI not only provides material benefits in the form of unconditional financial support, but it is also beneficial because of how it symbolically challenges the myth of meritocracy, which underlies the ubiquitous stigma of unemployment. By decoupling a minimum income from employment, UBI sends a message that all individuals are deserving of a basic income and implicitly recognizes that the labor market is not the only arbiter of value and does not always produce a fair or desirable outcome. This policy message alone may help chip away at the persistent stigma we have seen throughout this book. More immediately, the very process of advocating for a policy like UBI may stimulate a much-needed societal discussion and critical analysis of dominant cultural assumptions of what makes a person worthy of dignity or what qualifies a person to be seen as an equal and not as tainted or stigmatized. In other words, it would challenge the core assumptions beneath the myth of meritocracy and its dark underside of the stigma trap.

Why Does the Unemployment Stigma Endure?

The workers discussed in this book pose a profound challenge to the myth of meritocracy. They went to college, often to very elite colleges, had successful careers, acquired valuable work experience, and yet find themselves unable to get professional jobs. They are no different from any reader of this book, including those who are currently quite successful. The experiences reported by these long-term unemployed workers—as they interact with others in their lives—can help us understand how the flipside of the myth of meritocracy is a cruel stigma. We see a consistent pattern repeat in various contexts, with stigma showing up whether we are exploring how recruiters react to unemployed jobseekers, or the experiences of unemployed jobseekers when seeking support from colleagues, friends, spouses, coaches, or government policies.

The ubiquity and enduring force of the unemployment stigma in the United States is powered by the myth of meritocracy. But how is it that this myth is sustained and endures given that all around us we see outcomes that do not reflect meritocracy?

One way to understand the tenacious staying power of this myth is to consider the role of culture and institutions. Scholars of American culture have long shown that we are swimming in a cultural sea of individualism, with its assumption that individuals, though their effort and skill, are the masters of their own fates—in the labor market as well as anywhere else.[19] This cultural assumption is institutionalized at the core of American capitalism with employer hiring practices of ostensibly evaluating and selecting candidates on the basis of merit. From a young age, our educational system prepares us for this process by naturalizing testing and ranking. Starting in elementary school, we are encouraged by teachers and parents to work hard and to believe that our grades reflect our effort and abilities—or lack thereof.[20] By the time we move from school to work, we have been groomed to see employer evaluations and selections as akin to grades reflecting our merit.[21]

One cannot grow up in the United States without internalizing the myth of meritocracy.[22] The wide acceptance and internalization of this myth is not only facilitated by the culture of individualism and by the educational institutions that structure our upbringing, but also by the role of government in American society. In the American version of capitalism, the government reinforces the myth by its actions and inactions. In Western European countries, especially in Scandinavian countries such as Denmark and Sweden, generous government policies provide a material safety net and, in this way, symbolically communicate an alternative standard of valuation—universally granting value and support to all individuals, regardless of how they make out in the capitalist labor market. By contrast, in the this country, the absence of a meaningful safety net reinforces the legitimacy and naturalness of equating a person's value to their labor market outcomes.[23]

To understand the tenacity of the myth of meritocracy, dominant cultural messages and institutions are of course significant, but equally so is the fact that we tend to mobilize—and thereby reproduce—the myth of meritocracy in our everyday lives because it seems helpful in dealing with the uncertainty and precarity of living under American capitalism. In other words, we all live and breathe this myth as part of our everyday life because it helps us feel just a bit less anxious as we play the societal game we are stuck playing, even as our very playing helps reproduce this game.[24]

In the context of American capitalism, with its extreme precarity and inequality, the myth of meritocracy can seem reassuring. The struggles of the people discussed in this book are terrifying to all those around them, precisely because of their impressive accomplishments. If *their* careers can go off the cliff, so can *anyone's*. To avoid this upsetting conclusion, we are motivated to find some reason why *they* are at fault for their unemployment—something *they've* done wrong that we can make sure to do right. As this book shows over and over again, we try to find what explains their case, rather than letting ourselves think about how their case challenges our comforting assumptions that our hard work and skills will protect us.[25] As Max Weber, one of the founders of sociology, famously observed: "The fortunate is seldom satisfied with the fact of being fortunate. Beyond this, he needs to know that he has a right to his good fortune. He wants to be convinced that he 'deserves' it, and above all, that he deserves it in comparison with others. He wishes to be allowed the belief that *the less fortunate also merely experiences his due*."[26]

We may know that in American capitalism we are all playing in a rigged game and that meritocracy is a myth, and yet we may nonetheless be tempted by this myth as the path of least anxiety—comforting ourselves and teaching our kids mantras about how outcomes reflect hard work and talents. With sky-high levels of precarity and inequality, it is not surprising that we are intensely fearful about our fates and seek soothing beliefs. In the United States stress and anxiety are common across the economic spectrum, including the upper middle class, for whom the fear of falling off the ladder of success (or of having one's children fall) is as intense as the fear of not making it.[27] We therefore desperately seek to hold on to the belief that, as Weber puts it, we "deserve" our good fortunes. The myth of meritocracy may be a strategy adopted, consciously or not, under conditions of duress, but it has very serious consequences—the stigmatizing of those who do fall, or even just slip—or in Weber's words the belief that the "*less fortunate merely experience[es] his due*."

We are all trapped by the fact that by acting and thinking in ways that may be comforting in our individual cases, at least in the short run, we are unwittingly reproducing, along with everyone else, a myth that causes great harm. At a societal level, we are reproducing a cultural understanding that blames individuals for societal shortcomings while leaving the shortcomings themselves untouched. At an interpersonal level, we judge and stigmatize each other, even our friends and loved ones, instead of providing empathetic support when it's most needed. And belief in the myth sets us up as individuals for feeling shame and self-blame when we experience any setbacks over which we have limited control, and as this book shows, ultimately risks devastating our sense of self.

The only way out is by confronting the myth of meritocracy and its attendant stigma head on. A first step is to recognize our internalized assumptions about ourselves and others and the larger social forces from which those assumptions arise. This form of recognition is not beyond our grasp. Recall the sociological form of support described for unemployed jobseekers in Chapter 6, in which critical awareness was facilitated by open discussions with peers, and which helped jobseekers see more clearly that their challenges are not attributable to individual shortcomings but to broader social forces. To move toward larger social change, these sociologically informed peer discussions cannot be limited to support settings for unemployed jobseekers. They are sorely needed at dinner tables across the United States, in classrooms, at work, and ultimately in the political sphere. This is where both you—the reader—and I, as members of this society, have an important role to spark these conversations with our family and friends, in our places of worship, in our workplaces, and in our political community.

Acknowledgments

This book would not have been possible without the time and energy of countless people. First, I want to acknowledge and thank all the people who agreed to be interviewed for this book, and who in many cases shared some of the most painful experiences of their lives. Your stories are the core of this book. Also at the heart of this book, and the larger project of supporting and researching the challenges facing long-term unemployed jobseekers, are the many coaches and counselors who volunteered their time to the Institute for Career Transitions (ICT) and provided support to unemployed jobseekers including: Cath Amory, Mark Biddle, Arleen Bradley, Deborah Burkholder, Catherine Butler, Matt Casey, Mo Chanmugham, Arnold Clickstein, Tess Dedman, Joanne Dennison, Leigh Doherty, Robert Dolan, Suzy Drapkin, Nancy Dube, Deb Elbaum, Marion Estienne, Melinda Fabiano, Debra Faith House, Deborah Federico, Maggie French, Allyn Gardner, Wendy Gawlik, Tammy Gooler Loeb, Suzanne Greenwald, Anne Grieves, Melanie Hamon, Clare Harlow, Kit Hayes, Dale Hinshaw, Jan Hodges, Richard Johnson, Cindy Key, Rachelle Lappinen, Pam Lassiter, Ed Lawrence, Lauren Lemieux, Gail Liebhaber, Debbie Lipton, Amy Mazur, Tom McDonough, Wilma Nachsin, Dorthy O'Beirne, Shannon O'Brien, Sara Pacelle, Bonnie Petrovich, Martha Plotkin, Jennifer Riggs, Ilene Rudman, Karen Samuelson, Lisa Shapiro, Robin Slavin, Jan Stewart, Jennifer Straton, Tish Wakefield, Patricia Weitzman, and Lou Yelgin. In addition, I would like to thank Fred Studley of Transition Solutions who donated the time of seven career consultants to the ICT.

I want to particularly recognize the enormous contributions of Deborah Burkholder and Amy Mazur who played key leadership roles in the ICT, helped recruit many of the career coaches and counselors to this project, and in so many other ways made the ICT happen. Deborah Burkholder's efforts and organizational genius were the only reason numerous ICT events happened, and Amy Mazur's deep expertise in counseling played a pivotal role in developing the nature of the support offered by the ICT.

Michelle Rosin deserves special recognition for her instrumental role in helping me kickstart the ICT. Michelle created our first website, wrote and disseminated surveys, matched jobseekers with coaches, and much more. I am also extremely grateful to Alexandra Vasquez who conducted many of the initial interviews with jobseekers and helped analyze early interview data. Toward the end of the project some of the career coaches and counselors and others also helped with interviewing jobseekers including Amy Mazur, Allyn Gardiner, Rachelle Lappinen, Martha Plotkin, Tammy Gooler-Loeb, Tish Wakefield, Deb Elbaum, Ed Lawrence, Robin Slavin, Michele Murphy, and Gail Liebhaber. I also want to thank Gokce Basbug who helped design the initial selection process for participants in this study, design the surveys of jobseekers, and analyze the survey data. Likewise I am grateful for support in analyzing data or for other research help from Rand Ghayad, Dale Hinshaw, and Sara Wedeman.

David Blustein has been a key ally in supporting the work of the ICT and in leading the Work Intervention Network (WIN) which trains career coaches and counselors in providing support to unemployed jobseekers that includes the critical consciousness and sociological perspective discussed in Chapter 6. Key support to the ICT and this project was also provided by Susan Joyce, who taught me so much about the challenges facing unemployed jobseekers and introduced me to many of the recruiters I interviewed for this book, as well as to Dick Bolles.

I will be forever grateful for the extremely helpful feedback at various stages of this manuscript from my colleagues at UMass Amherst, and specifically for many rich conversations with Amy Schalet, Cedric de Leon, Fareen Parvez, Brian Sargent, and Millian Kang. I also appreciate the feedback and insightful comments of Ilana Gershon, Dawn Norris, Annette Nierobisz, Aliya Rao, Patrick Sheehan, and Sabina Pultz. Conversations with many others helped shape my thinking on unemployment including Gerry Crispin, Alex Freund, Jerry Rubin, and Elizabeth White.

I am grateful for the wonderful editing of John Elder who helped reduce my reliance on sociological jargon and made this book more readable. I also received helpful editing from Deborah Burkholder, Amy Mazur, and Ed Lawrence. My terrific transcriptionist Cherie Potts also deserves a special thank you, as does Alexcee Bechthold, the anonymous reviewers, and the whole team at Oxford University Press. In particular James Cook made extremely helpful suggestions and never wavered in his support of this book.

Thank you also to the AARP Foundation for a grant that provided crucial early funding for this project.

Finally, no words can fully express my gratitude to my children, Avilev, Talia, and Eliyah, for their loving support throughout this project, and especially for putting up with me as the deadline for this book was approaching.

APPENDIX

The Story Behind This Book and Methodology

The research for this book was designed to both generate new knowledge about long-term unemployment and to support the unemployed workers who participated in the research and made this book possible. To recruit interviewees to participate in this research I offered to match them with support that is free and which takes a sociological approach instead of the dominant self-help approach. For my prior book I studied a self-help support organization that focused on the message that finding a job is simply a matter of improving one's search skills and maintaining a positive attitude, a message that implicitly blames and stigmatizes jobseekers for their unemployment. Having seen the harms of the self-help approach, I determined that any further research on unemployment that I conduct include the provision of an alternative form of support, one that is sociologically informed, and which explicitly aims to combat the stigma of unemployment.

The project began in the summer of 2013 when I started to reach out to career coaches and counselors (which I will refer to collectively as "coaches") in the Boston area by attending professional association conferences, e-mail listservs, and word-of-mouth. By 2013 the highly visible wave of unemployment that came with the Great Recession was trending downward, but in the shadows and out of the public spotlight millions of people remained long-term unemployed at historically high rates.[1] As I reached out to the coaches I highlighted the magnitude of the ongoing crisis of long-term unemployment and discussed the findings of my then newly released book that self-help forms of support can exacerbate the challenge of long-term unemployment. Having described this background, I then asked the coaches if they were willing to volunteer their time to provide support for free, and adjust their practice to take account of my research findings. I also asked to have the outcomes of their support efforts researched. In the fall of 2013, I hosted several meetings of coaches in my living room in which I explained in more detail the shortcomings of the self-help support, as described at the start of Chapter 6, and how it tends to intensify the internalization of stigma. I also shared other sociological research findings about long-term unemployment, including audit studies showing employer discrimination against long-term unemployed jobseekers and other studies showing the emotional toll of long-term unemployment. By November 2013, 42 volunteer coaches agreed to have me match them with long-term unemployed jobseekers and to provide three months of free support.[2] After the project's initial launch more coaches volunteered to join.

Ultimately a total of 63 volunteer coaches participated in this project to provide support to 539 unemployed jobseekers. The coaches did not receive compensation for providing this support but were motivated by the opportunity to help long-term unemployed workers directly through support and indirectly via research. A key factor to my ability to enlist the help of such a large number of volunteers was that I provided the coaches with an opportunity to participate in the research process from its earliest stage. I shared with the coaches my own prior research findings, but I also asked for their input, as professionals on the front lines of supporting jobseekers, what they have learned and how they understand the struggles of unemployed workers. The coaches were motivated to help research that would ultimately provide an opportunity to improve the way support is provided and an opportunity for professional development.

With the help of Michelle Rosin, who at the time was a recent graduate from Wellesley College, from fall of 2013 to spring of 2015, 170 long-term unemployed jobseekers were matched with coaches and received either weekly one-on-one support or weekly small group support for a 3-month period. Starting in the spring of 2015 the form of support shifted to intensive 2-day or 1-day "re-bootcamps," which brought together between 50 to 100 jobseekers for interactive workshops led by volunteer coaches and me. Over the course of five re-bootcamps during 2015–2017, support was provided to an additional 320 jobseekers. Finally, in 2017 the format of support shifted again, this time to a more intensive program called the "Collaboratory" which combined support with a co-working environment for small cohorts of jobseekers to engage in job searching in the context of a community. A total of 49 jobseekers participated in the "Collaboratory," during the time I collected data for this book. While the forms of support evolved over time certain, key features of the support, most importantly its sociologically informed practices, were consistent and are described in detail in Chapter 6.

From among the 539 unemployed jobseekers who received support between 2013 and 2018 a total of 139 jobseekers were interviewed in-depth, including 51 who were interviewed both before and after receiving support, 35 who were only interviewed prior to receiving support, and 53 who were interviewed after receiving support. The ultimate number of interviews was determined by saturation; the point at which further interviews provided little new and surprising information.[3] The interviews were conducted directly by me as well as initially by Alexandra Vasquez, who at the time was a graduate student at Brandeis University. At a later stage a number of the volunteer coaches also conducted interviews with jobseekers (whom they did not directly support) including Amy Mazur, Allyn Gardiner, Rachelle Lappinen, Martha Plotkin, Tammy Gooler-Loeb, Tish Wakefield, Deb Elbaum, Ed Lawrence, Gail Liebhaber, and Robin Slavin.

In addition to traditional interviews, starting in 2015 I began collecting data by asking jobseekers to conduct peer-to-peer interviews in another attempt to blend research with support. Prior to attending a re-bootcamp event, jobseekers were randomly matched with peers and set up to have a one hour phone conversation. In the first 30 minutes one jobseeker asked another a few broad questions about their experiences with job searching and unemployment, and then in the next 30 minutes they switched roles. A total of 32 jobseekers participated in peer-to-peer interviews that were recorded and transcribed. These peer-to-peer interviews yielded important and unique data that I would not have otherwise obtained. For example, as discussed in Chapter 4, in their peer-to-peer interview Steven asks Liam how he feels about going to the gym during the workday to which Liam responds by sharing that he feels self-conscious being in public and not working. Steven's question is not one that I would have thought to ask, as it arose directly from his own experience of internalized stigma, which in the same peer-to-peer interviews he reveals by discussing his hesitation to step outside his home during the workday to get the mail for fear as being seen by neighbors. In addition to unique data, the peer-to-peer interviews also served as a form of peer support. One jobseeker put it this way: "My peer interview helped make me not feel so alone. We have similar circumstances." At the end of another peer-to-peer interview one of the jobseekers states, "Thank you for listening. It was very supportive having somebody willing to listen to me." In this book I only draw on the peer-to-peer interviews of jobseekers who were also separately in-depth interviewed.

Recruitment and Sample

To recruit long-term unemployed jobseekers to participate in this research I reached out to Boston-area career centers, networking groups, and libraries, and asked these organizations to share with jobseekers information about the opportunity to receive free job search support in exchange for agreeing to participate in research. Interested jobseekers who reached out to me by email were asked to complete a short survey in order to determine whether they met the following eligibility criteria: (i) unemployed 6 months or longer, (ii) between the ages of 40 and 65, (iii) previously employed in a white-collar occupation, and (iv) looking for work in the Boston area.

Before discussing the rationale for these specific criteria, the issue of self-selection bias should be acknowledged. Given that the interviewees were recruited with the promise of free job search support, it is likely that the sample consists of jobseekers with some level of motivation to continue with their job search and receive job search support. This means that the sample may underrepresent long-term unemployed workers who are either highly discouraged and therefore are not motivated to seek support, or highly confident and therefore do not think they need support. Because the self-selection bias likely means an under-representation of both highly discouraged and the highly confident jobseekers, I do not expect that this self-selection systematically affects the key findings of this book around the experience of stigma.

In terms of the basic demographics of the interviewees, they had a mean age of 56, were 52% male and 48% female, and 64% of the interviewees were married. The interviewees were 89% white, 4% African American, 4% Asian, 2% Hispanic, and 1% "other." This compares to an estimate of American white-collar workers nationally being 81% white, 7% African American, 5% Hispanic, and 4% Asian,[4] and suggests that the sample over-represents unemployed white jobseekers and under-represents unemployed African American and Hispanic jobseekers.

In terms of the specific eligibility criteria for participating in the research, the four criteria listed above reflect a purposive recruiting approach, which is appropriate when seeking to understand particular processes or extend theories.[5] The research focused on white-collar workers, who are largely college educated and in many cases have advanced degrees, and who are trapped in long-term unemployment. This particular focus was motivated by my interest in examining the processes and forces forming the stigma trap in the case of workers who by most sociological accounts would seem most immune to it. I sought to figure out the puzzle of how and why workers—who by standard sociological categories would be classified as privileged in terms of class, education, social and cultural capital, and in many cases race and gender—nonetheless are stigmatized and excluded from the labor market. Existing sociological theory does not offer ready explanations for the economic precarity and struggle of, for example, highly educated white men. And yet, prior research does show that both stigma and the internalization of stigma is prevalent among this group of workers,[6] and in fact that once unemployed, highly educated workers are either as likely or more likely to get trapped in long-term unemployment as workers with less formal education.[7]

The research focused on older workers, between the ages of 40 and 65, because prior studies show that older workers are more likely than younger workers to get trapped in long-term unemployment,[8] and an important goal of this research was to understand the forces that create this trap. Finally, I limited the sample to jobseekers searching for work in the Boston area for two reasons. First, labor market conditions can vary greatly by geographical region, which may in turn shape the experience of unemployment. Since in this research I was looking for patterns of experiences among the long-term unemployed jobseekers, I sought to limit the extent to which factors, such as varied geographic locations, shaped the results. Second, having the jobseekers in the Boston area was important for practical reasons since the research involved receiving support from Boston-area coaches, and this was largely provided in person.

The ultimate sample for this study was highly educated and with impressive professional backgrounds. In term of their prior fields and occupations, the most common fields were technology and biotech, healthcare, sales and marketing, finance and insurance, corporate or nonprofit management, and education. Within their fields, 52% of the interviewees characterized their role as being "experienced individual contributors," 26% characterized their role as "management," and 22% characterized their role as "executive." The mean number of years of work experience is 27 years. A majority of the jobseekers had held only one or two full-time jobs over the preceding 10 years. In other words, the jobseekers in our sample are not chronically unemployed workers or otherwise workers who might be negatively characterized as "job hoppers" by employers.[9] Reflecting the fact that nearly half the sample consisted of professionals in managerial or professional levels, and with many years of experience in their most recent full-time jobs, 50% of the respondents were earning between $50,000 and $99,000, 42% were earning more than $100,000 a year. Only 8% were earning less than $50,000 a year.

In terms of the duration of unemployment, all the jobseekers were at least six months unemployed. With 29% being unemployed 6 months to a year, 35% being unemployed 1 to 2 years, and 36% being unemployed more than 2 years.

Interviews and Coding

All the interviews were semi-structured and were conducted in person, by telephone, or by videoconference. The interviews lasted between 60 and 120 minutes. In interviews conducted prior to the jobseeker's receiving support, jobseekers were asked questions regarding their experience looking for work, including interactions with potential employers and networking, and the effects of unemployment on their emotional well-being and important personal relationships. In interviews conducted after receipt of support, jobseekers were asked similar questions as well as a set of questions about the effect of the support they had received. The interviews were recorded, transcribed, and coded using NVivo software. The coding initially used broad concepts drawing on existing theories such as "stigma" (Goffman 1963) or "self-blame" (Sharone 2013), as well as other concepts that inductively emerged from the interview data such as "beggar" or "used-car salesman." Codes that corresponded to significant amounts of data were subsequently broken down into several subcodes.

Interviewing Recruiters and MIT Sloan Alumni

To supplement my data and provide context for the experiences and obstacles faced by long-term unemployed jobseekers, I also interviewed 20 recruiters whose job involves reviewing and vetting applications for a broad range of white-collar positions. I reached out to recruiters to participate in this research through introductions from coaches, career centers, and most of all my long-time collaborator Susan Joyce who at the time ran a well-known website for jobseekers and has extensive ties among recruiters. In terms of self-selection bias, the recruiters who agreed to participate in this research knew that the research focus was understanding the obstacles and challenges facing older long-term unemployed workers. Since they were motivated by a desire to support research on such challenges it is reasonable to assume that if there is any self-selection bias among the recruiters it would cut in the direction of the recruiters being more empathetic to the plight of long-term unemployed jobseekers, and who may experience above average social desirability pressures to discuss how they treat these particular jobseekers fairly. As such, this potential bias only bolsters the findings reported in Chapter 2 regarding employer stigmas and how they lead to the systematic exclusion of both older and long-term unemployed workers.

In my interviews of recruiters I asked about their general process of reviewing applicants, and specifically what meanings they might attach to unemployment, including long-term unemployment; a worker being older; a worker applying for jobs that are at a lower level than their most recent job; or a worker seeking to switch careers in midlife. I also asked them how they might understand existing research findings showing that older workers, regardless of education and credentials, are the most likely to become trapped in long-term unemployment.

Finally, to recruit MIT Sloan alumni for the interviews about networking reported in Chapter 3, I used a complete list of all recent alumni obtained from the MIT Sloan Alumni Office and randomly selected 18 of them to reach out to. I introduced myself as a current professor at MIT Sloan (which I was at the time) who is doing research about networking within the Sloan Alumni network. The vast majority, 15 of 18, agreed to short phone interviews during which I asked them how they respond to typical networking messages from fellow Sloan alumni or current students, and then specifically how they might respond to a Sloan alumnus who has been unemployed for a year. Given the random selection of interview subjects and the high response rate it is unlikely that the findings are shaped by a self-selection bias.

Notes

Chapter 1

1. Long-term unemployment is only one form of precarity, though perhaps the most intense. For discussions of precarity and insecurity more generally see, for example, Kalleberg (2018) and Pugh (2015).
2. Surveys show that an overwhelming majority of American workers are worried about job security (Van Horn 2013). See also Gershon (2017).
3. Studies showing that the likelihood of getting trapped in long-term unemployment is the same or higher for college-educated workers include Krueger, Cramer, and Cho (2014); Van Horn (2013); EPI (2020); Lopez and Philips (2019); Norris (2016); and Executive Office of the President (2014). For example, both Krueger, Cramer, and Cho (2014), drawing on Current Population Survey data, and a report by the Executive Office of the President (2014), using Bureau of Labor Statistics data, show that the long-term unemployed are equally or slightly more educated than short-term unemployed workers. See also Sharone et al. (2015); Stettner and Wenger (2003); and Mishel, Bernstein, and Allegretto (2007). The finding that even the most highly educated, credentialed, and experienced workers can be trapped in long-term unemployment—and paradoxically at the same or even higher rates than less formally educated workers—showed up in an interesting way in the process of recruiting jobseekers for this research. To participate in this research, jobseekers needed to fill out a short survey with basic information including their educational background and their length of unemployment. Initially, 800 unemployed jobseekers completed the sign-up survey, but many of them could not be invited to participate in the research because they were unemployed for *less* than 6 months. Looking at the information provided in the sign-up process, my colleague Gokce Basbug noticed that from among the 800 people who signed up those who were unemployed for longer than 6 months were in fact more likely to have advanced degrees than those who were short-term unemployed. Specifically, from among the respondents to our initial sign-up survey, 6.3% of the long-term unemployed have doctoral degrees compared to 3.4% of the short-term unemployed, and 12.5% of the long-term unemployed jobseekers held professional degrees compared to only 7.7% of the short-term unemployed jobseekers (Sharone et al. 2015).
4. The demographics of short-term unemployed workers and their long-term counterparts are generally very similar except that long-term unemployed workers are disproportionately older and more likely to be African American. With respect to age, Van Horn (2013) shows that laid-off older workers were much more likely to become long-term unemployed compared younger workers, even controlling

for health, education, and income. See also Monge-Naranjo and Sohail (2015), Evangelist and Christman (2013), and Schwartz Center for Economic Policy Analysis (2018). Historically the proportion of unemployed workers who are over 55 years old and who get trapped in long-term unemployment is significantly higher than for the general population. This trend became more pronounced during and after the Great Recession when over 50% of unemployed workers who were over 55 years old were long-term unemployed, and this figure remained in the 40% to 50% range through 2021 (Schwartz Center for Economic Policy Analysis 2018; AARP 2021). In addition to being older, another predictor of long-term unemployment is being African American. For example, in 2014, 39.6% of unemployed African Americans were long-term unemployed compared to 31.5% of whites (Pedulla 2020; see also Mitchell 2013). The rise of long-term unemployment that came with the recent Covid-19 pandemic largely fit this historic demographic pattern, with the fastest rise in long-term unemployment found for older workers between the ages of 45 and 64, African American workers, but also unexpectedly, Asian American workers (Pew Research Center 2021).

5. See, for example, the findings of Pedulla (2020). For the public articulation of this stigma by politicians, see Damaske (2021).

6. Faberman et al. (2017); McDonald et al. (2019); Atkinson, Giles, and Meager (1996).

7. See, for example, Kroft, Lange, and Notowidigdo (2013); Pedulla (2020); Ghayad (2013); and Faberman et al. (2017). In Farber, Silverman, and von Wachter (2016), the researchers do not find a negative effect from unemployment for females applying for administrative support positions but do show a negative effect if the applicant is over the age of 50.

8. Internalized stigma, self-blame, and feeling "flawed" were an important focus of my prior book *Flawed System/Flawed Self* (Sharone 2013), which found that such experiences were particularly prevalent among American white-collar workers. Similar results showed up in the survey of 125 long-term unemployed jobseekers who initially signed up to participate in this research and a majority agreed with the statement "Sometimes I fear there is something wrong with me that is preventing me from finding work." The finding of self-blame among unemployed American workers was also found by Blustein (2019, 188) who reports that "the self-blame theme that was evident in Sharone's work was replicated here and is integral to the causal connection between unemployment and mental health problems." Other studies point to the link between self-blame and depression (e.g., Peterson, Schwartz, and Seligman 1981); self-blame and negative health outcomes (e.g., Rantakeisu, Starrin, and Hagquist 1999; Eales 1989; Creed and Bartrum 2007) and self-blame and job search discouragement (e.g., Kanfer, Wanberg, and Kantrowitz 2001; Kaufman 1982). The prevalence of self-blame is also supported by the findings of Newman (1999); Smith (2001); Cottle (2001); Uchitelle (2006); Chen (2015); Norris (2016); Rao (2020); Zukin, Van Horn, and Stone (2011), and Komarovsky (1940). Damaske (2021) and Lane (2011) both find that self-blame is more common among women than men. Lopez and Phillips (2019) interviewed unemployed American jobseekers after the Great Recession and found a mix of reactions including both self-blame and the blaming of external

factors such as an unfair hiring system. In a study focusing on African Americans, Lamont et al. (2019, 98) find that most of their interviewees "embrace self-reliance and self-blame when faced with unemployment." Beyond the context of unemployment Lamont et al. (2019) also discuss research showing self-blame among workers for not being able to finish college and among African Americans who embrace individualist explanations of racial inequality over structural explanations. Lamont et al. (2019) link this broad pattern of self-blame to neoliberalism and the myth of meritocracy discussed in Chapter 1. Similarly, Cech (2021, 11) links neoliberalism and "meritocratic ideology" to self-blame, claiming that "neoliberalism promotes the idea that individuals are solely responsible for their own economic and social success." She specifically reports that when college students experience difficulties in finding jobs that they are "passionate" about, they tend to "frame these as the result of their own decisions, even when structural obstacles were evident" (Cech 2021, 175).

9. A number of excellent books have recently explored how the experience of unemployment varies by gender, how it affects spouses and families, and how it shapes our identities (Lane 2011, Gershon 2017, Norris 2016, Damaske 2021, and Rao 2020). My own prior book (Sharone 2013) explores how these experiences vary cross-nationally. This book is the first to focus on the role of stigma in shaping the long-term unemployment experience in various realms of life and how these combine to form an unemployment trap that is difficult to escape.

10. Goffman (1963, 3). Link and Phelan (2001, 367) provide a four-part definition of stigma as occurring when (1) "people distinguish and label human differences," (2) the labeled persons are linked to "undesirable characteristics," (3) the "labeled persons are placed in distinct categories" to create "separation of 'us' and 'them,'" and (4) the "labeled persons experience status loss and discrimination." Karen and Sherman (2012, 849) similarly define stigma as a "mark that designates the individual as defective and deserving of less valued treatment," and note that of the three categories of stigma recognized by Goffman—including "tribal stigmas" such as race, "abominations of the body" such as physical disabilities, and "blemishes of character"—unemployment falls into the third category.

11. Lamont et al. (2019, 59). In an important cross-national comparative study of stigma experienced by racial and ethnic minorities in three countries, Lamont et al. (2019) distinguish stigma from discrimination and point out that while discrimination involves a denial of access to material opportunities and is usually a violation of law, stigma is more pervasive, omnipresent, and profoundly influential in shaping everyday life.

12. As Link and Phelan (2001, 367) point out, "The vast majority of human differences are ignored and therefore socially irrelevant." The few differences that are picked out as salient vary dramatically depending on time and place. It is therefore important to consider what social forces in a particular historical context render specific differences, such as employment status, salient targets of stigma.

13. Foucault (2004, 44–47).

14. In linking the unemployment stigma to institutions of neoliberal capitalism, in addition to Michel Foucault, I am building on the work of Tyler and Slater (2018,

727) who theorize that stigma "cannot be disentangled from the political and economic imperatives of financial capitalism." This perspective emphasizes how stigma
"reproduces existing inequalities" (732) by naturalizing such inequalities and blaming
those at the bottom of society's ladder for their social location. Also theorizing this
connection are Karen and Sherman (2012, 849–850) who claim that the reason unemployment is stigmatized as a "blemish of character" is precisely because of the
core assumption of neoliberal capitalism that the unemployed "are to blame," or have
"caused their unemployment."

15. While the myth of meritocracy is not limited to the American context, much research
shows that it is distinctly strong in the United States. Sandel (2020) discusses survey
data showing that 77% of Americans compared to only half as many Germans believe
that hard work brings success. On the flipside, 70% of Americans believe the poor can
make it out of poverty on their own, as compared to only 35% of Europeans. Lewis
(1978, 7–8) similarly finds that in the United States, most people ignore the role of
social structures in determining outcomes and only focus on the individual; therefore the "dominant interpretation of disadvantage" is "ineptness" or "misbehavior."
Lamont (2019, 668–669) reports data showing that "belief in meritocracy—that who
gets ahead in society is decided by hard work—is considerably higher in the United
States than in France, Germany and the UK." Similar findings are reported in Alesina,
Stantcheva, and Teso (2018), showing that survey respondents in the United States
are much more likely than in Sweden, the UK, France, and Italy to believe that effort
is the main reason for individual success. In the same study, Americans were found to
overestimate the likelihood that a person born into the lowest 20% of household income would end up in the highest 20% of household income, whereas respondents in
Sweden, the UK, France, and Italy underestimated those chances for someone in their
countries.

16. Kallberg (2018). Cech (2021, 164) defines neoliberalism as follows: "Neoliberalism is
a political and economic ideology that advocates radical free market capitalism under
the presumption that economic and social well-being is best achieved by scaling back
social programs and resisting collective or redistributive processes that would restrict
the free market in any way."

17. For example, Cech's (2021) recent study of college students reveals the persistent belief that the lack of success of others is the outcome of lack of drive. Older studies reveal the same pattern and consistently find that majorities of Americans believe that
hard work is the most important determinant of individual success (see Kluegel and
Smith 1986, Schlozman and Verba 1979).

18. For discussions of this pattern, see Kalleberg (2018) and Pugh (2015). Farber (2008)
analyzes Current Population Survey (CPS) data from 1973 to 2006 and concludes
that "the structure of jobs in the private sector has moved away from long-term
relationships." The change in the structure of private sector jobs can be seen in the
rapid and dramatic decline of long-term employment for men. The data are not as
clear for women, but as Farber (2008) explains, this is only due to an offsetting increase in women's attachment to the labor force during the past half century.

19. The neoliberal era, which took hold in the 1980s, has been described as requiring a "one way honor system," where workers are still expected to be dedicated to their employers, but employer layoffs of workers are a part of everyday life (Pugh 2015). For a broader historical discussion of the transformation to neoliberalism and the rise of job insecurity, see also Krugman (2007), Osterman (1999), and Reich (2007).

20. Damaske (2021).

21. The rate of long-term unemployment began to be tracked by the Bureau of Labor Statistics in 1948. From 1948 until 2000 the share of the unemployed who became long-term unemployed rarely exceeded 15%, and this occurred for only brief periods following steep recessions (Mitchell 2013). However, the proportion of the unemployed who are long-term unemployed has been rising in the past two decades. Specifically, since the start of the 2000s the share of the unemployed who are long-term unemployed has not dipped below 15% (Mitchell 2013). It rose to a record high of 45% in the aftermath of the Great Recession (Mitchell 2013) and remained elevated at above 20% until the Covid-19 Pandemic hit in March 2020 when an unprecedented spike in new unemployment temporarily lowered the proportion of the long-term unemployed.

Chapter 2

1. In some cases, company policy dictates that at the moment of layoff the worker must immediately gather his or her personal belongings and be escorted from the premises without a chance to say goodbye to colleagues (Damaske 2021).

2. In our survey of 125 long-term unemployed jobseekers who signed up to receive sociologically informed support (as discussed in Chapter 6), layoffs were by far the most common reason for job loss. Eighty-four percent of the interviewees were laid off while only 9% quit, 4% were fired, and 3% reported that a contract position had expired.

3. E.g., Rivera (2015); Finlay and Coverdill (2002); Huo, Huang, and Napier (2002).

4. McDonald et al. (2021).

5. Damaske (2021, 40) discusses how Americans have stigmatized unemployed workers going back to the 1800s, seeing them as "lazy" and "immoral." Research shows that this stigma shapes hiring decisions. For example, a study by the New York Federal Reserve (Faberman, et al. 2017) shows that unemployed job applicants are significantly less likely to receive positive responses to applications than otherwise similar employed applicants. Specifically, this study showed that jobseekers who are currently employed were more likely to receive invitations to interviews than unemployed jobseekers despite the fact that the unemployed jobseekers were searching seven times harder than those currently employed. See also Kroft, Lange, and Notowidigdo (2013); Pedulla (2020); Ghayad (2013); McDonald et al. (2019); and Atkinson, Giles, and Meager (1996).

6. Similar finding about the preference for passive jobseekers is reported by Pedulla (2020) and McDonald et al. (2019).

7. In an audit study, Pedulla (2020) finds that white males are invited to interviews 10.4% of the time if they are full-time employed but an otherwise identical applicant who has been unemployed for 12 months receives an interview invitation only 4.2% of the time. Pedulla (2020) explains that employers are concerned by unemployment and that this concern increases the longer one is unemployed, citing a range of stereotypes such as laziness and incompetence. See also Kroft, Lange, and Notowidigdo (2013).

8. This is what Foucault (2004, 44–47) means by the market in neoliberalism being an institution of "veridiction" (as discussed in Chapter 1).

9. Pedulla (2020, 46), likewise finds an expression of concern from hiring professionals that unemployed workers have been "doing nothing."

10. A similar finding is reported in Gershon (2017), who finds that when candidates are evaluated, there is an assumption that their resumes—and which companies they worked for—are completely under the jobseekers' control. Similarly, Pedulla (2020) also finds that recruiters pay attention to the overall unemployment rate but do not dig any deeper than this metric. As Pedulla (2020, 39) puts it, recruiters interpret resumes by "placing responsibility on workers themselves rather than focusing on broad structural economic changes."

11. Beyond the in-depth interview data, in a survey of 125 long-term unemployed jobseekers who signed up to participate in this study, 78% reported that since the start of their search they have "broadened their search in terms of industries," and 76% reported being open to a lower salary (Sharone et al. 2015).

12. An anonymous reviewer of this book astutely noted that among the frustrating aspects of job searching is the contradictory advice that jobseekers receive. On the one hand, jobseekers are encouraged to be strategic in their self-presentation and highlight only their more marketable dimensions; on the other hand, they are also urged to be their authentic selves. This latter is advice is further discussed in note 22 of Chapter 3 .

13. In recent years, the US economy has created more short-term and contract positions as firms increasingly outsource many functions that used to be performed internally (Weil 2014). For long-term unemployed jobseekers, these contract positions are often relatively appealing as a way to get their toe back into professional work. Yet, as recruiters explained, by taking contract jobs the jobseeker may send unintended signals that they are not interested in a long-term job. For example, a recruiter, Sherry, explained the logic that creates a distinct trap for workers who take contract jobs. Essentially, she explains, no matter the reason the worker took a contract position (and regardless of whether they had actually preferred a permanent position and only took a contract job because that was the only thing available) they will be perceived by employers as risky investments who are "likely to move on" from a permanent position. And given this perception, hiring them for a permanent position, and spending time and resources on training them, would be seen as "a waste." For this reason, workers who take several contract jobs may find themselves unable to find anything but more contract jobs.

14. This dilemma is discussed in detail in Sharone (2017) and Gershon (2017). Sharone (2017) explores how the design of social networking sites such as LinkedIn limits the

capacity of jobseekers to segregate their audiences (Goffman 1959), which leads to what boyd (2014, 31) calls "context collapse." Another related force is the pressure on all jobseekers to create a consistent brand (Vallas and Commins 2015).

15. For example, see Lahey (2005); Chou and Choi (2011); Neumark, Burn, and Button (2017); Roscigno et al. (2007); and Oesch (2019).

16. See discussion of research on age and long-term unemployment in note 4 of Chapter 1.

17. Zhang (2011).

18. Pedulla (2020) likewise notes the lack of opportunity to rebut employers' negative perceptions.

19. Marlowe, Schneider, and Nelson (1996); Ruffle and Shtudiner (2013); Ladders (2012); Caers and Castelyn (2011).

20. Moreover, profiles on LinkedIn are categorized as "incomplete" if they are missing pictures, and incomplete profiles are less likely to come up near the top on searches by recruiters.

21. The biases and stigmas discussed in this book are not the only institutional obstacles facing unemployed jobseekers. For other important studies of hiring practices and institutional barriers facing jobseekers see Pedulla (2020), Cappelli (2012), Rivera (2015), and Finlay and Coverdill (2002). More recently, scholars have discussed the challenges created by the increasing use of algorithms in reviewing applicants (Bogen 2019).

Chapter 3

1. Wanberg, Kanfer, and Banas (2000, 492) define networking as "individual actions directed towards contacting friends, acquaintances, and other people to whom the jobseeker has been referred for the main purpose of getting information, leads, or advice on getting a job."

2. Sharone (2014) discusses how the use of networks to find a job is an age-old phenomenon, and sociological studies have focused on the use of networks going back to at least the 1930s (De Schweinetz 1932). A vast literature examines the relationship between networking and career outcomes (e.g., Cross and Cummings 2004; Higgins and Kram 2001; Mcguire 2007; Mcguire and Bielby 2016; Wolff and Moser 2009; Forret and Dougherty 2001; Kanfer, Wanberg, and Kantrowitz 2001; Van Hoye, van Hooft, and Lievens 2009; Wanberg, Kanfer, and Banas 2000).

3. For example, Granovetter's (1974; 1973, 1371) canonical explanation of the strength of weak ties focuses on the distinctly useful information that can be gained from such ties: "Those to whom we are weakly tied are more likely to move in circles different from our own and will thus have access to information different from that which we receive." In other words, it is the access to new information about job opportunities that makes weak ties strong (Sharone 2014).

4. Granovetter's assumptions—and that of much of the traditional networking literature that focuses on networks as a way to share *information* about job openings—need to be revisited. Consistent with my findings, Gershon (2017) also notices that jobseekers

no longer worry about discovering job openings but rather are focused on getting someone to notice their resume. As Rivera (2015) shows in the case of elite jobs, network referrals are critically important as a way to communicate the applicant's cultural fit with the company.

5. Jobseekers are keenly aware of the need to network. Gershon (2017) finds that some workers invest more time in networking than in developing their skills.

6. Link and Phelan (2001, 374) discuss how people who have been stigmatized for being hospitalized for mental illness "may act less confidently and more defensively," and the "result may be strained or uncomfortable social interactions." My interviews reveal that stigma works in a very similar way in the context of unemployment.

7. Gershon (2017).

8. As will be discussed in note 13 of Chapter 4Burke and Stets's (2009) book *Identity Theory* predicts Sam's strategy of switching identities from one that is stigmatized (being unemployed) to one that is celebrated (being retired). Although it may be comforting to switch to an identity that receives more external validation, in the case of unemployed jobseekers such a switch comes at the great cost of undermining their ability to mobilize support for their job search.

9. Granovetter's (1974) seminal book on the use of networks, *Getting a Job*, expects that networking can only succeed with preexisting ties, but this is contrary to most current jobseekers' understanding and practices.

10. Sharone (2014), Gershon (2017).

11. Casciaro, Gino, and Kouchaki (2014).

12. For a brief discussion of contract work, see Chapter 2, note 13.

13. Pultz and Sharone (2020).

14. The inability to set up in-person meetings is one of the difficulties that jobseekers discuss in trying to network during the Covid-19 pandemic (Sharone 2021).

15. This sentiment is consistent with the advice given in networking workshops which suggest that jobseekers not directly ask for a job and instead maintain ambiguity about the direct goals of the interaction (Pultz and Sharone 2020; Gershon 2017).

16. One way the personal cost of networking is discussed in prior research is to recognize that networking entails various forms of emotion work (Hochschild 2012; Pultz and Sharone 2020).

17. Bellah et al. (1985), Schalet (2011).

18. Letkemann (2002, 511) discusses how coping techniques for dealing with stigma can "generate additional stigma," which he refers to as "derivative stigmata." This refers to stigma that arises from "practices of stigma management rather than from the initial stigma itself (2002, 511)."

19. Burke and Stets (2009, 117) define "self-authenticity" as the "feeling that one is being one's true self," and identify it as one of the bases for self-esteem. As an example of a case of individuals not feeling self-authenticity, Burke and Stets (2009) discuss the flight attendants in Hochschild's (2012) well-known study who were required to perform the emotional labor of conjuring up feelings of warmth even in situations where they otherwise would have felt frustration and anger. Burke and Stets's (2009) example of the flight attendants suggests that acting with authenticity means revealing

one's feelings as they arise and not engaging in the intentional emotional labor of conjuring up other feelings.

20. The analogy between job searching and dating comes up repeatedly in this book. At various points, jobseekers themselves bring up the comparison to dating, and at other points I raise it as a way of capturing some of the typically overlooked aspects of the experience of job searching. The analogy is useful because both dating and looking for work are processes of searching for a compatible connection with others (whether romantic or professional), and as such typically involve some degree of what Goffman (1959) calls "impression management," or presenting oneself in the best possible light. In both cases the search may involve the attempt to fulfill a strong need (whether for income or companionship). Moreover, while we usually think of the professional and romantic aspects of our lives as unrelated and operating in separate spheres, noticing the similarities in these two search processes can highlight how looking for work can be as deeply personal and generate as much vulnerability as one's romantic life, which is typically seen as the epitome of vulnerability.

21. This is likely why Letkemann (2002, 518) reports that coping with stigma leads unemployed workers to feel like "deceitful and duplicitous characters," which can be "damaging to self-worth."

22. Unfortunately, most support settings and coaching for unemployed jobseekers ignore these tensions. Networking workshops and career coaches typically emphasize the importance of being authentic in one's networking interactions (Gershon 2017; Pultz and Sharone 2020), while ignoring how the context of unemployment creates strong pressures on jobseekers to act in ways that do not feel authentic. This is similar to the broader tension facing American workers as described by Cech (2021), who observes the strong cultural push in the United States for workers to be passionate and self-expressive in their career pursuits while ignoring the structural constraints to such pursuits. The workshops, coaching, and broader cultural push to be authentic and passionate under all circumstances likely contribute to the feelings of shame and self-blame we hear from Sharon and other jobseekers when they find themselves acting in ways that do not feel authentic.

23. Just over half of those who eventually found professional jobs report that networking was helpful in some way. Gershon (2017) had a similar finding, reporting that among the unemployed white-collar workers she studied, nearly half of those who found professional jobs did so with the help of network contacts, most commonly former coworkers, bosses, or clients.

Chapter 4

1. Burke and Stets (2009) show how the concept of identity links individuals and society. They define identity as "the set of meanings that define who one is when one is an occupant of a particular role in society, a member of a particular group, or claims particular characteristics that identify him or her as a unique person" (2009, 3).
2. Cooley (1922).

3. Burke and Stets (2009, 68–69) explain that one sure way to upset someone is to "tell them that they are not who they think they are." Individuals experience negative emotions whenever they are not able to verify their identities in their interactions with others. Long-term unemployed jobseekers tend to experience their job search as a repeated denial of their identities as good and worthy professionals. In her study of unemployment and identity Norris (2016) discusses "feedback mismatches" and the process by which unemployment experiences, and the perceived feedback that comes with it, undermine unemployed jobseekers' sense of identities as good workers. One of Norris's key arguments, with which I agree, is that these identity mismatches are more important to the stress and mental health challenges of unemployment than is typically recognized. This book, and particularly this chapter, builds on Norris's work by pointing out the variety of ways that identity is undermined by unemployment and centering the role of stigma in this experience.

4. Newman (1999), Smith (2001), and Sharone (2013) all find that unemployed jobseekers harbor conflicting perspectives on their own unemployment, both self-blaming and, at the same time, recognizing external barriers. This finding is also consistent with Norris's(2016) description of jobseekers who intellectually know that middle-class jobs are decreasing but who in their hearts still expect that a college education means they will be immune from unemployment. Beyond the context of unemployment, similar finding are reported by Lamont et al. (2019) regarding the response of African Americans who struggle with economic mobility. In what they (2019, 98) call a "paradoxical" response, and one revealing a dual consciousness, a majority of African Americans in their study believed that mobility results from individuals' efforts and at the same time they recognized that structural factors limit their mobility. This was in contrast to black Brazilians or ethnic minorities in Israel who were far less likely to focus on the role of individual effort. Lamont et al. (2019, 117) link this American tendency to self-blame to neoliberalism in the United States and poignantly note that "although aware of racism and other forces that shape their lives, African-Americans take responsibility for their fate, and, like Sisyphus, aim to push the stone up the mountain against all odds."

5. Goffman (1963) also observed the tendency of the stigmatized to internalize the stigma.

6. In discussing the centrality of work to American identity, Cech (2021) astutely notes that American kids are not asked what they hope to do for work when they grow up but rather who they want to *be*. When those kids grow up, as Sennet (1998, 119) observes, career setbacks may be experienced as a "failure to live rather than merely exist."

7. Scheff (2011, 2000).

8. Van Horn's (2013, 78) survey of long-term unemployed workers found that 74% of jobseekers reported feelings of shame or embarrassment.

9. This pattern is consistent with studies dating back to the 1930s. For example, Komarovsky's (1940, 74) study of long-term unemployment in the Great Depression finds that "man experiences a deep frustration because in his own eyes he fails to fulfill what is the central duty of his life, the very touchstone of his manhood—the role of

family provider." A very similar finding is reported by Newman's (1999, 139) research of unemployed white-collar workers in the 1980s: "Unemployment strikes at the heart of the masculine ideal. . . . [Having] failed at the task that most clearly defines his role, he suffers a loss of identity as a man." The finding is also supported by the more recent findings of Norris (2016, 63–67) who reports that most men talked about the connection between unemployment and a threat to their masculinity, and that breadwinning is central to men's identities. In Chapter 5 we will see that the interruption in breadwinning posed by unemployment is a greater challenge for married men than married women, a finding that is also supported by Rao's (2020) book on the effects of unemployment on marriages. See also Killewald (2016) and Inanc (2018). An exception to this pattern is the findings of Lane (2011), whose unemployed male interviewees reported that unemployment did not undermine their masculinity and in fact it was bit of a badge of honor to be "man enough" not to be threatened in their gender identity. Lane's findings may reflect the age of her participants, as she was interviewing younger men than the ones that I interviewed for this book or that Norris (2016) interviewed for hers. In terms of survey studies, some find no difference between the experience of men and women—see, for example, Broman et al. (1995) and Leana and Feldman (1991)—but a meta-analytic review of the literature claims that in terms of health and well-being men are more negatively affected by unemployment than woman (Paul and Moser 2009).

10. See the discussion of internalized stigma and self-blame in note 8 of Chapter 1 discussing, among others, findings by Sharone (2013), Blustein (2019), Newman (1999), Smith (2001), Cottle (2001), Uchitelle (2006), Chen (2015), Norris (2016), Rao (2020), and Zukin, Van Horn, and Stone (2011).

11. Strikingly, this exact form of self-blame was found in a study of unemployment experiences among men during the Great Depression. Discussing a case study of an unemployed worker, Komarovsky (1940, 27) reports that "he blames himself for being unemployed, while he tries all day long to find work and would take anything, he feels that he would be successful if he had taken advantage of opportunities in his youth and had secured an education."

12. The loss of self-esteem and the challenge to identity are related experiences. In Burke and Stets's *Identity Theory* (2009, 79–80), the authors explain that when individuals experience difficulties in validating or "verifying" their identity, this challenges their self-esteem, which is defined as the "evaluation of the self, made by the self."

13. Burke and Stets's *Identity Theory* (2009, 41) predicts that if an individual's identity has not been validated by the response of others, that person can be expected to shift their focus to another identity that is more likely to receive validation. Norris (2016, 78–79) applies this theory to the context of unemployment and discusses how some unemployed jobseekers engage in "identity work" to shift their central identity away from the work identity that is under threat to another identity that may be available—such as stay-at-home mom.

14. Norris (2016, 89) finds, consistent with my interview data, that not everyone has the same access to opportunities to shift their locus of identity; in particular, it is easier for women than men to shift their identities to a focus on parenting as "women were

assumed to be normal when not working"—that is, being a full-time homemaker/mother—but this is not the case for men.

15. Blair-Loy (2003).

16. In our survey of 125 long-term unemployed jobseekers who initially signed up to participate in this research, 78% reported that financially their current situation is "difficult," 23% reported receiving assistance from family or friends, and 6.5% reported receiving food stamps. Although a majority (61%) of the long-term unemployed jobseekers had either a savings or a retirement account to provide some cushion at the start of their unemployment, it did not take long for this cushion to be depleted. Half of the jobseekers who had such a financial backup reported that the account contained less than $20,000. Van Horn's (2013) survey of jobseekers reports the lingering financial effects of prolonged unemployment. Using repeated surveys to follow a group of workers who had experienced long-term unemployment, Van Horn (2013) finds that after 2 years, only 7% managed to climb back to their original standard of living. An Urban Institute study (Johnson and Gosselin 2018) shows that more than half of American adults who had full-time jobs with a long-term employer as they turned 50 subsequently experienced an involuntary separation and that, among this group, only 10% ever regained their previous income.

17. Van Horn's (2013) survey reports that about a third of long-term unemployed jobseekers had to change their living arrangements as a result of their unemployment.

18. Schalet (2011).

19. Blustein (2019) reports that the rate at which unemployed jobseekers suffer from mental health issues is more than double the rate of the general population. In Van Horn's (2013) survey of long-term unemployed jobseekers, the majority discussed feelings of depression and anxiety. Meta-analytic reviews consistently show that unemployed individuals suffer from significantly higher levels of mental health challenges compared to employed individuals (McKee-Ryan et al. 2005), and as the duration of unemployment increases, so does the negative emotional toll and the risk for mental health issues (Paul and Moser 2009). Studies show similarly negative effects of unemployment on physical health—for example, see Sullivan and von Wachter (2009), McKee-Ryan et al. (2005), Paul and Moser (2009), Strully (2009), and Brand (2015).

20. Norris (2016).

21. This finding is consistent with Blustein's (2019, 175, 187) description of unemployment as an experience filled with an "inescapable sense of precariousness" and "abject terror."

22. Retirement savings accrue slowly over many years, so the rapid spending down of retirement savings by older unemployed workers is among the lasting harms arising from long-term unemployment; recovering from this loss is extremely difficult, even if one is fortunate enough to ultimately regain a full-time professional job. As we can hear in Sharon's quote, the loss of retirement savings changes one's outlook toward the future and gives rise to a sense of dread about how one will financially survive in older age.

23. This interview, as with a few others, greatly concerned me about Eric's immediate well-being and safety and led me to connect Eric with mental health support.

24. Scheff (2011, 455) discusses this pattern as a form of "emotion trap" as "one becomes ashamed of one's feelings in such a way that leads to further emotion."

25. As discussed in note 22 in Chapter 3 networking workshops and coaches encourage jobseekers to be authentic (Gershon 2017; Pultz and Sharone 2020) while ignoring the cross-pressures to suppress negative emotions as well as the broader cultural expectation in the United States for all workers to be self-expressive and authentic under all circumstances (Cech 2021).

26. See note 19 in this chapter for a discussion of research showing mental health challenges from unemployment.

27. Goffman (1963).

28. Blustein (2019).

Chapter 5

1. Van Horn (2013) finds in a large survey that 90% of long-term unemployed jobseekers experience stress in relationships.

2. Existing research shows that, overall, married unemployed individuals are in a better psychological state than single unemployed individuals (Cooke and Rousseau 1984; Leana and Feldman 1991), but also that economic hardships tend to create conflicts in married couples (Conger, Rueter, and Elder 1999; Hoffman and Duncan 1995).

3. The most in-depth analysis of the gendered dynamics among unemployed heterosexual couples is Rao's (2020) book based on interviews with both unemployed workers and their spouses. Rao finds strikingly gendered differences in unemployment experiences. The expectations of breadwinning and complete devotion to finding work, which Rao calls "the ideal job-seeker norm," apply much more strongly to men than women. Norris (2016) also finds gendered breadwinner expectations and reports that overall, women in relationships are the least distressed by unemployment and that men in relationships are the most distressed. Single men and women fall in between. The particular way in which breadwinning expectations create tensions for men in their marriages was vividly documented by Komarovsky's research of unemployed men during the Great Depression. For example, Komarovsky (1940, 37) quotes one woman who calls her husband "a big lug" who "failed to make something of himself." Another woman likewise explicitly blames her husband: "If he had a better education and a better personality he would not be in his present state" (1940, 25). Analyzing her interview data, Komarovsky (1940, 42) observes: "In most of the cases the unemployed man was doomed by the very fact of unemployment.... [H]is failure as a provider and loss of money undermined his status . . . [and] lowered the prestige of the man in the eyes of his wife." Komarovsky (1940, 43) poignantly concludes: "The unemployed husband who has suffered a loss of status with his wife is a tragic figure. Defeated in the outside world, he feels the ground slipping under his feet within the home as well." More recent support for the finding that breadwinner expectations in

heterosexual married couples are disproportionately placed on husbands is shown in a study drawing on American survey data showing that male breadwinning is important for marital stability and is a "central component of the marital contract for husbands" (Killewald 2016, 716). See also Inanc (2018, 555) drawing on British data and finding that "coupled individuals' well-being is highly contingent upon men's fulfilment of the bread-winner role." For more discussion of masculinity and unemployment, see note 9 in Chapter 4 discussing research by Komarovsky (1940), Norris (2016), Rao (2020), and Lane (2011), among others.

4. Goffman (1963, 30) observed that married couples are even intertwined in terms of being stigmatized. The marriage "leads society to treat both individuals in some respects as one," and therefore spouses "are obliged to share some of the discredit of the stigmatized person to whom they are related." This is sometimes referred to as "courtesy stigma," or stigma by association.

5. Rao (2020) likewise finds tensions among heterosexual couples around the intensity of the unemployed persons' search, most commonly with wives feeling that their husbands could search more intensely.

6. Other studies find a gendered pattern regarding household work and unemployment. For example, both Damaske (2021) and Rao (2020) find that unemployed women increase their contribution to household work more than unemployed men.

7. A 2021 survey finds that nearly half of all Americans (49%) report having three or fewer friends (Cox 2021), and in the United States, non-work contacts decline with age (McDonald, Chen, and Mair 2015).

8. Kelly and Moen (2020).

9. Zelizer (2005).

10. This sentiment supports Wacquant's (2008, 30) observation that in American society a certain level of consumption has become a "passport to personhood" and essential for social dignity.

11. The pain from social comparisons can be most acute for jobseekers who previously held elite positions and whose social circles therefore typically consist of other elite professionals (Rao 2020).

12. Thereby perfectly fitting Goffman's (1963) definition of stigma as classifying someone as an "other" *and* as "inferior."

13. Goffman (1963). The association between unemployment and contagious disease is discussed in Letkemann (2002).

14. Supporting this finding of a gendered pattern of friendships among the unemployed, Rao (2020) finds that women are able retain their friends during unemployment more than men.

15. Friends may be available for occasional or short-term emotional support, but my interviewees are enduring long-term unemployment, and therefore my findings suggest that after some period of time—which may vary in length—friends are less willing to provide emotional support.

16. Komarovsky's (1940) study of unemployment among men during the Great Depression reveals the feedback loop of negative emotions from unemployment leading to relationship tensions which then lead to more negative emotions.

Komarovsky (1940, 47) observed this typical pattern: "Unemployment calls forth some action or attitude on the part of the husband. The wife reacts to it in a manner which aggravates the original attitude of the husband. He hits back and so the two are caught in a mounting wave of bitterness."

Chapter 6

1. Sharone (2013), Sheehan (2022), Ehrenreich (2005).
2. Sharone (2013).
3. Similar findings are reported in Sheehan's (2022) study of self-help workshops in Texas. Sheehan (2022, 1165) finds that coaches aiming to help unemployed job seekers put the entire focus on the unemployed person's attitude, positive thinking, and finding their passion, which means that "failure is a failure of the self" and an indicator of self-sabotage.
4. Cech (2021, 33) refers to Bolles's book as a "pillar of the career-related self-help genre."
5. Bolles's focus on a self-inventory as the key to escaping unemployment is consistent with Sheehan's (2022, 1165) recent findings in a study of coaches where the most common solution offered for career challenges is "more self-awareness."
6. Sandel (2020).
7. Sandel (2020, 79) discusses the message in a speech by former President Obama in which he pronounces that "this is a country where no matter what you look like, or where you come from, if you're willing to study and work hard you can go as far as your talents will take you. You can make it if you try." This view is widely shared. As discussed in Chapter 1 note 15, a majority of Americans (by contrast to Europeans) believe that hard work brings success, and someone who is poor can make it out of poverty on their own, and that individuals alone, and not larger social structures, determine their life outcomes (e.g., Lewis 1978; Cech 2021).
8. Beyond the culture of American individualism this approach is likely also encouraged by research in psychology on the issue of "learned helplessness." This line of research shows that under certain conditions people come to believe that they have less control over a situation than they actually do, and as a result they can become discouraged and cease taking helpful actions. Applied to this context, self-help forms of support likely assume that jobseekers have more control than they believe they do and that by emphasizing jobseeker control the support will help jobseekers overcome learned helplessness.
9. Sandel (2020, 25–26) discusses how under the "meritocratic ethic" and its implicit premise of individual control and that you can "you can make it if you try," it is "hard to escape the thought that failure is not [one's] own doing." It leads to the denigration of those who struggle "in their own eyes" (Sandel 2020, 46). Blustein (2019, 202–203) discusses how viewing oneself as an "architect of one's life" may under certain conditions be motivating, but for unemployed jobseekers it can also result in self-blame. See also Lewis (1978) for a discussion of how assumptions of individual control can lead to self-doubt.

10. Sapolsky (1994, 268).
11. Sapolsky (1994, 404).
12. This research was previously discussed in chapters 1 and 2.
13. I note that the generally positive response to the open sharing of difficult emotions was not universally shared, and a few unemployed jobseekers found it disturbing to hear the distress of others. Lisa, for example, shared experiencing "a lot of negative vibes" and that "all that trauma and drama that was going on did not help my emotional situation at all." Lisa was among a small minority of unemployed jobseekers who reacted negatively to the open sharing of emotions. To minimize negative experiences of this sort, support that utilizes a sociological approach should be upfront in explaining the nature of this approach so that people who would not be helped by open sharing of negative emotions can opt out.
14. See Sharone (2013) and Ehrenreich (2005).
15. Scheff (2000).
16. Scheff (2003); Brown (2007).
17. To increase the likelihood of jobseekers experiencing the feeling of being in the "same boat," it would be helpful to group together unemployed workers with similar lengths of unemployment because there are significant differences in unemployment experiences depending on length. For example, in small group support settings, Michelle, who is 1 year unemployed, describes in negative terms being with others who are much longer-term unemployed jobseekers: "In some ways it was depressing. I was in a group of three. Two other women, all of us in our 50s. I just kept looking at these other two women and I'd say to myself, 'They're not employable. How are they going to get jobs? I wouldn't hire them. You compare them to the competition applying for the jobs they say they're interested and qualified for. There's no way anybody is going to hire them.' And then I look at me and I say, 'Am I like them?'"

   As Michelle's experience suggests, finding oneself with others who are much *longer* term unemployed than oneself can feel discouraging. This effect is the flipside of the above-discussed experience of being in the same boat with "impressive" others, which allows jobseekers to see themselves in a new light and as potentially impressive as well. Workers who were very long-term unemployed suggested also that a group made up exclusively of longer-term unemployed workers would be more effective because it could focus on their specific challenge, such as financial survival. For example, Susan explained, "When you become long-term unemployed, financial stuff becomes huge, and there is a need for information about electing to take social security early, SNAP, subsidized housing, [health care], free lunch for kids, how to ask family for financial help." Another longer-term unemployed jobseeker, Rachel, focused on the challenge of "how we get along with other people. How to respond to siblings and friends when they ask why we don't have a job?"
18. Blustein (2019, 163–164) draws on the work of Paolo Freire (2000) to define critical consciousness as the "capacity to reflect on the causes of social injustice," which helps unemployed jobseekers "not blame themselves for their experience of marginalization."
19. Brown (2007).

20. Hing (2013) shows that for members of a stigmatized group, being aware of potential barriers to employment, such as employer discrimination, means that when facing negative outcomes they are less likely to blame themselves. See also Blustein (2019), Brown (2007), Sharone and Vasquez (2016), and Scheff (2000).

21. Sharone (2013).

22. Beyond these examples, sociological coaching can draw on a broad range of other studies that focus on hiring practices (e.g., Finlay and Coverdill 2002; Pedulla 2020; Cappelli 2012; Rivera 2015; Gershon 2017), which may give jobseekers a better understanding of employers' practices and suggest possible strategies.

23. While sociologists rightly focus on how some aspects of the know-how required for effective networking is deeply internalized as habitus, giving a hidden advantage to those who possess certain cultural capital (e.g., Ilouz 2007), the interviews suggest that an important dimension of this know-how can be learned and put into practice.

24. In a similar vein, Norris (2016) discusses how effective job search support groups may help unemployed jobseekers maintain their professional identity.

25. Prior research on unemployment reveals that job search discouragement is a common issue. After a long string of labor market rejections, and without effective support, jobseekers may cease to believe that continued searching will bring positive results and wish to avoid the pain of likely future rejections (e.g., Sharone 2013; Komarovsky 1940).

26. The importance of countering internalized stigma is also emphasized by Lamont (2009, 152): "How individuals interpret and deal with" stigmatization, particularly whether or not stigma is internalized, "is a key intervening factor" in effects on mental and physical health.

27. From among the jobseekers who signed up to participate in this research in the first year of the ICT, and who fit the eligibility criteria in terms of being 40 to 65 years old, long-term unemployed, and in white-collar occupations (as described in more detail in the methodological appendix at the end of this book), we randomly selected 102 long-term unemployed jobseekers to be matched with free ICT support for 3 months, and at the same time also randomly selected 22 otherwise similar long-term unemployed jobseekers whom we were not able to support but who were paid to complete surveys and serve as a small control group. After 4 months, 30% percent of the unemployed jobseekers who were matched with ICT support found a full-time job compared to only 18% of the jobseekers not in the support group. Because of the small numbers, these findings are not statistically significant but the difference in the rate of finding a job between those receiving ICT support and those not receiving support is suggestive that this form of support can make a meaningful practical difference. There is an even more stark difference between the group receiving support and the small control group in terms of internalized stigma. Prior to anyone receiving ICT support, 61% of the long-term unemployed jobseekers we surveyed either agreed or strongly agreed with the statement: "I fear there is something wrong with me." But in a follow-up survey that was administered 10 weeks after the start of support, the fear that "something is wrong with me" decreased to 41% percent among jobseekers receiving support but increased to 84% among the small control group. Again, because

of the small numbers, these differences were not statistically significant, but they are consistent with the interview data discussed in this chapter showing that sociologically informed support helps unemployed jobseekers in their struggle to resist internalizing stigma. To fully explore the effects of sociological support would require a larger experimental study that would compare jobseekers receiving sociologically informed support to those receiving the more typical self-help support and to compare both of those groups to jobseekers receiving no support at all.

28. Cooley (1922).
29. https://www.bc.edu/content/bc-web/schools/lynch-school/sites/win.html.
30. Autin et al. (2022).
31. See Sharone (2007), Schlozman and Verba (1979).

Chapter 7

1. Goffman (1963, 7) observed that "the stigmatized individual tends to hold the same beliefs" and perceive their "own attributes as being a defiling thing to possess."
2. Goffman (1963, 6).
3. The link between being stigmatized and being perceived as contagious was also observed by Goffman (1963) and Letkemann (2002).
4. The feedback loop—whereby negative emotions arising from unemployment lead to relationship tensions which in turn lead to more negative emotions—was keenly observed in Komarovsky's study of unemployment among men during the Great Depression. As Komarovsky (1940, 40) found: "Changes in the man's personality may affect his relations with the family, and changes in his relationship with the family may affect his personality."
5. Goffman (1963, 53).
6. See the discussion of Lamont (2019) and Sandel (2020), among others, in Chapter 1 and other parts of this book.
7. Foucault (2004, 44–47). See the discussion of Foucault (2004) in Chapter 1.
8. Exceptions to the 6-month time limit are sometimes made during severe recessions.
9. The ever-present anxiety of such conditions was vividly captured by Sennet and Cobb (1972, 72) who described how blue-collar workers' lives are "infect[ed]" by the "fear of being summoned before a hidden bar of judgement and *being found inadequate*." The centrality of the myth of meritocracy in the fears of workers about losing their job is described with particular sharpness in the classic book *The Hidden Injuries of Class* (Sennet and Cobb 1972). Here is how Sennet and Cobb (1972, 72) describe shame stemming from precarity among blue-collar American workers: "No one could blame a father for losing a job during the Depression—but the more one talks to these men the more one senses a fear in each that he will be blamed now, he will be failing the others, if he loses his job."
10. To develop a more general theory of stigmas that arise in the context of neoliberal capitalism it would be helpful if future research undertook a comparative study of different kinds of stigmas, explored their similarities and differences, and considered the

factors that may shape variations. As an example of what this kind of comparison may look like, consider the findings of Lamont et al. (2019) on the experience of stigma among African Americans. There are striking similarities and differences in the experiences of stigma rooted in racism compared to the experience of stigma among the long-term unemployed workers discussed in this book. Two striking similarities are the ubiquity of the stigma and the tendency for the stigma to be internalized. Just as the stigma of unemployment comes up in every relationship Lamont et al. (2019) describe how incidents revealing racist stigma likewise arise in a plethora of contexts including with friends, colleagues, neighbors, and sometimes family. And just as with unemployed jobseekers, Lamont et al. (2019) report that African Americans often internalize this stigma and may harbor conflicting individualistic and structural explanations for the challenges they face. Some of the ways that stigma is experienced is also similar. In both cases, subtle incidents of stigma include being excluded from informal networks or being misunderstood. One of their study's African American interviewees reported being looked at "like I've got two heads" (Lamont et al. 2019, 66), while one of my unemployed interviewees felt that an interviewer looked at them "like I had 10 heads." But there are also important differences in how the stigma comes up and the response to it. A majority of African American interviewees in the Lamont study reported being explicitly insulted or disrespected by, for example, being called the N word or told to go back to Africa. By contrast, explicit insults were rare for the long-term unemployed, suggesting an important difference in the kinds of feelings underlying each form of stigma or in the degree of social permission to hurl insults at the stigmatized individual. There is also a clear difference in how African Americans and unemployed jobseekers respond to stigma. According to Lamont et al. (2019) the most common response to stigma among African Americans is to confront the stigmatizer. These researchers theorize that confronting stigmatizing behavior is enabled by the wide availability of cultural scripts about the historically racist character of the United States. These cultural scripts stem from decades of civil rights activism and protest movements that have strengthened the general awareness of racism, helped shape a collective memory of a shared racist history, and fostered an "unambiguous sense of groupness" (2019, 110). By contrast, in my study there are only rare instances of an unemployed jobseeker confronting a stigmatizer. Strikingly, all the factors that Lamont et al. theorize as enabling of confrontation in the case of racist stigma are absent in the unemployment context. There are no cultural scripts, no collective memories, and usually no sense of being part of a group. The absence of wide cultural understanding of the unemployment stigma means that unemployed jobseekers face a barrier that is similar to what Lamont et al. (2019) observe with re-spect to class-based forms of stigma. As discussed in Chapter 1, neoliberal discourses and the myth of meritocracy mean that unemployment is widely seen as the fault of the unemployed worker and reflective of their lack of merit. These differences in the cultural contexts of the stigma likely shape the response to this stigma, and in this case the typical absence of confrontation. It is also important to note that unlike the more typical situation for African Americans who live with families and in communities that collectively experience stigma, most long-term unemployed jobseekers do not know others who are facing similar challenges, and as such endure their challenge in relative isolation.

11. As discussed in note 10 of this chapter, engaging in resistance to stigma is facilitated by the availability of cultural scripts that recognize the depth and history of the particular stigma. The case of the racism stigma suggests that such cultural scripts only become widely available after prolonged periods of protest and activism (Lamont et al. 2019).

12. *Los Angeles Times* article on January 31, 2014, "CEOs pledge not to discriminate against the long-term unemployed." https://www.latimes.com/business/la-fi-obama-jobs-20140201-story.html

13. Using a composite measure of unemployment insurance generosity, Kalleberg (2018) finds that among the six countries studied, the United States had among the least generous levels of benefits.

14. Schroder (2013). In the United States the replacement rate varies by state, with a range of 32% to 56%, and a rate of 46% in the Commonwealth of Massachusetts where the data for this study were collected. The duration also varies by state and may be temporarily extended during peaks of recessions.

15. Damaske (2021) discusses the role of stigma in informing unemployment insurance policies, citing the example of a recent Pennsylvania governor publicly suggesting that unemployed workers were drug users.

16. Wanberg et al. (2020) compare the effects of different levels of unemployment insurance benefits in the United States, Germany, and the Netherlands, and find that more generous levels of benefits are associated with better mental health outcomes and higher quality of re-employment. For creative discussions of the benefits of enhanced unemployment insurance and ways to improve and expand unemployment insurance, see Damaske (2021) and Uchitelle (2006).

17. One limitation of the ICT's support was its focus on white-collar college-educated workers. This segmented approach to support is double edged. It may make it easier to generate the recognition among jobseekers that similar others are in the "same boat," but by creating silos of support for different kinds of occupations, it deprives workers of the opportunity to recognize that the barriers they are facing are shared across the lines of class and occupations.

18. The potential appeal of this policy may have been foreshadowed by the unexpectedly strong showing of Andrew Yang, whose single-issue candidacy in the 2020 Democratic primary focused on UBI. Blustein (2019) discusses universal basic income as a policy that may reduce the stress for workers in precarious occupations and which may make possible engagement in meaningful non-market activities like hobbies, caregiving, and creative pursuits. For more discussion of the potential benefits of a universal basic income, see also Van Parijs and Vanderborght (2017), Bregman (2017), and Stern (2016).

19. E.g., Newman (1999), Chen (2015), Bellah et al. (1985), Lewis (1978), Sandel (2020).

20. Lamont (2019, 671) discusses how American parents "cultivate a strong belief in meritocracy" in their children, citing a study by Demerath (2009) showing that a large

majority of students believe effort is the most important factor determining their future.

21. Sharone (2004).
22. Sandel (2020), Lamont (2019), Newman (1999), Chen (2015).
23. Foucault (2004) describes how in American neoliberalism, economic analysis is used as the lens for understanding everything, including who deserves to be valued and who does not. (For further discussion of Foucault, see Chapter 1.) Also see Sandel (2020, 59) noting that "our public culture in recent decades reinforces the idea that we are responsible for our fate."
24. Burawoy (1979).
25. For a discussion of the particular strength of the belief in the myth of meritocracy in the United States see note 15 in Chapter 1.
26. Weber (1946, 271). The same observation is made by Sandel (2020, 36) who points out that the meritocratic way of thinking gives rise to hard attitudes toward those who suffer misfortunes, and that the more acute the suffering, the more we suspect the victims have brought it on themselves.
27. E.g., Dhingra (2020) and Lamont (2019).

Appendix

1. Long-term unemployment remained at historically high levels through 2015, and then declined to the levels that are more typical in recent decades, with an overall trend of increased risk of long-term unemployment and precariousness (Kalleberg 2018).
2. Thirty-five of the forty-two coaches individually agreed to provide their service pro bono, and seven worked for an outplacement company, which as an organization volunteered to provide their coaches' time for the research.
3. Small (2009).
4. Harrington et al. (2015).
5. Becker (1998), Burawoy (1998), Trost (1986).
6. Newman (1999), Sharone (2013).
7. See discussion of education and long-term unemployment in note 3 of Chapter 1.
8. Krueger et al. (2014); Roscigno, Lassus, and Lopez (2015).
9. Bills (1990).

References

AARP. 2021. "Many Older Workers Trapped in Long-Term Unemployment." https://www.aarp.org/work/careers/older-workers-long-term-unemployment/.

Atkinson, John, Lesley Giles, and Nigel Meager. 1996. *Employers, Recruitment and the Unemployed*. Brighton, UK: Institute for Employment Studies.

Alesina, Alberto, Stefanie Stantcheva, and Edoardo Teso. 2018. "Intergenerational Mobility and Preferences for Redistribution." *American Economic Review* 108(2): 521–554.

Autin, Kelsey, Blake Allan, David Blustein, Saliha Kozan, Ofer Sharone, Brian Stevenson, Rachel Cinamon, Joaquim Ferreira, and Mindi Thompson. 2022. "The Work Intervention Network (WIN): Foundations of a Holistic Vocational Intervention." *Journal of Career Assessment*. https://doi.org/10.1177/10690727221138619.

Becker, Howard S. 1998. *Tricks of the Trade: How to Think about Your Research While You're Doing It*. Chicago: University of Chicago Press.

Bellah, Robert, Richard Madsen, William M. Sullivan, Ann Swidler, and Steven M. Tipton. 1985. *Habits of the Heart: Individualism and Commitment in American Life*. Berkeley: University of California Press.

Bills, David. B. 1990. "Employers' Use of Job History Data for Making Hiring Decisions: A Fuller Specification of Job Assignment and Status Attainment." *Sociological Quarterly* 31(1): 23–35.

Blair-Loy, Mary. 2003. *Competing Devotions: Career and Family among Women Executives*. Cambridge, MA: Harvard University Press.

Blustein, David. 2019. *The Importance of Work in an Age of Uncertainty: The Eroding Work Experience in America*. New York: Oxford University Press.

Bogen, Miranda. 2019. "All the Ways Hiring Algorithms Can Introduce Bias." *Harvard Business Review*. https://hbr.org/2019/05/all-the-ways-hiring-algorithms-can-introduce-bias.

boyd, danah. 2014. *It's Complicated: The Social Lives of Networked Teens*. New Haven, CT: Yale University Press.

Brand, Jennie. 2015. "The Far-Reaching Impact of Job Loss and Unemployment." *Annual Review of Sociology* 41:359–375.

Bregman, Rutger. 2017. *Utopia for Realists*. London: Bloomsbury.

Brown, Brene. 2007. *I Thought It Was Just Me (But It Isn't)*. New York: Avery.

Broman, Clifford, Lee Hamilton, William S. Hoffman, and Roya Mavaddat. 1995. "Race, Gender, and the Response to Stress: Autoworkers' Vulnerability to Long-Term Unemployment." *American Journal of Community Psychology* 23(6): 813–842.

Burawoy, Michael. 1979. *Manufacturing Consent*. Chicago: University of Chicago Press.

Burawoy, Michael. 1998. "The Extended Case Method." *Sociological Theory* 16(1): 4–33.

Burke, Peter, and Jan Stets. 2009. *Identity Theory*. Oxford: Oxford University Press.

Caers, Rafl, and Vanessa Castelyn. 2011. "LinkedIn and Facebook in Belgium: The Influences and Biases of Social Network Sites in Recruitment and Selection Procedures." *Science and Computer Review* 29(4): 437–448.

Cappelli, Peter. 2012. *Why Good People Can't Get Jobs*. Philadelphia: Wharton Digital Press.

Casciaro, Tiziana, Francesca Gino, and Maryam Kouchaki. 2014. "The Contaminating Effects of Building Instrumental Ties: How Networking Can Make Us Feel Dirty." *Administrative Science Quarterly* 59(4): 705–735.

Cech, Erin. 2021. *The Trouble with Passion: How Searching for Fulfillment at Work Fosters Inequality*. Berkeley: University of California Press.

Chen, Victor. 2015. *Cut Loose: Jobless and Hopeless in an Unfair Economy*. Berkeley: University of California Press.

Chou, Rita, and Namkee Choi. 2011. "Prevalence and Correlates of Perceived Workplace Discrimination among Older Workers in the United States of America." *Ageing & Society* 31(6): 1051–1070.

Conger, Rand, Martha Rueter, and Glen Elder. 1999. "Couple Resilience to Economic Pressure." *Journal of Personality and Social Psychology* 76(1): 54–71.

Cooley, Charles. 1922. *Human Nature and the Social Order*, rev. ed. New York: Charles Scribner's Sons.

Cooke, Robert A., and Denise M. Rousseau. 1984. "Stress and Strain from Family Roles and Work-role Expectations." *Journal of Applied Psychology* 69(2): 252–260.

Cottle, Thomas. 2001. *Hardest Times: The Trauma of Long-Term Unemployment*. Amherst: University of Massachusetts Press.

Cox, Daniel. 2021. "The State of American Friendship: Change, Challenges and Loss." In Survey Center on American Life. Accessed January 19, 2023. https://www.americansurveycenter.org/research/the-state-of-american-friendship-change-challenges-and-loss/.

Creed, Peter, and Dee Bartrum. 2007. "Explanations for Deteriorating Wellbeing in Unemployed People: Specific Unemployment Theories and Beyond." In *Unemployment and Health: International and Interdisciplinary Perspectives*. Edited by Thomas Kieselbach, Anthony Winefield, and Carolyn Boyd. Bowen Hills: Australian Academic Press.

Cross, Rob, and Jonathon N. Cummings. 2004. "Tie and Network Correlates of Individual Performance in Knowledge-Intensive Work." *Academy of Management Journal* 47(6): 928–937.

Damaske, Sarah. 2021. *The Tolls of Uncertainty: How Privilege and the Guilt Gap Shape Unemployment in America*. Princeton, NJ: Princeton University Press.

Demerath, Peter. 2009. *Producing Success: The Culture of Personal Advancement in an American High School*. Chicago: University of Chicago Press.

De Schweinetz, Dorothea. 1932. *How Workers Find Jobs*. Philadelphia: University of Pennsylvania Press.

Dhingra, Pawan. 2020. *Hyper Education: Why Good Schools, Good Grades, and Good Behavior Are Not Enough*. New York: New York University Press.

Eales M. 1989. "Shame Among Unemployed Men." *Social Science and Medicine*. 28(8): 783–789.

Economic Policy Institute. 2020. "Understanding Long-Term Unemployment." https://www.epi.org/multimedia/understanding-long-term-unemployment/.

Ehrenreich, Barbara. 2005. *Bait and Switch: The (Futile) Pursuit of the American Dream*. New York: Metropolitan Books.

Evangelist, Mike, and Anastasia Christman. 2013. "Scarring Effects: Demographics of the Long-Term Unemployed and the Danger of Ignoring the Jobs Deficit." NELP Briefing

Paper. Washington, DC: National Employment Law Project. http://nelp.3cdn.net/4821 589f87f6c502e1_nem6b0xjt.pdf.

Executive Office of the President. 2014. "Addressing the Negative Cycle of Long-Term Unemployment." Washington, DC: White House. https://obamawhitehouse.archives. gov/sites/default/files/docs/wh_report_addressing_the_negative_cycle_of_long-term _unemployment_1-31-14_-_final3.pdf

Faberman, Jason, Andreas Mueller, Aysegul Sahin, Rachel Schuh, and Giorgio Topa. April 5, 2017. "How Do People Find Jobs?" Federal Reserve Bank of New York. Liberty Street blog.

Farber, Henry. 2008. "Employment Insecurity: The Decline in Worker-Firm Attachment in the United States." Center for Economics Policy Studies (CEPS) Working Paper No. 172, Princeton University, Princeton, NJ.

Farber, Henry, Dan Silverman, and Till von Wachter. 2017. "Factors Determining Callback to Job Applications by the Unemployed: An Audit Study." *RSF: Journal of the Social Sciences* 3(3): 168–201.

Finlay, William, and James Coverdill. 2002. *Headhunters: Matchmaking in the Labor Market.* Ithaca, NY: Cornell University Press.

Foucault, Michel. 2004. *The Birth of Biopolitics.* New York: Palgrave Macmillan.

Forret, Monica, and Thomas Dougherty. 2001. "Correlates of Networking Behavior for Managerial and Professional Employees." *Group and Organization Management* 26(3): 283.

Freire, Paulo. 2000. *Pedagogy of the Oppressed.* New York: Continuum.

Ghayad, Rand. 2013. "The Jobless Trap." Working paper. Center for Labor Markets, Northeastern University, Boston, MA.

Gershon, Ilana 2017. *Down and Out in the New Economy: How People Find (or Don't Find) Work Today.* Chicago: University of Chicago Press.

Goffman, Ervin. 1963. *Stigma: Notes on the Management of Spoiled Identity.* New York: Simon and Schuster.

Goffman, Ervin. 1959. *The Presentation of Self in Everyday Life.* New York: Doubleday Anchor Book.

Granovetter, Mark. 1974. *Getting a Job: A Study of Contacts and Careers.* Cambridge, MA: Harvard University Press.

Granovetter, Mark. 1973. "The Strength of Weak Ties." *American Journal of Sociology* 78(1): 1360.

Harrington, Brad, Fred Van Deusen, Jennifer Sabatini Fraone, and Iyar Mazar. 2015. "The New Dad: A Portrait of Today's Father." Boston College Center for Work & Family. https://www.bc.edu/content/dam/files/centers/cwf/research/publications/research reports/The%20New%20Dad%202015_A%20Portrait%20of%20Todays%20Fathers

Higgins, Monica, and Kathy Kram. 2001. "Reconceptualizing Mentoring at Work: A Developmental Network Perspective." *Academy of Management Review* 26(2): 264–288.

Hing, Leane Son. 2013. "Stigmatization, Neoliberalism, and Resilience." In *Social Resilience in the Neoliberal Era.* Edited by Peter Hall and Michele Lamont. New York: Cambridge University Press.

Hochschild, Arlie. 2012. *The Managed Heart: Commercialization of Human Feeling,* 3rd ed. Berkeley: University of California Press.

Hoffman, Saul, and Greg J. Duncan. 1995. "The Effect of Incomes, Wages, and AFDC Benefits on Marital Disruption." *Journal of Human Resources* 30(1): 19–41.

Huo, Paul, Heh Jason Huang, and Nancy Napier. 2002. "Divergence or Convergence: A Cross-National Comparison of Personnel Selection Practices." *Human Resource Management* 41(1): 31–44.

Illouz, Eva. 2007. *Cold Intimacies: The Making of Emotional Capitalism*. Cambridge: Polity Press.

Inanc, Hande. 2018. "Unemployment, Temporary Work, and Subjective Well-Being: The Gendered Effect of Spousal Labor Market Insecurity." *American Sociological Review*, 83(3): 536–566.

Irwin, Neil. 2016. "The Real Jobless Rate Is 42 Percent?" *New York Times*, February 10, 2016.

Johnson, Richard, and Peter Gosselin. 2018. "How Secure Is Employment at Older Ages?" Washington, DC: Urban Institute.

Kalleberg, Arne. *2018. Precarious Lives: Job Insecurity and Well-Being in Rich Democracies*. Cambridge: Polity Press.

Kanfer, Ruth, Connie Wanberg, and Tracy Kantrowitz. 2001. "Job Search and Employment: A Personality–motivational Analysis and Meta-analytic Review." *Journal of Applied Psychology* 86(5): 837–855.

Karen, Ronald, and Kim Sherman. 2012. "Layoffs and Unemployment Discrimination: A New Stigma." *Journal of Managerial Psychology*. 27(8): 848–863.

Kaufman, Harold G. 1982. *Professionals in Search of Work: Coping with the Stress of Job Loss and Underemployment*. New York: John Wiley.

Kelly, Erin, and Phyllis Moen. 2020. *Overload: How Good Jobs Went Bad and What We Can Do about It*. Princeton, NJ: Princeton University Press.

Killewald, Alexandra. 2016. "Money, Work, and Marital Stability: Assessing Change in the Gendered Determinants of Divorce." *American Sociological Review* 81(4): 696–719.Kluegel, James R., and Eliot R. Smith. 1986. *Beliefs about Inequality: Americans' Views of What Is and What Ought to Be*, 2nd ed. Piscataway, NJ: Aldine Transaction.

Komarovsky, Mirra. 1940. *The unemployed man and his family*. New York, NY: Octagon Books.

Kroft, Kory, Fabian Lange, and Mathhew Notowidigdo. 2013. "Duration Dependence and Labor Market Conditions: Evidence from a Field Experiment." *Quarterly Journal of Economics* 128(3): 1123–1167.

Krueger, Alan, Judd Cramer, and David Cho. 2014. *Are the Long-Term Unemployed on the Margins of the Market?* Brookings Institute. Accessed December 14, 2020. https://www.brookings.edu/bpea-articles/are-the-long-term-unemployed-on-the-margins-of-the-labor-market/.

Krugman, Paul. 2007. *The Conscience of a Liberal*. New York: Norton.

Ladders 2012. "Keeping an Eye on Recruiter Behavior." http://cdn.theladders.net/static/images/basicSite/pdfs/TheLadders-EyeTracking-StudyC2.pdf.

Lahey, Joanna. 2005. "Do Older Workers Face Discrimination?" Boston College Center for Retirement Research. https://crr.bc.edu/wp-content/uploads/2005/07/ib_5-33_5 08x.pdf.

Lamont, Michele. 2009. "Responses to Racism, Health, and Social Inclusion as a Dimension of Successful Societies." In *Successful Societies: How Institutions and Culture Affect Health*. Edited by Peter Hall and Michele Lamont. New York: Cambridge University Press.

Lamont, Michele. 2019. "From 'Having' to 'Being:' Self-worth and the Current Crisis of American Society." *British Journal of Sociology* 70(3): 660–707.

Lamont, Michele, Graziella Moraes Silva, Jessica Welburn, Joshua Guetzkow, Nissim Mizrachi, Hanna Herzog, and Elisa Reis. 2019. *Getting Respect: Responding to Stigma and Discrimination in the United States, Brazil & Israel*. Princeton, NJ: Princeton University Press.

Lane, Carrie. 2011. *A Company of One: Insecurity, Independence, and the New World of White-Collar Unemployment*. Ithaca, NY: Cornell University Press

Leana, Carrie, and Daniel Feldman. 1991. "Gender Differences in Responses to Unemployment." *Journal of Vocational Behavior* 38(1): 65–77.

Letkemann, Paul. 2002. "Unemployed Professionals, Stigma Management and Derivative Stigmata." *Work, Employment and Society* 16(3): 511–522.

Lewis, Michael. 1978. *The Culture of Inequality*. Amherst: University of Massachusetts Press.

Link, Bruce, and Jo C. Phelan. 2001. "Conceptualizing Stigma." *Annual Review of Sociology* 27(1): 363–385.

Lopez, Steven, and Lora Phillips. 2019. "Unemployed: White-Collar Job Searching after the Great Recession." *Work and Occupations*: 46(4): 470–510.

Marlowe, Cynthia, Sandra Schneider, and Carnot Nelson. 1996. "Gender and Attractiveness Biases in Hiring Decisions: Are More Experienced Managers Less Biased?" *Journal of Applied Psychology* 81(1): 11–21.

McDonald, Steven, Amanda Damarin, Hannah McQueen, and Scott Grether. 2021. "The Hunt for Red Flags: Cybervetting as Morally Performative Practice." *Socio-Economic Review*. https://doi.org/10.1093/ser/mwab002.

McDonald, Steven, Amanda Damarin, Jenelle Lawhorne, and Annika Wilcox. 2019. "Black Holes and Purple Squirrels: A Tale of Two Online Labor Markets." *Research in the Sociology of Work* 33: 93–120.

McDonald, Steven, Feinian Chen, and Christine A. Mair. 2015. "Cross-National Patterns of Social Capital Accumulation: Network Resources, Gender, and Aging in the United States, China, and Taiwan." *American Behavioral Scientist* 59(8): 914–930.

Mcguire, Gail. 2007. "Intimate Work: A Typology of the Social Support That Workers Provide to Their Network Members." *Work and Occupations* 34(2): 125–147. doi:10.1177/0730888406297313.

Mcguire, Gail, and William Bielby. 2016. "The Variable Effects of Tie Strength and Social Resources: How Type of Support Matters." *Work and Occupations* 43(1): 38–74.

McKee-Ryan, Frances, Zhaoli Song, Connie R. Wanberg, and Angelo J. Kinicki. 2005. "Psychological and Physical Well-being during Unemployment: A Meta-analytic Study." *Journal of Applied Psychology* 90(1): 53–76.

Mishel, Lawrence, Jared Bernstein, and Sylvia Allegretto. 2007. *The State of Working America 2006/2007*. Ithaca, NY: Cornell University Press.

Mitchell, Josh. 2013. "Who Are the Long-Term Unemployed?" Urban Institute. https://www.urban.org/sites/default/files/publication/23911/412885-Who-Are-the-Long-Term-Unemployed-.PDF.

Monge-Naranjo, Alexander, and Faisal Sohail. 2105. "The Composition of Long-Term Unemployment Is Changing toward Older Workers." *Regional Economist*. Federal Reserve Bank of St. Louis.

Neumark, David, Ian Burn, and Patrick Button. 2017. "Age Discrimination and Hiring of Older Workers." Federal Reserve Bank of San Francisco. https://www.frbsf.org/economic-research/publications/economic-letter/2017/february/age-discrimination-and-hiring-older-workers/.

Newman, Katherine. 1999. *Falling from Grace: Downward Mobility in the Age of Affluence.* Berkeley: University of California Press.

Norris, Dawn. 2016. *Job Loss, Identity and Mental Health.* New Brunswick, NJ: Rutgers University Press.

Oesch, Daniel. 2019. "Discrimination in the Hiring of Older Jobseekers: Evidence from Two Survey Experiments in Switzerland." Lives Working Paper 81: http://dx.doi.org/10.12682/lives.2296-1658.2019.81.

Osterman, Paul. 1999. *Securing Prosperity: The American Labor Market, How It Has Changed and What We Can Do about It.* Princeton, NJ: Princeton University Press.

Paul, Karsten, and Klaus Moser. 2009. Unemployment Impairs Mental Health: Meta-Analyses. *Journal of Vocational Behavior* 74: 264–282.

Pedulla, David. 2020. *Making the Cut: Hiring Decisions, Bias, and the Consequence of Nonstandard, Mismatched, and Precarious Employment.* Princeton, NJ: Princeton University Press.

Peterson, Christopher, Stanley Schwartz, and Martin Seligman. 1981. "Self-Blame and Depressive Symptoms." *Journal of Personality and Social Psychology* 41(2): 253–259.

Pew Research Center. 2021. "Long-Term Unemployment Has Risen Sharply in the U.S. amid the Pandemic Especially among Asian Americans." https://www.pewresearch.org/fact-tank/2021/03/11/long-term-unemployment-has-risen-sharply-in-u-s-amid-the-pandemic-especially-among-asian-americans/.

Pultz, Sabina, and Ofer Sharone. 2020. "The Intimate Dance of Networking: A Comparative Study of the Emotional Labor of Young American and Danish Jobseekers." *Research in the Sociology of Work* 34: 33–58.

Pugh, Allison. 2015. *The Tumbleweed Society: Working and Caring in an Age of Insecurity.* New York: Oxford University Press.

Rao, Aliya. 2020. *Crunch Time: How Married Couples Confront Unemployment.* Oakland: University of California Press.

Rantakeisu, Ulla, Bengt Starrin, and Curt Hagquist. 1999. "Financial Hardship and Shame: A Tentative Model to Understand the Social and Health Effects of Unemployment." *British Journal of Social Work* 29 (6): 877–901.

Reich, Robert. 2007. *Supercapitalism: The Transformation of Business, Democracy, and Everyday Life.* New York: Knopf.

Rivera, Lauren. 2015. *Pedigree: How Elite Students Get Elite Jobs.* Princeton, NJ: Princeton University Press.

Roscigno, Vincent, Sherry Mong, Reginald Byron, and Griff Tester. 2007. "Age Discrimination, Social Closure and Employment." *Social Forces* 86: 313–334.

Roscigno, Vincent, Laura Lassus, and Steven Lopez. 2015. "Aging Workers and the Experience of Job Loss." *Research in Social Stratification and Mobility.* DOI:10.1016/j.rssm.2015.01.001.

Ruffle, Bradley, and Ze'ev Shtudiner. 2013. "Are Good-Looking People More Employable?" SSRN. http://ssrn.com/abstract=1705244.

Sandel, Michael. 2020. *The Tyranny of Merit: Can We Find the Common Good?* New York: Farrar, Straus and Giroux.

Sapolsky, Robert. 1994. *Why Zebras Don't Get Ulcers.* New York: W. H. Freeman.

Schalet, Amy. 2011. *Not under My Roof: Parents, Teens, and the Culture of Sex.* Chicago: University of Chicago Press.

Scheff, Thomas. 2000. "Shame and the Social Bond: A Sociological Theory." *Sociological Theory* 18(1): 84–99.

Scheff, Thomas. 2003 ."Shame in Self and Society." *Symbolic Interaction* 26(2): 239–262.

Scheff, Thomas. 2011. "Social-emotional origins of violence: A theory of multiple killing." *Agression and Violent Behavior* 16: 453-460.

Schlozman, Kay Lehman, and Sidney Verba. 1979. *Injury to Insult: Unemployment, Class and Political Response*. Cambridge, MA: Harvard University Press.

Schröder, Martin. 2013. *Integrating Varieties of Capitalism and Welfare State Research: A Unified Typology of Capitalisms*. Basingstoke: Palgrave Macmillan.

Schwartz Center for Economic Policy Analysis. 2018. "38% of 1.1 Million Jobless Older Workers Left Out of Unemployment Rates Are Poor." https://www.economicpolicyr esearch.org/jobs-report/june-2018-unemployment-report-for-workers-over-55.

Sennet, Richard. 1998. *Corrosion of Character: The Personal Consequences of Work in the New Capitalism*. New York: Norton.

Sennet, Richard, and Jonathan Cobb. 1972. *The Hidden Injuries of Class*. New York: Norton.

Sharone, Ofer, Rand Ghayad, Gocke Basbug, Alexandra Vasquez, and Michelle Rosin. 2015. "Supporting Experienced Long-Term Unemployed Professionals." In *Transforming U.S. Workforce Development Policies for the 21st Century*. Edited by Carl Van Horn, Todd Green, and Tammy Edward. Washington, DC: Federal Reserve.

Sharone, Ofer and Vasquez, Alexandra. 2017. "Sociology as a Strategy of Support for Long-Term Unemployed Workers." *The American Sociologist* 48: 246–265.

Sharone, Ofer. 2013. *Flawed System/Flawed Self: Job Searching and Unemployment Experiences*. Chicago: University of Chicago Press.

Sharone, Ofer. 2017. "LinkedIn or LinkedOut? How Social Networking Sites Are Reshaping the Labor Market." *Research in the Sociology of Work* 30:1–31.

Sharone, Ofer. 2014. "Social Capital Activation and Job Searching: Embedding the Use of Weak Ties in the American Institutional Context." *Work and Occupations* 41(4): 409–439.

Sharone, Ofer. 2004. "Engineering Overwork: Bell-Curve Management at a High-Tech Firm." In *Fighting for Time: Shifting Boundaries of Work and Social Life*. Edited by Cynthia Fuchs Epstein and Arne L. Kalleberg. New York: Russell Sage Foundation.

Sharone, Ofer. 2021. "Networking When Unemployed: Why Long Term Unemployment Will Likely Persist Long After the Covid-19 Pandemic Recedes." *American Behavioral Scientist*. https://doi.org/10.1177/00027642211066032.

Sharone, Ofer. 2007. "Constructing Unemployed Job Seekers as Professional Workers: The Depoliticizing Work-Game of Job Searching." *Qualitative Sociology* 30(4): 403–416.

Sheehan, Patrick. 2022. "The Paradox of Self-Help Expertise: How Unemployed Workers Become Professional Career Coaches." *American Journal of Sociology* 127(4): 1151–1182.

Small, Mario Luis. 2009. "'How Many Cases Do I Need?': On Science and the Logic of Case Selection in Field-Based Research." *Ethnography* 10(1): 5–38.

Smith, Vicki. 2001. *Crossing the Great Divide: Worker Risk and Opportunity in the New Economy*. Ithaca, NY: Cornell University Press.

Stern, Andy. 2016. *Raising the Floor: How a Universal Basic Income Can Renew Our Economy and Rebuild the American Dream*. New York: Public Affairs.

Stettner, Andrew, and Jeffrey Wenger. 2003. "The Broad Reach of Long-Term Un- employment." Economic Policy Institute Issue Brief 194 (May 15). http: // www .epi.org / publication / issuebriefs_ib194 / .

Strully, Kate. 2009. "Job Loss and Health in the U.S. Labor Market." *Demography* 46(2): 221–246.

Sullivan, Daniel ,and Till von Wachter. 2009. "Job Displacement and Mortality: An Analysis Using Administrative Data." *Quarterly Journal of Economics* 124(3): 1265–1306.

Trost, Jan. 1986. "Statistically Nonrepresentative Stratified Sampling: A Sampling Technique for Qualitative Studies." *Qualitative Sociology* 9(1): 54–57.

Tyler, Imogen, and Tom Slater. 2018. "Rethinking the Sociology of Stigma." *Sociological Review Monographs.* 66(4): 721–743.

Uchitelle, Louis. 2006. *The Disposable American: Layoffs and Their Consequences.* New York: Knopf.

Van Horn, Carl. 2013. *Working Scared (or Not at All): The Lost Decade, Great Recession, and Restoring the Shattered American Dream.* Lanham, MD: Rowman and Littlefield.

Van Hoye, Greet, Edwin A. J. van Hooft, and Filip Lievens. 2009. "Networking as a Job Search Behaviour: A Social Network Perspective." *Journal of Occupational and Organizational Psychology* 82(3): 661–682. doi:10.1348/096317908X360675.

Van Parijs, Philippe, and Vanderborght, Yannick. 2017. *Basic Income: Radical Proposal for a Free Society and a Sane Economy.* Cambridge, MA: Harvard University Press.

Vallas, Steven, and Emily Commins. 2015. "Personal Branding and Identity Norms in the Popular Business Press: Enterprise Culture in an Age of Precarity." *Organization Studies* 36(3): 293–319.

Wacquant, Loic. 2008. *Urban Outcasts: A Comparative Sociology of Advanced Marginality.* Cambridge: Polity Press.

Wanberg, Connie, Ruth Kanfer, and Joseph Banas. 2000. "Predictors and Outcomes of Networking Intensity among Unemployed Job Seekers." *Journal of Applied Psychology* 85(4): 491–503. doi:10.1037/0021-9010.85.4.491.

Weber, Max. 1946. "The Social Psychology of the World Religions." In *From Max Weber: Essays in Sociology.* Edited by H. H. Gerth and C. Wright Mills. Oxford: Oxford University Press.

Weil, David. 2014. *The Fissured Workplace.* Cambridge, MA: Harvard University Press.

Wolff, Hans-Georg, and Klaus Moser. 2009. "Effects of Networking on Career Success: A Longitudinal Study." *Journal of Applied Psychology* 94(1): 196–206. doi:10.1037/a0013350.

Zelizer, Viviana. 2005. *The Purchase of Intimacy.* Princeton, NJ: Princeton University Press.

Zhang, Ting. 2011. "Workforce Investment Act Training for Older Workers: Toward a Better Understanding of Older Worker Needs during the Economic Recovery." US Department of Labor/Employment and Training Administration, Research & Publication, No. EATAOP 2011-10.

Zukin, Cliff, Carl Van Horn, and Charley Stone. 2011. "Out of Work and Losing Hope: The Misery of Bleak Expectations of American Workers." John J. Heldrich Center for Workforce Development, Rutgers University. https://www.heldrich.rutgers.edu/work/out-work-and-losing-hope-misery-and-bleak-expectations-american-workers

Index

For the benefit of digital users, indexed terms that span two pages (e.g., 52–53) may, on occasion, appear on only one of those pages.